Nineteenth-Century Music: The Western Classical Tradition

Jon W. Finson

University of North Carolina at Chapel Hill

D1410896

Upper Saddle River, New Jersey 07458

Library of Congress Cataloging-in-Publication Data

FINSON, JON W.

    Nineteenth-century music : the western classical tradition / Jon W. Finson
      p. cm.
    Includes bibliographical references (p.) and index.
    ISBN 0-13-927179-1 (pbk.)
    1. Music—19th century—History and criticism   I. Title: 19th-century music. II. Title.

ML196.F56 2002
780'.9'034—dc21

                             2001036166

Senior acquisitions editor: *Christopher T. Johnson*
Editorial assistant: *Evette Dickerson*
Project manager: *Carole R. Crouse*
Prepress and manufacturing buyer: *Benjamin Smith*
Copy editor: *Carole R. Crouse*
Marketing manager: *Sheryl Adams*
Cover designer: *Joseph Sengotta*
Cover art: Klimt, Gustav, "Music I," 1895, oil on canvas, 37 × 45 cm.
         In the collection of the Neue Pinakothek, Munich.

This book was set in 10.5/12 New Baskerville by Stratford Publishing Services
and was printed and bound by Hamilton Printing Company.
The music was set by MPT Music Engraving.
The cover was printed by Phoenix Color Group.

© 2002 by Pearson Education, Inc.
Upper Saddle River, New Jersey 07458

Printed in the United States of America

10 9 8 7 6 5 4 3 2 1

ISBN 0-13-927179-1

PEARSON EDUCATION LTD., *London*
PEARSON EDUCATION AUSTRALIA PTY, LIMITED, *Sydney*
PEARSON EDUCATION SINGAPORE, PTE. LTD.
PEARSON EDUCATION NORTH ASIA LTD., *Hong Kong*
PEARSON EDUCATION CANADA, LTD., *Toronto*
PEARSON EDUCACÍON DE MEXICO, S.A. DE C.V.
PEARSON EDUCATION--JAPAN, *Tokyo*
PEARSON EDUCATION MALAYSIA, PTE. LTD.
PEARSON EDUCATION, *Upper Saddle River, New Jersey*

For Samuel Mages, Marjory Irvin,
Barbara Kinsey Sable, and Abraham Chavez,
extraordinary teachers all

Contents

7 *THE DIVERSITY OF NATIONALISM*   231

8 *THE NEW LANGUAGE AT CENTURY'S END*   283

INDEX   305

Preface

The nineteenth century retains a singular place in the history of Western music. It marks the advent of many features in musical life we still take for granted, among them the recognized distinction between "classical" and "popular" music, the rise of widespread subscription concerts, the emergence of the middle classes as the primary consumers of music, and the establishment of international musical copyright. Not the least of the nineteenth century's legacy is a body of classical music so diverse and compelling that it dominates modern concert life.

The musical diversity of the nineteenth century presents the historian with myriad choices, the first of which concerns coverage. The "complete" approach demands a kind of detail that will verge at times on the trivial, and in an age blessed with two truly fine encyclopedias of music (*The New Grove Dictionary of Music and Musicians* in its second edition and the revised *Musik in Geschichte und Gegenwart*) there seems little point to this strategy. I mean this book, moreover, to address mainly students taking a survey course in music history. They deserve a study that will acquaint them with music they will most likely play or hear. For both of these reasons I have decided to write a selective introduction to the period focusing primarily on "classical" music. It would be a mistake, however, to present the notion of a "classical" music as somehow inevitable or divinely inspired, especially for a century that developed the concept of "classical" music. We can explore this construct as an aspect of history just like any other.

An introduction to nineteenth-century classical music invariably engages the issues surrounding "the canon." My quotation marks around "the" as well as "canon" highlight a misconception on the part of some music historians, that we can identify one monolithic central repertory upon which all would (mysteriously) agree. In fact, there are several canons, one for the concert hall, one for the opera, a different one for the radio, one for academics, and so forth. Even these generalizations would apply locally to the United States. Different core repertories would appear in Europe, and vary, in fact, from country to country. Though these various standard repertories overlap, to be sure, I mean to address an American audience in this book, and I will sample both the publicly performed and the academic canons. To give an example of the contrast between the two, Tchaikovsky's orchestral music plays a relatively large role in the canon of the concert hall but receives fairly brief treatment in most academic accounts, whereas Meyerbeer's opera, rarely performed on these shores, nevertheless plays a prominent role in academic accounts because of its influence. The concept of a canon aids a historian: It helps him or her reduce the vast repertory of the nineteenth century to manageable size. Were there no canon, we would need to create one, for such constructs are inevitable in the writing of art history. But we need not pretend that "the canon" is irrevocable or universally valid.

This book takes one convenient approach to dividing music history, based on calendar chronology. We could make a very good argument for beginning such a history around 1750, including all of the nineteenth century, and ending around 1950. Most expectations of genre, many fundamental aesthetic premises, and a set of common compositional assumptions (in spite of widely divergent style) would be valid for much of the music written during this two-hundred-year period. If style diverges drastically toward the end of it, it must be seen as just that: deviating for artistic reasons from some commonly accepted norm known to all composers. But in the end, a two-hundred-year history would be either unwieldy or cursory, and thus I have chosen the simple expedient of beginning about 1800 and leaving off about 1900, as arbitrary as that may seem. In the end, Carl Dalhaus's suggestion that a coherent segment begins around 1814 and ends around 1914, for all its political logic, produces no better results than the seemingly more arbitrary calendar approach.

I have pointedly avoided suggesting a cohesive nineteenth-century aesthetic theme like that found in books such as Leon Plantinga's worthy *Romantic Music*. A study on musical Romanticism should probably start with the 1780s. After all, most of the aesthetic tenets of Romanticism appear in the late eighteenth century. And no less than E. T. A. Hoffman considered the older Haydn and the mature Mozart Romantic, while finding the acme of Romanticism in Beethoven. Charles Rosen's recently acclaimed *The Romantic Generation* would be more aptly titled *The Second Romantic Generation*. Music throughout the period exhibits both "Romantic" and "Classic" qualities, and in a sense the concept of one requires the other to define it. Fredrick Blume's view of "Classic" and "Romantic" as two complementary antitheses in an ongoing synthesis proves in the end the most satisfactory conceptualization, the only one that allows us to embrace composers as diverse as Beethoven, Rossini, Mendelssohn, Verdi, Brahms, and Mahler in one period. But such a solution only emphasizes the problems inherent in trying to find one pervasive, aesthetic "spirit of the times" in the nineteenth century.

Finally, musicologists have recently encountered some criticism from within their own ranks for ignoring the emotional impact and sonic beauty of music. I will not be shy about reflecting what I find moving and beautiful about nineteenth-century music. By this same token, I will feel free to point out what I consider to be the great music of this period. The sophisticated edifice of theory, aesthetics, composition, history, and performance constitutes one of Western civilization's most magnificent intellectual constructs. We encounter many striking achievements of Western art music in the works of Beethoven, Schubert, Rossini, Berlioz, Chopin, Schumann, Wagner, Verdi, Brahms, and the other composers of the nineteenth century. The magnitude of their accomplishments deserves, indeed demands, recognition among the *gesta humanorum*.

ACKNOWLEDGMENTS

There are many colleagues whose advice I sought on this book, from John Nádas, who encouraged me to take the project on and looked over some of my musings on Italian opera, to Evan Bonds, with whom I traded ideas about how a textbook should work. Thanks also go to my students, and particularly to the proudly British Tom Geddes, who suggested "For He Is an Englishman" as the most appropriate expression of Victorian nationalism. Various others unknowingly aided and abetted me, including John Daverio and Kern Holoman. Many thanks go to Dan Zager and Diane Pettit for helping with permissions for various sources, and to Sarah McClosky and Eva Boyce, who helped to locate various errant volumes from the Hill Music Library. Thanks go to Stephen Zank (University of Illinois, Champaign-Urbana), David Whitwell (California State University–Northridge), and Joseph Sylvan (New Mexico State University) for their thoughtful review of the manuscript. Mrs. Carole Crouse spent many valuable hours editing the initial copy, using her vast knowledge of music and foreign languages to keep me in the straight and narrow way. Finally, I should like to give Bud Therien and Chris Johnson at Prentice Hall a nod for supporting this project along the way.

Jon Finson

Nineteenth-Century Music:
The Western
Classical Tradition

CHAPTER 1

Nineteenth-Century Music: Overview and Background

Any account of nineteenth-century music must come quickly to grips with the obvious fact that this body of work constitutes our present as much as it records our past. No other repertory of art music from any historical period in Western civilization currently enjoys as much prominence, whether in the concert hall, or on the stage, or over the airwaves (at least on fine-arts stations). We hear very little music from before 1700 today, less than the tip of the iceberg from the eighteenth century (selected Bach, Handel, Haydn, Mozart, and an infrequent handful of others), and audiences unfortunately flee most music after 1914. But the works of Beethoven, Schubert, Rossini, Donizetti, Bellini, Schumann, Mendelssohn, Berlioz, Wagner, Verdi, Brahms, Musorgsky, Dvořák, Tchaikovsky, Mahler, and myriad other nineteenth-century composers still occupy a central place in our everyday experience. Even for those who never darken the doors of a concert hall or an opera house, nineteenth-century music or musical style often provides the framework for the experience of television and film.

The centrality of nineteenth-century music to our present-day listening has prompted many distinguished historians to seek in its art a pervasive "spirit of the times" that explains its attraction. Scholars often consider "Romanticism" to be the aesthetic glue that holds the century together, and many distinguished writers, from Jacques Barzun to Alfred Einstein to Leon Plantinga, make strong arguments for this notion. But in the end the search for a pervasive "spirit of the times" entails so broad a meaning for "romantic" that the term tends to lose its usefulness. We cannot deny that Romanticism constitutes one of the most important aesthetic themes during the first half of the century, but we must also give realism, naturalism, and empiricism during the second half of the century their due.

By the same token, no one social change accounts for the centrality of nineteenth-century music to present-day listeners. The German musicologist Carl Dahlhaus designates the nineteenth century as the age of middle-class music. But just a brief glance will show that many nineteenth-century composers enjoyed the benefits of aristocratic patronage at some point—Beethoven, Liszt, Mendelssohn, Wagner, and Mahler among them. Although the nineteenth century witnessed the institutionalization of many a middle-class concert society and subscription series, it also saw the continuation of court opera companies and even a few private, aristocratic orchestras.

If no single factor accounts for the continued vitality of nineteenth-century music, however, we can still list the multifaceted influences—political, industrial, social, and aesthetic—that marked the years from 1800 to 1900. In this way we can behold our modern world of music emerging out of the confluence of activity during this period. It provided an artistic diversity that was not yet entirely chaotic, a demand for novelty and invention that did not prevent the formation of stable and enduring institutions, and a notion of progress that was not rootless.

THE CREATION OF MODERN EUROPE

A look at any map of Europe in the first fifteen years of the nineteenth century would reveal a strikingly unfamiliar picture from the one we see today. On the Continent, France under Napoleon Bonaparte dominated Spain, Portugal, Italy, Belgium, the Netherlands, Denmark, Norway, much of Germany, Poland, and a good part of the northern Balkans. By marriage Napoleon counted the Hapsburgs as allies; their territories included Austria, Hungary, and the Czech and Slovakian lands. Only Russia in the east and the mercantile empire centered on the island of Britain in the west retained complete independence.

The first step toward redrawing the map of Europe came after Russia, England, Austria-Hungary, and Prussia (located in the northeastern part of modern Germany) defeated Napoleon in battle and established new boundaries for Europe at the Congress of Vienna in 1815. This map of continental Europe would look just slightly more familiar to a modern viewer. France, Spain, Portugal, Denmark, Norway, and Sweden all took more or less their modern form. The Netherlands included present-day Belgium. In place of present-day Germany, the map would show many small principalities and a few large ones (Bavaria, Prussia, Saxony), and the Hapsburg Empire still included Austria, Bohemia, Hungary, much of the northern Balkans, and the northern part of Italy. Russia enfolded all of Ukraine, Belarus, and Georgia, and vast holdings to the east. Poland disappeared, divided between the Russians on the east, the Prussians on the west, and the Austrians to the south.

The map of Europe drawn at the Congress of Vienna in 1815 lasted for almost forty years, but uprisings across Europe around midcentury resulted in a trend toward national consolidation. By the early 1870s a map of the continent would look much more familiar to a modern observer. Germany and Italy both became unified nations in their modern sense (with somewhat different boundaries), and Belgium had seceded from the Netherlands. Only Austria-Hungary, with its control over the Czech republic, Slovakia, Bosnia, Herzegovina, Slovenia, Croatia, part of Romania, and Poland, would look entirely unfamiliar to us. Internal unrest in the Hapsburg Empire, however, indicated that it was not long for this world. One more convulsion, in 1914, would finally establish something very much like the map of twentieth-century Europe by breaking Austria-Hungary into its constituent parts. Over this same period the United States would expand across the North American continent, almost completing its final form.

INDUSTRIALIZATION

Just as modern European polities began to emerge in the nineteenth century, modern habits of industry coalesced during this period. Although agrarian pursuits would continue to occupy a large part of the population in Europe, the wealth of nations would increasingly consist of what they manufactured. Steam engines, which initially allowed the pumping out of deeper coal mines for energy, powered faster manufacturing equipment and also created a revolution in transportation. With the coming of steamships and railroads travel that had taken a day at the beginning of the century took an hour by midcentury and even less at century's close. The faster transportation of goods and supplies in turn quickened the pace of commerce. Hand in hand with speedy transportation came almost instantaneous communication, first in the form of the telegraph (1837) and later in the form of the telephone (1876).

We may smile at the thought that industrialization might directly affect the making of music, but it had a profound influence. Rotary steam presses could print much more music than hand presses had, and improved transportation could speed the greater supplies of printed music to a wider audience. Manufacturers began to apply the techniques of mass production to musical instruments as well, most notably to the piano. The English instrument maker Broadwood was one of the first to use cast iron for the frame of its pianos and to produce them on an assembly line. Instead of making fifty pianos a year at the end of the eighteenth century, a firm could make five hundred a year by the second decade of the nineteenth century, five thousand by midcentury, and fifty thousand or more by the last quarter of the nineteenth century. The unit price of these instruments came down accordingly, and their iron frames made them much more reliable for use in the larger number of households that could afford them. Manufacturers also applied technological advances in the form of elaborate keys and valves to wind instruments, developed the modern action for the harp, and modified the design of the violin family to lend its members more acoustical projection. Manufacturers invented new instruments as various as the tuba (1835), the saxophone (1840), and the celesta (1886) during the nineteenth century. And the end of the nineteenth century also saw remarkable advances in mechanical reproduction of sound, ranging from development of the simple music box into a device as elaborate as the reproducing piano (1890s) to actual sound recording invented by Thomas Edison in 1877. Through these technologies merchants distributed music to wider audiences than ever before.

From reading novelists such as Charles Dickens, we may tend to think of nineteenth-century industrialization as grimy and unpleasant. The process drew large masses of people into urban surroundings, where they were subjected to poor sanitation, pollution, and overcrowding. But these real and substantial drawbacks aside, the industrial revolution created and spread wealth more widely in European civilization than ever before. This wealth greatly expanded the middle classes, and it also allowed them more leisure in which to enjoy the performing arts.

MUSIC IN SOCIETY

Although the expanding middle classes were the driving force behind musical developments in the nineteenth century, the old order of feudal aristocracy persisted in most European countries. Its traditional institutions, including opera companies and a small number of court orchestras, retained their viability and prestige. Wagner's music dramas would be unthinkable without the generous patronage of the Bavarian King Ludwig, Mendelssohn worked for a time as a Prussian court Kapellmeister and stood high in the favor of England's Queen Victoria, and Liszt could not have composed his orchestral works without his position as Weimar's court Kapellmeister. Tchaikovksy received a stipend from the tsar, Brahms spent some time writing for the Detmold court wind ensemble, Strauss held his first conducting appointment with the Meiningen court orchestra, and Mahler spent much of his career directing the Hungarian and Austrian court operas.

Lacking both the traditional authority and the financial means to support institutions as opulent as the grand opera, the expanding middle classes created new institutions as expressions of their power and prestige. These were often nonprofit organizations, such as London's Philharmonic Society (1813),

Vienna's Gesellschaft der Musikfreunde (1812), and Boston's Handel and Haydn Society (1815). In such associations, middle-class and (in Europe) aristocratic connoisseurs often combined with artists to support concert series by subscription and by donations of their time or wealth. It did not take musicians long to realize that they could also profit from this model, and they banded together to form such concert-giving associations as the Vienna and New York Philharmonics in 1842 or the Parisian Société Nationale de Musique in 1871. Middle-class entrepreneurs or artist-businessmen increasingly turned concerts into commerce, offering series of orchestral concerts, or chamber-music concerts, or recitals by instrumental and vocal soloists. Although there had long been public concerts in Europe, the nineteenth century saw a vast expansion in their number, their regularity, and the dependability of their organization. When a country turned to democratic rule as France did after 1870, the trappings of aristocratic power generally transferred to middle-class bureaucratic authorities. They administered traditional strongholds of music such as opera companies in the name of the government. Finally, some wealthy middle-class patrons, especially in France, held private musical performances in "salons"—evening gatherings in their homes to which they invited their friends and prominent musicians as performers.

As the audience for music expanded, so did the number and size of venues for performance. The nineteenth century saw the construction of many large halls and theaters still in use today, including Vienna's "Golden Hall" at the Gesellschaft and Semper's Opera, the Palais Garnier in Paris, New York's Carnegie Hall, Leipzig's new Gewandhaus (replacing the old guild hall), London's Royal Albert Hall, and Amsterdam's Concertgebouw. The larger-sized halls in turn demanded larger ensembles employing more musicians, and these expanded auditoriums also prompted the technological developments in instruments mentioned in the previous section.

The middle classes viewed music, both "popular" and "classical," as commerce. Increasingly, widespread wealth and leisure fed the need for diversion, not only in the form of public concerts, but also in the form of music for the home. "House music" required in turn instruments on which to perform it and lessons for people who wanted to sing or play. For much of the century, music businesses integrated vertically to conduct their trade. To take just one example, the firm of Breitkopf in Leipzig printed music, manufactured instruments, maintained the retail outlets that sold their music and instruments, and even arranged for people to receive instruction (lessons) in how to use musical products. Although some firms did specialize in one trade or another, separation of music publishers from instrument makers and from retail outlets for music occurred only slowly over the course of the century.

In the commerce of musical style and musical goods a social division gradually became apparent. Though we cannot draw an absolute dividing line, the professional middle classes (those who received university degrees and went on to become lawyers, doctors, engineers, and educators) tended to be consumers of "classical" music, a term they invented. This was supposed to be a music of superior intellectual content (and therefore increased sophistication) that survived transient stylistic fads and conferred on its adherents a higher social status. If these listeners could not claim nobility through familial heritage, they simply created their own elevated tradition to demonstrate their superior standing. A number of critic-composers took a hand in this exercise, including such estimable figures as E. T. A. Hoffmann (a lawyer, critic, and composer), Robert Schumann (who studied law but became both critic and composer), and Hector Berlioz (who studied medicine before he turned to composition, criticism, and conducting).

The lofty and inaccessible "classical" music in turn left a niche open for a less esoteric, more accessible "popular" music that appeared increasingly around midcentury. This music offered the novelty of changing fashion, and it often served the commercial middle class, whose members generally did not attend universities to learn their trade. Because of its immediate accessibility, popular music also slowly widened its appeal to the working classes.

AESTHETIC TRENDS

The various aesthetic movements in art music of the nineteenth century unfolded against the backdrop of emerging national identity, burgeoning industrial development, and more leisure for an increasingly influential professional middle class. The earliest aesthetic trend, Romanticism, finds its roots and beginnings in the late eighteenth century, and it maintained full sway into the first half of the nineteenth. But at midcentury Romanticism gave way to other sensibilities, most notably a complex involving artistic realism, naturalism, and empiricism. Various elements from all of these fed artistic historicism and nationalism, both of which surfaced sporadically throughout the century but became most salient toward its close.

Romanticism

In many ways Romanticism arose in response to the eighteenth-century Enlightenment view of a rationally ordered universe governed by immutable laws. Enlightenment thinkers believed that human beings could understand the world around them primarily by using their rational faculties. These philosophers tended also to be cosmopolitan (believing that knowledge transcended national boundaries) and anticlerical (especially suspicious of the Roman Catholic Church). Perhaps no undertaking is so typical of Enlightenment thought as the Denis Diderot's *Encyclopédie* (1751–72), to which a number of

French "philosophes" contributed articles. This compendium sought to rationalize, categorize, define, and assemble all useful knowledge. (Another famous example of this activity appeared as the Encyclopædia Britannica, 1768–71.) Other important figures of the Enlightenment included the French philosopher Voltaire, the German philosopher Immanuel Kant, the British philosopher David Hume, and Americans such as Thomas Jefferson. The Enlightenment systematization of knowledge extended from the sciences (Isaac Newton's laws of physics, for instance) to government (our own Constitution, for example). In music, theorists such as Rameau tried to order harmony rationally in his *Traité de l'harmonie* (1722), and the German writer Heinrich Christoph Koch in his composition manual (*Versuch einer Anleitung zur Composition*, 1782–93) treated music as if it were a variety of rational speech.

The Romantics believed that Enlightenment rationalism *by itself* did not provide a sufficiently realistic view of the universe and human nature. Admitting that rationalism displayed one aspect of the world as we encounter it, Romanticism placed as much emphasis on intuition as on logic, on sentiment as on reason, on the supernatural as on the physical, and on diversity as on universality. The seeds of Romanticism began in the writings of the French philosopher Jean-Jacques Rousseau (1712–78). His emphasis on the freedom of the individual and his famous dictum, "I felt before I thought," resonated across Europe with such writers as Johann Gottfried von Herder (1744–1803) and Johann Wolfgang von Goethe (1749–1832).

The word "Romanticism" derives from *romance,* a medieval term for a fanciful tale. Many of the important Romantics were novelists or poets, including Friedrich Schiller (1759–1805) and E. T. A. Hoffmann (1776–1822) in Germany, and William Wordsworth (1770–1850), Samuel Coleridge (1772–1834), Lord Byron (1788–1824), and Sir Walter Scott (1771–1832) in England. The Romantic writers active in the first half of the nineteenth century tended to focus on fantastic stories that blurred the distinction between the supernatural and physical worlds or that took place in settings distant in either time or location. Local color and exoticism were the stock-in-trade of these authors.

German writers were particularly important for musical Romanticism. Drawing on the tenets of Platonic Idealism (in which a transcendent world of ideas or essences presented a superior reality to physical existence), authors such as Friedrich Schelling (1775–1854), August Wilhelm Schlegel (1767–1845), Wilhelm Heinrich Wackenroder, and Ludwig Tieck (1773–1853) began to regard music as the most direct expression or even manifestation of a spiritual realm. They saw a glimpse of this supernatural world revealed in the music of Haydn and Mozart. But they discovered the quintessentially Romantic composer in Beethoven, whose music, E. T. A. Hoffmann wrote, "opens the colossal and immeasurable for us" and "tears the listener irresistibly away into the wonderful spiritual realm of the infinite." Romanticism placed a premium on originality, distinctiveness, and idiosyncrasy that the Viennese composers, especially

Beethoven and Schubert, were at great pains to cultivate. But Romanticism did not completely discard the art of the Enlightenment, either in literature or in music. Rather, the Romantics extended the forms and the language of the late eighteenth century, constructing their new edifice on the foundations previously built.

The influence of Romanticism persisted throughout the first half of the nineteenth century. It had a profound effect on a second generation of authors such as Heinrich Heine (1797–1856) and Joseph Freiherr von Eichendorff (1788–1857) in Germany, Victor Hugo (1802–85) and Théophile Gautier (1811–72) in France, Alessandro Manzoni (1785–1873) in Italy, Alexander Pushkin (1799–1837) in Russia, and Washington Irving (1783–1859) and Edgar Allen Poe (1809–49) in America. The second generation of Romantic composers included the likes of Mendelssohn, Schumann, Liszt, Chopin, Bellini, and Donizetti, and many others. For all these artists the lure of fantastic, exotic, or highly fanciful subject matter and local color proved irresistible, and they perpetuated the philosophical Idealism that had marked earlier Romanticism.

Empiricism, Realism, Naturalism

The Romantics' call to take the full range of reality into account carried within it the seeds of movements that blossomed in the second half of the nineteenth century. The underlying principle that all knowledge originates in experience (the philosophy known as "empiricism") led to realism and naturalism. In the sciences this meant a new trend toward experimentation that brought, among other things, significant advances in biology and medicine. In aesthetics, empiricism and its allied realism and naturalism meant that certain key parts of Romanticism began to drop away, particularly the love of the fantastic and mystical. Some elements of Romanticism remained, however, especially the notion that the universe was a diverse and disorderly place.

As with Romanticism, realism and naturalism found their first adherents in the arts among writers, such as Prosper Merimée (1803–70) and Charles Murger in France, Charles Dickens (1812–70) in England, and, later, Mark Twain (1835–1910) in America. Novellas such as Merimée's *Carmen* (1845) and novels such as Murger's *Scènes de la vie de bohème* (1849), Dickens's *Oliver Twist* (1839), or Twain's *Tom Sawyer* (1876) tend to focus on the life of working classes in all its gritty, sometimes squalid actuality. It may seem at first that the Romantic interest in exoticism governs such works. But in fact, a more compelling motivation for authors of realist fiction lay in addressing the actual hardships of the poor or the life of everyday people. For that reason, a good deal of violence permeates realist literature, which begins to feature slang and expressions from common speech. Naturalism usually explores the same social milieu through the lens of pathological psychology, and it comes rather later in the works of Russian authors such as Dostoyevsky.

Realism and naturalism manifested themselves in music in various ways. We can see a turn to realistic subject matter in opera easily enough: the lady of ill repute in Verdi's *La traviata,* the working-class woman in Bizet's *Carmen,* or even the psychological and social naturalism in Musorgsky's *Boris Godunov.* Less obvious but just as important was a turn to empiricism in aesthetics and music theory, which tended to split the adherents of instrumental music into two camps. A work such as Eduard Hanslick's *On the Beautiful in Music* (1854) denied the idea that music "expressed" anything beyond itself: it consisted of nothing but patterns in sound that might well act on the mind psychologically but contained no emotions or "spirit" (as Romantic Idealists maintained). This empirical view of music found resonance in theorists such as Hermann Helmholtz (1821–94), who suggested in *The Sensations of Tone as a Physiological Basis for the Theory of Music* (1863) that the aesthetics of music was grounded in the ear's mechanical ability to detect the wave motions of sound. Such aesthetic and theoretical tracts bolstered adherents of "absolute" music, such as Johannes Brahms. On the other hand, Franz Liszt and his followers, also prompted by the notion of realism, came to quite different conclusions about the aesthetic value of music. The concept moved them to a more literal view of music's content in which words or visual images translated into musical "tone poems." At the extreme end of "programmatic" composition, Richard Strauss once remarked that he could "set a glass of beer to music." Although the debate between absolute and program music has lasted into the twenty-first century, the Romantic view of music with supernatural "spirit" has largely disappeared.

Historicism and Nationalism

Two major themes running through the nineteenth century have existences independent of Romanticism, realism, naturalism, and empiricism, and fit themselves comfortably into all these aesthetic trends. Both have their roots in the Enlightenment's interest in encyclopedic knowledge, and various aesthetic movements appropriated and transformed them for their own purposes.

We can see quite clearly a new interest in music history taking shape during the second half of the eighteenth century in works such as John Hawkins's *General History of the Science and Practice of Music* (London, 1776), Charles Burney's *General History of Music from the Earliest Ages to the Present Period* (London, 1776–89), and Johann Forkel's *Allgemeine Geschichte der Musik* (*General History of Music;* Leipzig, 1788–1801). The Romantics easily converted the encyclopedic impetus behind such enterprises into something more fantastic: affection for the fabled past or for tales of artistic heroes from previous ages performing superhuman feats of creativity. The decision by German composers and scholars to unearth J. S. Bach's forgotten works or by the Caecilian movement to seek the roots of Roman Catholic chant have as much of legend as of science about them (however much they uncovered material of concrete value).

The latter part of the nineteenth century, with its empiricist bent and literal-mindedness, converted the historical impulse yet again into neoclassicism. We can see this quite obviously in Brahms's allusions to Baroque style in pieces ranging from his *a cappella* motets to his serenades for orchestra to his use of a chaconne in the last movement of his Fourth Symphony. Neoclassicism also appears in Tchaikovsky's suites for orchestra and even some of his ballets. The historical impulse may be less evident but is no less important in a composition such as Wagner's *Meistersinger von Nürnberg*, with its invocation of bar form and use of melody by an actual sixteenth-century songwriter, Hans Sachs. The study of music history, of course, was formalized in the second half of the nineteenth century with university professorships and enterprises such as George Grove's *Dictionary of Music and Musicians*.

The elements of nationalism undergo a similar progression during the eighteenth and nineteenth centuries. Originally centered on encyclopedic interest in popular culture, collections of national "folk" music during the eighteenth century were legion, ranging from William Thomson's *Orpheus Caledonius, or a Collection of the Best Scotch Songs* (London, 1725) to Jean-Benjamin de La Borde's *Choix de chansons mises en musique* (Paris, 1773). These activities in turn gave rise to the German Romantic interest in such collections, promoted by Herder, Goethe, and, later, Clemens Brentano partly as a reflection of things ancient and fabled, partly as a product of minds unspoiled by formal education.

The Romantics found national folk music attractive because it gave proof of what they regarded as the irrationality and diversity of human culture. Whether it came in the form of the Grimms' fairy tales, Robert Burns's Scottish poetry, Nikolay Alexandrovich Lvov's and Johann Gottfried Pratsch's Russian folk songs, or Thomas Moore's *Irish Melodies*, the folk music of different ethnic groups reflected "the characteristic." Carl Dahlhaus defines the "characteristic" as "the idiosyncratic rather than the general or typical, the exception rather than the rule, 'interesting' and 'striking' rather than 'nobly simple,' coloristic rather than statuesque." Merged with the resistance to the Napoleonic Empire at the beginning of the nineteenth century, nationalistic music also took on political overtones. Romantic love of exotic material and political nationalism combined in pieces as various as Liszt's Hungarian Rhapsodies or Chopin's mazurkas and polonaises to elicit powerful patriotic sentiments.

As Romanticism waned after midcentury, some of these nationalistic elements made themselves equally at home in the age of empiricism and realism. For one thing, the study of folk music was formalized in more thorough and "scientific" collections such as Erk and Böhme's *Deutscher Liederhort* (1893–94), Francis James Child's *English and Scottish Popular Ballads* (1882–98), Champfleury's *Chansons populaires des provinces de France* (1860), and Lopatin and Prokunin's *Sbornik russkikh narodnïkh liricheskikh pesen* (*Collection of Russian Lyric Folksongs;* 1889). The diversity of culture formerly regarded as exotic simply became natural. Human beings organize themselves into groups sharing common cultural backgrounds, and experience would suggest that they should organize themselves politically according to their respective ethnic affinities. This resulted not from some mysterious force but from simple observation: Nationalism in art music after midcentury had roots in a realism that impelled the various linguistic groups of Europe to separate themselves politically from one another.

The art music of European civilization during the nineteenth century, then, embraced a number of aesthetic tenets, some inherited from the eighteenth century, some that ran throughout the nineteenth century, some that appeared and disappeared in the manner of all intellectual fashions. We find these various themes woven through the fabric of composers' lives and their music, but not seamlessly. Where one thread leaves off, another begins. The history of art is not so much an attempt to show a logical progression from one event or piece to another as an exercise revealing the kaleidoscopically changing patterns that appeared during a particular period. The rich variety of motivations and materials that intersected in nineteenth-century music render the constant arrangement and rearrangement of artistic elements a deep and continual source of delight to this day.

CHAPTER 2

The Viennese Ascendancy

BEETHOVEN

Max Klinger's famous statue of Beethoven (Figure 2.1) must be the most unusual representation of a composer ever created. Sculpted between 1886 and 1902, the statue employs several iconic traditions to depict its subject as viewed by the end of the nineteenth century. Beethoven sits enthroned as Olympic Zeus, heroically confronting the eagle symbolizing the power of that god. Further reinforcing his divine nature, cherubim emerge in relief on the back of his throne. The pose for Zeus in turn draws on another iconic tradition, one in which the god is shown seminude, draped in philosopher's robes spilling from one knee toward the ground. Klinger means to tell us that Beethoven possesses the stature of a godlike thinker, that his music constitutes divine thought.

What could possibly have led to such a remarkable view of a composer? Some would say that Beethoven was in the right place at the right time. As a pianist heavily invested in instrumental music, he benefited from a change in the prevailing German aesthetic that placed a new premium on the abstract power of music to manifest the spiritual world. This view ranked music highest among the arts, specifically *because* of its inability to represent physical objects or phenomena. Others might claim that Beethoven, through his loss of hearing, gained "the sympathy vote." Still others would argue that Beethoven received

Figure 2.1   Statue of Beethoven as divine philosopher by Max Klinger, 1902 (Leipzig, Museum der bildenden Künste). Courtesy Art Resource, NY; photo: Erich Lessing.

very good press, that he was the first major product of what Virgil Thomson once called "the German propaganda machine."

All these explanations for Beethoven's commanding position in nineteenth-century music contain an element of truth, and yet none of them alone can explain satisfactorily why such exalted honors are not accorded other composers. "Hype" might account for some of Beethoven's status, but it cannot explain entirely why artists such as Klinger continued to hold him in awe after the passage of almost a century, why theorists based whole systems of analysis on his work, or why that work became the measure of performers' abilities. Beethoven did happen on the scene at an opportune moment, but he also had the goods. The "myth of Beethoven" has a basis in his music, which combined features that continue to command the respect of performers, listeners, theorists, and historians.

Three primary traits helped Beethoven to establish his position. One was his extraordinary, intuitive command of the psychology of musical time. Another was his remarkable ear for sonority. And the third was his proclivity for musical insistence. This last seems to have found its roots in a personality trait that in its turn may account in part for the fact that Beethoven's life seems closely bound to his artistic output. As we explore his life, we can also explore these traits in selected pieces from his nineteenth-century oeuvre. A bit of background will help prepare the way.

A Brief Sketch of the Early Viennese Years

The musical life of Vienna at the end of the eighteenth and the beginning of the nineteenth century was in a state of flux. As an imperial city and capital of the only major power in central Europe, it offered the potential for substantial support of the arts. But traditional financial support for music became somewhat uncertain as the higher nobility, beset by financial woes, reduced the size of their private musical establishments or dismissed them altogether. Annual subscription series catering to the upper middle classes had yet to be established.

Vienna attracted talented composers and performers from a wide area, including eastern Europe and Italy, and it had just witnessed the dual glories of Mozart and Haydn. But Mozart was dead by 1792, and Haydn belonged to a previous generation. A new artist who could follow in the Viennese tradition established by these two masters and negotiate the cataracts of the changing musical economy might do quite well. Partly through opportune timing, partly through talent, and partly by design, Ludwig van Beethoven (1770–1827) was well positioned to succeed in the Viennese milieu. As a solo pianist he could easily accept one-time engagements at the homes of various noblemen or give specially arranged public concerts. And Haydn himself had already agreed to tutor the young composer in the Viennese tradition.

Beethoven obviously came with very good connections. His employer, the Elector of Bonn, was the Austrian emperor's uncle. Beethoven's protector in Bonn, Count Waldstein, also had influence in Vienna. The doors to the salons of the music-loving Viennese nobility opened to the young Beethoven, whose ability as a virtuoso pianist and improviser became immediately evident. Not only did he play for the Esterházy family, Prince Lobkowitz, Baron van Swieten, Count Razumovsky, and many other members of the high nobility, he also took up lodging in one of the houses owned by Prince Lichnowsky.

Despite all the fuss made over him by the nobility, Beethoven proved to be highly independent. When he had a falling-out with Haydn, he simply switched teachers to study counterpoint with Albrechtsberger (and later the art of vocal composition with Salieri). When the money supporting his study stopped arriving from Bonn (in 1794 as the result of the Elector fleeing the French), he began a career as a virtuoso performer and freelance composer. This existence, which eschewed employment as a full-time salaried retainer of a single prince, had become increasingly common in the last decades of eighteenth-century Vienna. Mozart embarked upon it and was about to make a success of it when he died, and Haydn pursued it after the death of Nikolaus Esterházy. Beethoven became the model of the freelance musician, but it was not a matter of living only by performing and composing. He also accepted the largesse of several noble patrons without being in their employ, a circumstance that would continue all his life.

Beethoven's compositions in the last decade of the eighteenth century reflect very much his preoccupation with establishing himself in the salons of wealthy Viennese patrons. He wrote a good deal of chamber music for piano and various combinations of instruments: some trios (including opp. 1 and 11), a number of sonatas (for two cellos, op. 5; for violin, op. 12; for horn, op. 17), a piano quartet rearranged for piano and winds (op. 16), and a fair number of variations on well-known tunes, two taken from Mozart's *Magic Flute* (WoO 46 and op. 66). There were a scattering of chamber-music pieces for other combinations—string trios (op. 9), a serenade for string trio (op. 8), a string quintet (op. 4), a mixed septet (op. 20), and wind sextets (opp. 71 and 81b). Above all, there were many songs (most of them published later without opus numbers) and a long series of pieces for piano solo, including brilliant variations and a breathtaking succession of piano sonatas.

Beethoven found publishers for the solo piano pieces easily, and they must also have served to show off his prodigious technique when he played them at soirées. The sonatas in particular invested this genre with an unprecedented weight of both sonority and musical thought. Rarely do they rely only on a simple cantilena (a songlike melody) supported by a subordinate accompaniment. Instead, the musical ideas are instrumentally conceived to use the piano idiomatically, especially its abilities to play chords and create full textures. The intricate motivic working combined with dramatic use of sound lends the pieces a virtuosic aura, both pianistically and compositionally.

Only toward the end of his first decade in Vienna did Beethoven take on the musical genres whose august traditions demanded full artistic maturity. They included the six string quartets, op. 18 (1798–1800), dedicated to Haydn. These demonstrate amply that Beethoven had absorbed Haydn's technique of distributing motivic working equally throughout all four instruments. The composer also fashioned two fine symphonies—the first (op. 21; 1800) replete with Haydnesque wit and verve and the second (op. 36; 1801–2) intimating the more formidable style that would mark later symphonies. In these years Beethoven had his first public, theatrical success with a ballet entitled *The Creatures of Prometheus* (op. 43; premiered at the Burgtheater, 1801), the subject matter taken signally from the story of the defiant, long-suffering Titan. Although this piece would not be counted today among the composer's greatest, it did much to establish his reputation among a wider audience and also played an important role in the symbolism of his career during the first decade of the nineteenth century.

Beethoven's "Heroic" Period

If the history of nineteenth-century music rightly has a starting point, it must begin with Beethoven's "middle" or "heroic" period about 1803, lasting a decade until 1812 or 1813. Writers have characterized it as "heroic" for a number of reasons, including the relatively large output, the aggressive style of the pieces, and the large dimensions of these works. But key to the later understanding of this period and its portrayal in the literature is Beethoven's defiant struggle with his progressive loss of hearing.

Beethoven may have begun to notice his gradual deafness as early as 1796, but he first mentions it to friends in correspondence from June of 1801: "I must confess that I am living a miserable life. For almost two years I have ceased to attend any social functions, just because I find it impossible to say to people: I am deaf." As a performer and composer increasingly sought after by publishers, the relatively young man felt this anguish keenly. He hints at suicide in an unsent letter to his brothers, the so-called "Heiligenstadt Testament," dated October 6, 1802, and found only after his death in 1827. Yet through the depths of a depression bordering on despair, he increased his productivity, offering defiance in the face of the cruelest fate to befall a musician. The works of this period are also characterized as heroic because of this personal struggle: The composer seemed determined to exit the world of hearing in the proverbial "blaze of glory."

To gain an idea of how the adjective "heroic" might translate into musical terms, we might do well to look at the piano sonata, a genre Beethoven had cultivated much by the time he arrived in 1803. One of the most singular pieces from this period is Sonata No. 21, op. 53 (composed 1803–4), also called "The Waldstein" sonata because of its dedication to the composer's longtime patron in Bonn. Writers often talk of its "symphonic" conception, referring first to its proportions: an expansive exposition in the first movement, a development section as long and intricate as that found in most symphonies, and a coda almost as long as the development. The texture of the writing also borders on the orchestral—thick, closely spaced chords in low tessitura set the tone from the start (see Example 2.1). The main theme exhibits two of Beethoven's compositional hallmarks. The first has to do with the perception of musical time, for the composer presents us with what later analysts call a *Satz* (or "sentence"). He creates a four-measure musical unit (mm. 1–4), then repeats that unit in sequence (mm. 5–8). From this cell he detaches a fragment—the idea of the high-pitched descending scale. And over increasing harmonic motion, he dissolves this fragment further to lend the impression of acceleration (mm. 9–13), concluding with an open-ended half cadence. The psychological effect achieved by progressive fragmentation and increased harmonic motion creates an excitement that propels the listener into the rest of the movement.

Beethoven uses the technique of progressive fragmentation constantly, in main and secondary themes, in more loosely knit sections such as the ensuing transition (mm. 14–34), and most prominently in development sections. The device lends Beethoven's music its overwhelming drive. Coupled with his penchant for insistence (who but Beethoven would dare to fashion a motive from an unrelentingly repeated chord?), the technique gives the music its rhetorical force and leads to the thought that it "has something to say." The second theme (mm. 35–49), with its initial hymnlike block chords (Example 2.2) in a very distant major mediant key, further intimates that this "something" might also be "divine."

We cannot leave the *Waldstein* entirely before listening just briefly to the beginning of the last movement, which exemplifies Beethoven's love of unusual sonorities (the third prominent trait in his music). He expresses it here not only in the delicate tracery of arpeggios supporting the cross-hand theme but also in the pedaling, which allows chords to blur into one another (especially in mm. 13–22). The effect is light and impressionistic, not muddy, and its airiness stands in direct contrast to the roiling episode that follows (m. 62). Even if Beethoven progressively lost his hearing, he did not lose his appreciation for the subtleties of sonic texture and spacing in this sonata.

An extraordinary concern for sonority also marks the central monument of the heroic style, the *Sinfonica Eroica*, Beethoven's Third Symphony, op. 55 (composed 1803). The first two hammerstroke chords announce a fuller and grander orchestral texture than any of Beethoven's Viennese predecessors had ever produced, even though they had often used much the same instrumentation in their works from the 1790s. Beethoven regularly detaches the cellos from the basses and gives the winds unprecedented melodic prominence. (Contemporary critics complained that Beethoven's symphonies sounded like "band music.") Beethoven's approach to sonority provided the foundation of

EXAMPLE 2.1 Initial "sentence" from Beethoven's *Waldstein* Sonata, op. 53, 1803–4

EXAMPLE 2.2   Initial period from second theme of Beethoven's *Waldstein* Sonata, op. 53, 1803–4

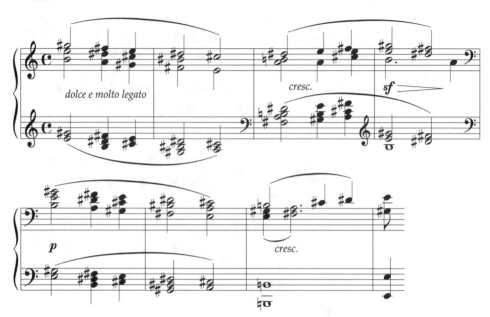

the nineteenth century's expanded orchestra and still sounds satisfyingly rich and full today.

The symphony can be called "Heroic" on other counts, including the grand proportions exemplified in its first movement. With the repeated exposition performed at a reasonable tempo, the movement runs approximately seventeen minutes, almost as long as the whole of an earlier Haydn or Mozart symphony. Beethoven achieves this length in a number of ways, especially by introducing two new motivic ideas in an expansive transition (mm. 37–82). He treats these ideas, along with the simple arpeggiated main theme (mm. 3–36) and secondary theme (mm. 83–99), to the same process of fragmentation as he did the main theme of the *Waldstein* Sonata, lending this first movement the same aura of excitement and forward motion.

The propulsive force of progressive fragmentation is most evident in the development of the first movement, and here too it helps Beethoven sustain a section of extraordinary length. Beethovenian developments typically fall into three parts: an initial bridge, a core, and a retransition (see Table 2.1). The bridge usually marks time and maneuvers into tonal position. Even though it participates in the developmental activity of fragmenting and recombining material from the exposition, it leaves the impression of "the calm before the storm." The core usually sees the storm break, and Beethoven marks it here with

TABLE 2.1   Schematic for the Development Section of Beethoven's Third Symphony

SECTION	EVENT	CONTENT (FROM EXPO.)	MEASURES
Bridge 1	short sequences	Mth, m. 45 ff.	152–185
Core	Model 1	Mth, m. 65 ff.	186–197
	sequence		198–209
	fragment (1 × 4)		210–213
	fragment (2 × 2)		214–217
	liquidation (2 × 1)		218–219
Bridge 1 (repeated)		m. 45 ff.	220–235
	Fughetta	m. 113 ff.	236–247
	Model 2	m. 113 ff.	248–253
	sequence		254–259
	sequence		260–265
	sequence		266–271
	fragment (2 × 2)		272–275
	liquidation		276–283
	Model 3	Mth varied	284–291
	sequence		292–299
	Model 4	Mth	300–311
	fragmentation (irregular)		312–321
	Sequence of Model 3 (cont.)		322–329
	fragment (3 × 2)		330–335
	liquidation		336–337
	Model 5	Mth	338–341
	sequence		342–345
	sequence		346–349
	sequence		350–353
	sequence		354–357
	sequence		358–361
	sequence		362–365
Retransition:	modulation and dominant pedal		366–397

the *fortissimo* entry of the basses and cellos playing a motive from the main theme in counterpoint to a motive from the transition. These initial eight measures, together with a soft tag (mm. 194–197), form a twelve-measure "model" repeated in sequence, then fragmented by omitting the initial eight measures, then dissolved into a series of one-measure units.

We can find this process of progressive fragmentation in almost all Beethoven developmental cores. But this core is remarkable for its large number of different models (five in all) plus a section of fughetta (m. 236 ff.). And one of the models even seems to present a "new melody" (m. 284 ff.) In fact,

Beethoven uses a customary sleight of hand here: As Leon Plantinga observes, the composer places a varied portion of the main theme in the second violins and cellos while posing a prominent countermelody in the first oboe. This latter melodic figure predominates and wins Beethoven new melodic space, even as he technically follows the "rules" of a coherent development. The episode is all the more prominent for appearing again in the coda (m. 581), which continues the process of progressive fragmentation. In short, we find an unusual breadth of creativity in the first-movement development of the *Eroica*.

The inner movements of the Third Symphony are equally impressive. The composer designates the second movement as a "funeral march," pairing it with the customary trio in major mode (m. 69 ff.) and introducing topics of the sacred and eternal into the symphony. Every strain of the march repeats with varied instrumentation, the most striking effect appearing in the form of the basses imitating muffled drums at the beginning. The introduction of such serious material into the symphony reinforces the weight of the first movement. The third movement presents a kinetic scherzo that touches on the hunt in its trio of three horns (m. 167). The vastly contrasting moods of each movement imbue the work with an almost novelesque air that would prompt later nineteenth-century commentators to supply the piece with a program.

The story of the *Eroica*'s dedication urged commentators even more toward a programmatic interpretation. The original title page bore an inscription to Napoleon Bonaparte, which Beethoven later crossed out. One story from his friend Ferdinand Ries runs that the composer decided against this dedication when the French consul crowned himself emperor. In fact, it appears more likely that Beethoven dedicated the symphony to Napoleon when the composer contemplated moving to Paris. After he dropped this plan, and when Prince Lobkowitz requested rights to the piece in exchange for 400 ducats (the first performance took place in the Lobkowitz palace), Beethoven changed the dedication to his Viennese patron. But Beethoven may well have intended Napoleon as the "hero" of the title.

The music itself, however, may prompt a different conclusion about the identity of the "hero" from what the title page does. The last movement consists of a theme and variations, based on a set for piano, op. 35. The theme, in turn, originated in Beethoven's well-received ballet, *The Creatures of Prometheus* (later published as op. 43). The opening of the symphonic finale, like the piano variations, presents a conundrum, however. For after the theatrical flourish in the full orchestra, we do not hear the melody of the ballet theme but soft, pizzicato strings. Beethoven pointed to this conceit proudly in a letter to the publisher of the piano variations: "The introduction . . . begins with the bass of the theme and eventually develops into two, three, and four parts; and not till then does the theme appear, which again cannot be called a variation." The composer gains two advantages from this unorthodox beginning. First, he wins the extra compositional option of varying the bass line as well as the melody of his original. Double variations using a melody and its countermelody were one of the composer's favorite techniques. (We have already caught a glimpse in the development of the first movement.) In addition, the conceit relates directly to a Promethean myth (the subject of the ballet theme) in which the Titan creates animals and eventually humankind from clay. Fashioned from musical clay and assembled piece by piece before our ears, the seemingly endless and far-flung variations in the Third Symphony confront us with the composer's infinite creativity. In the last movement he draws the analogy between Prometheus, defiant before the fate decreed by the gods, and the heroic artist, none other than Beethoven himself.

The ensuing symphonies of the "Heroic" period are no less remarkable than the Third. Each assumes a strikingly different character—the introspective Fourth (op. 60; 1806), the tightly organized, overpowering Fifth (op. 67; 1807–8), the peaceful, reflective Sixth (op. 68; 1808), the rhythmic Seventh (op. 92; 1811–12), and the witty, ironic Eighth (op. 93; 1812). Beethoven elevates the tendency to idiomatic originality—already prominent in the last decades of the eighteenth century—to an imperative in these works, playing it adroitly against the need for clarity of presentation (a tension that becomes a hallmark of the nineteenth century).

The Fifth Symphony may best typify this tension. On the one hand it presents an extremely clear and logical structure that follows the tradition of the Viennese symphony closely. Beethoven presents four movements (sonata-allegro, slow variations, dance, and closing sonata-allegro), each bound together by succinct motivic repetition and strongly articulated tonal motion. On the other hand the symphony features a highly charged rhetoric, a transparent interrelation of the movements by motivic variation, transgression of internal form (Beethoven joins the third and fourth movements), and a highly dramatic progress from minor to major mode in the course of the piece. None of these devices was entirely new (all of them appear in Haydn and Mozart), but Beethoven asserts them with a demonstrative vehemence that is truly arresting.

It was this vehement mode of expression that led E. T. A. Hoffmann (lawyer, composer, author, and critic) to pen a famous encomium extolling Beethoven as the quintessentially "Romantic" composer and linking his music to the aesthetics of German Idealism. Idealism (sometimes called "Platonic Idealism" or "Neo-Platonism") held that ideas and things spiritual were every bit as "real" as physical objects or phenomena. Not only were ideas just as "real" as physical objects, but also the world of ideas was both prior and superior to the physical world, which imperfectly made concrete the shapes and forms of the Ideal. Idealism was a cornerstone of the Romantic movement. And music became the most "Romantic" of all the arts, because it could not represent objects in the physical world literally in the way that painting or sculpture could, or describe them as writing could. In a review of the Fifth Symphony Hoffmann writes, "Thus Beethoven's instrumental music opens to us also the realm of the monumental and immeasurable." Though Hoffmann recognizes the Romantic elements in Haydn and Mozart, "Beethoven's music sets in motion the levers of fear, awe, horror, suffering, and wakens just that infinite longing which is the essence of Romanticism." Through this kind of association and promotion, Beethoven's symphonies became the foundation of Idealism in music during the first half of the nineteenth century.

It would be a mistake to assume that the superiority granted the Ideal world excluded reference to the physical world in instrumental music, as Beethoven's Sixth Symphony (the *Pastoral*) demonstrates so strikingly. Rather, music had the power to reveal directly the spiritual essence of physical objects and phenomena, something that may seem perplexing at first. Beethoven endowed each movement of the *Pastoral* Symphony with a programmatic title suggesting some rustic scene. And a few touches here and there—birdcalls in the first and second movements, a stereotypical thunderstorm in the fourth movement, shepherds piping in the fifth movement—actually hearken back to the eighteenth century's love of musical imitation. The constant drones recalling folk instruments (bagpipes, hurdy-gurdies), the relatively static phrase structures, and the slow harmonic motion all result from this coloristic urge. Yet the composer would insist that the pastoral nature of the symphony was "more a matter of feeling than of painting." And underneath the five suggestive portraits lies the classic four-movement scheme: sonata-allegro, slow cantabile, scherzo, and rondo finale (the fifth movement with the fourth as bridge and dramatic introduction). Beethoven follows his usual proclivity for motivic manipulation, and the piece is largely comprehensible in the usual abstract instrumental terms.

As a result of their strong individual character expressed in classic forms, the symphonies of the "Heroic" period became the core of the orchestral repertory. This is all the more remarkable for the fact that there were no regular orchestral concerts in Beethoven's Vienna. His symphonies had their first performances either in the palaces of the nobility or in "academies," one-time concerts organized specifically for the playing of a composer's new works. When regular subscription concerts did become widespread, Beethoven symphonies often constituted the test by which conductors and ensembles were measured.

Beethoven's quartets from the "Heroic" period also form a central part of the literature, though more as abstruse experiments in texture, in the coherence of themes, and in formal proportions. The composer dedicated the three string quartets, op. 59, 1–3 (1805–6), to the Russian ambassador, Count Razumovsky, and included Russian folk themes in several movements. But the quartets were far from "popular" in tone, and audiences and players regarded them as inaccessible at first acquaintance.

The most delightful quartet from this period—surely more approachable for the audiences at the newly fashionable subscription chamber concerts in Vienna—bears the sobriquet *Harp* (op. 74; 1809) for its episodes of plucked, arpeggiated chords in the first movement. There is something magical in the way that Beethoven transforms the head motive of the sentimental slow intro-duction by fits and starts into the forceful chords that announce the main theme. The first phrase of the main theme is not, in turn, what we might expect: Instead of a forwardly propulsive Satz, Beethoven presents a lyrically irregular period (antecedent phrase mm. 27–31, consequent mm. 31–35; see Example 2.3). The secondary theme, most often a period in first movements from this time, takes the form of a contrapuntal Satz (mm. 52–56). The most remarkable gesture, however, appears in the retransition (mm. 125–138), where arpeggios ripple through all the parts, progressively accelerating into the recapitulation (m. 139).

The remaining movements of op. 74 present equally entertaining episodes, from the heartfelt *Adagio ma non troppo* to the *Presto* scherzo, which begins rather diabolically, only to reveal a strongly good-humored vein. This movement links directly to the charming final set of variations. Together with the three quartets of op. 59 and the more somber op. 95 (nicknamed the *Serioso*), Beethoven's quartets from this period establish him as a subtle as well as audacious chamber-music composer. This reputation is confirmed by the sonatas for violin of the middle period, especially the celebrated *Kreutzer* Sonata, op. 47, and the string trios, including the famous *Archduke* Trio for piano, violin, and cello, op. 97.

Archduke Rudolph, the dedicatee of the trio, became Beethoven's highest-born piano student sometime in 1803 or 1804, and together with the Princes Lobkowitz and Kinsky, he guaranteed Beethoven's living with an annuity begin-ning in 1809. Beethoven seems to have returned Rudolph's special regard, for he also dedicated his last two piano concerti to the archduke, and even wrote a special piano sonata, *Les adieux* or *Das Lebewohl* (op. 81a), at his departure before the invading French in 1809. The thoughtful Fourth Piano Concerto (op. 58; 1805–6) opens quietly with the peculiarly Beethovenian conceit of using repeated chords in the piano as the main ingredient of a theme. The alter ego of this work, the Fifth Piano Concerto (the *Emperor,* op. 73; ca. 1809), also begins with the piano, this time turning the first movement upside down by placing a cadenza first. The boisterous gesture heralds a work that exemplifies the assertiveness often found in pieces from the "Heroic" period. This pair of piano concerti, together with the lovely Violin Concerto, op. 61, enshrined Beethoven permanently in the repertory for soloist and orchestra.

Beethoven's only opera, *Fidelio* (op. 72), did not, on the other hand, earn him a place among the ranks of great opera composers. It may seem odd to end a discussion of the "Heroic" period with this piece, and yet it typifies many quintes-sentially Beethovenian traits and also provides a prime instance of how artistic accomplishment and circumstance combined to create the "myth of Beethoven."

Fidelio (*or Conjugal Love*) has a less-than-perfect libretto by Joseph Sonn-leithner, who adapted a French "rescue" play by Jean-Nicolas Bouilly in which

EXAMPLE 2.3   Initial period from main theme of Beethoven's *Harp* Quartet, op. 74, 1809

Leonore, disguised as a man named Fidelio, succeeds after much travail in saving her unjustly imprisoned husband, Florestan. The lofty vision of marital fidelity appealed to Beethoven, who sought an idealized spouse all his life in vain. But the realization in verse offered an uncomfortable mixture of "low" characters (Rocco, Marzelline, Jaquino) with noble ones (Leonore, Florestan, Don Fernando) and a stereotypical villain (Don Pizzaro). *Fidelio* proceeds from the tradition of the *Singspiel* (Mozart's *Magic Flute* falls in this same genre) and has a Singspiel's stock players and spoken dialogue.

The opera had a star-crossed history of performance at first. It premiered in November of 1805 during the French occupation, when theater attendance was poor. Beethoven tried again with a revised libretto in March and April of 1806, but *Fidelio* still fell on deaf ears. The climate was much better in 1814 after the allied victory over Napoleon. With a libretto newly revised by Georg Friedrich Treitschke, the opera appeared on stage again in May to great acclaim. *Fidelio* went on to enjoy sixteen performances in 1814 and to become a strong political symbol for Germans through the rest of the nineteenth century and well into the twentieth. (*Fidelio* was chosen, for instance, to reopen many German opera houses after World War II.)

The theme of triumph over political oppression does receive glorious moments in *Fidelio*: the two prisoners' choruses at the end of each act ("Ah, what delight, to breathe lightly again in the free air" and "Hail to the day, hail to the hour"), Leonore's heroic two-part aria ending in a declaration of hope, Florestan's vision of his valiant wife at the beginning of Act II, and the couple's reunion duet at the end of the opera ("O inexpressible joy"). There is also some musical dross and clumsy versifying mixed in with *Fidelio*'s riveting passages. The opera's eventual success and later canonization depended much upon the symbolism first attached to it in the celebratory atmosphere surrounding the defeat of Napoleon. Beethoven, supported much of his life through the largesse of noble and imperial patrons, nonetheless succeeded with *Fidelio* in making himself an icon for egalitarian sentiments.

Beethoven's Late Period

In the years following 1812, Beethoven's productivity fell off markedly. The reasons were manifold. The war with Napoleon had led to the devaluation of the Austrian currency in 1811, which reduced the value of Beethoven's annuity. Moreover, one of the guarantors (Kinsky) died in 1812, and another (Lobkowitz) suspended payments for lack of money. There was a secret passion for an "Immortal Beloved," suggested to be the married Antonie Brentano in Maynard Solomon's biography of the composer. She left Vienna in the autumn of 1812, never to return again. Also during this period the composer became clinically deaf, making his last public appearance as a performer in January of 1815.

And finally, his brother Caspar Carl became seriously ill with tuberculosis, naming Beethoven as co-guardian of his son Karl in 1812. Caspar Carl died in late 1815, initiating a bitter struggle between his wife and his brother over Karl's ultimate disposition.

Amid all these private reversals Beethoven ironically achieved his greatest popularity with the wider public. The few pieces he composed, such as *Wellington's Victory* (op. 91; 1813), the *Namensfeier* Overture (op. 115; 1814), and *The Glorious Moment* cantata (op. 136; 1814), all traded on the patriotic sentiments following Austria's victory (as did the revival of *Fidelio*). The topicality and easy accessibility of these pieces garnered public acclaim and made Beethoven the quasi-official composer of the Congress of Vienna from 1814 to 1815. There he was presented by Count Razumovsky and the Archduke Rudolph to the assembled crowned heads of Europe and received tributes from them. All this recognition proved to be short-lived, however, and by the end of 1815 Beethoven had fallen out of favor with the public. Aside from patriotic pieces, he had little substantive new composition to place before an audience, except for the Piano Sonata, op. 101 (1816), and the song cycle *An die ferne Geliebte,* op. 98 (1815–16).

Slowly in 1817—still enmeshed in litigation over the guardianship of his nephew, so deaf he had to carry on conversations in writing, and drinking heavily—Beethoven nonetheless recovered his compositional footing. He began with a four-movement piano sonata, the *Hammerklavier* (op. 106), continued with a mass dedicated to Archduke Rudolph (the *Missa Solemnis*), and eventually produced the Ninth Symphony, the *Diabelli Variations,* five more string quartets, two more substantial piano sonatas, and a number of shorter pieces. Here again the "myth" of Beethoven finds some basis in fact. A composer who practiced his art in the face of profound deafness and constant illness drew the admiration of his contemporaries and later biographers. Indeed, audiences are still astonished by the scope and daring of these works.

Beethoven's late style exaggerates all the characteristic features of his earlier compositions. Where he tended to expand the length of instrumental works from the very outset of his career, his pieces often grew to gigantic proportions at the end of his life. Where he had experimented constantly with novel sonorities in his earlier works, his late works explored and even exceeded the extreme ranges of both voices and instruments. Where he had often included short sections in contrapuntal texture in his works before 1817, after 1817 fugues appear with regularity. Where he had transgressed the normal limits both of overall formal plans (three-movement sonatas, four-movement symphonies, and so forth) and of the internal "fixed" forms in his previous output, in his last years he called the basic premises of these conventions into question.

Many of these stylistic traits appear in the *Missa Solemnis* (op. 123). Beethoven began this piece in 1818 with the intent of celebrating the creation of Archduke Rudolph as cardinal in 1819, then his elevation to archbishop in 1820. But the mass became longer and longer, assuming such vast proportions in the end that the composer did not have it ready for publication until 1823. By that point it had become far too long to form a practical part of an actual church service. The Kyrie runs about nine minutes, the Gloria almost twenty, the Credo over twenty minutes, and even the simple Agnus Dei up to fifteen minutes. In fact, the first performance of selected portions took place in Beethoven's last "academy," a public concert arranged specifically for the composer's works.

The length of the *Missa Solemnis* resulted not so much from a departure from traditional form: Beethoven followed the long-standing practice in orchestral masses of breaking subsections of the text into individual "movements." Rather, Beethoven expanded the dramatic weight and length of individual episodes. This is particularly evident in the fugues that end both the Gloria and the Credo. In the latter, Beethoven devotes more than two-thirds of the movement to just one phrase of text, *et vitam venturi saeculi. Amen.* ("[And I look for the resurrection of the dead] *and the life of the world to come. Amen.*"). These words unfold over a double fugue (one subject for the text *et vitam venturi saeculi* paired with another for *amen;* see Example 2.4) that presents a veritable catalogue of contrapuntal devices. After the exposition (mm. 309–327), we find inversion (m. 337 ff) and stretto (m. 352 ff). Then after a dramatic pause comes a lengthy section in diminution (mm. 373–398) before a return to regular time over a pedal (m. 399). The voices finally coalesce into a unison statement of the subject (m. 416) that breaks into four-part harmony (m. 420). The movement ends with a long section of amens (including one for the soloists) and a delicate parting comment: the head of the *et vitam* subject descending quietly over a chord held *pianissimo* in the orchestra. This finish leaves no doubt that the composer anticipated "the life of the world to come."

A portion of the Agnus Dei receives an equally grand treatment, this time theatrical in nature. In the midst of the setting for *dona nobis pacem* ("grant us peace"), the sound of distant drums and trumpets (m. 164) intrudes, eliciting a plea in recitative from the alto and tenor soloists, "Lamb of God who taketh away the sins of the world, Lamb of God have mercy upon us." The militaristic

EXAMPLE 2.4   Double-fugue subjects from Beethoven's *Missa Solemnis,* op. 123, 1818–23

tone is unmistakable, a memory of the composer's suffering in the French invasion, and it renders the surrounding pleas for "peace" all the more poignant. This militaristic drama returns at measure 326 before yielding finally to the closing reiterations of "peace."

Beethoven reinforces the drama of the *Missa Solemnis* with extraordinary effects, including extremely high ranges for the singers, intricate orchestral textures, and much use of syncopated entrances. Gestures such as the full chorus entering *forte* on the weak beat with the word "kyrie" or the *a cappella* shout of "gloria" at the end of the second section of the mass leave no doubt that the composer was painting his subject in vivid colors. He meant this mass to be something like the musical equivalent of Michelangelo's grand design for the ceiling and altar of the Sistine Chapel. And Beethoven was justifiably proud, characterizing it to the music publisher C. F. Peters as "the *greatest* work I have composed so far."

We might expect a symphonic mass to rely on counterpoint and drama for effect, but these same devices mark the late piano sonatas as well. Two of them, opp. 106 and 110, end with substantial fugues, a reference in the nineteenth century not only to learned but also to sacred style. And in the last sonata, op. 111 (1821–22), again dedicated to the Archduke Rudolph, Beethoven combines drama and counterpoint in the first movement to stunning effect. The opening of the slow introduction (see Example 2.5) comes as something of a shock, with an initial leap downward of a diminished seventh plunging yet an octave further into the lowest extremes of the piano's range. The loud diminished seventh chord that follows hardly provides reassurance, and the perfectly normal resolution, fading softly to the tonic chord, only to erupt again loudly in the dominant is equally unsettling. The slow introduction continues with these contrasting dynamic extremes until we reach the main theme (mm. 19–35). Its head motive sounds like a fugue theme, though it actually begins a wild, irregular Satz. But come the transition (mm. 35–49), Beethoven does treat this motive contrapuntally, and he extends this conceit further with a section of fughetta on the subject in the development, measure 76. Yet another bit of drama comes in the second key-area (m. 50 ff), which falls in the flat submediant (A-flat) instead of the mediant. After this stormy first movement, we expect a substantial group to follow, but the composer concludes with an extended variation set that encompasses all the moods of what would be the remaining movements.

Departure from the usual number of movements also characterizes a number of the late string quartets. Of the five, only opp. 127 and 135 present the usual plan. And Beethoven invested a good deal of serious counterpoint in all these quartets, the most extreme example of which appears in op. 130 (1825–26). The final fugue for this quartet was so lengthy that Beethoven ultimately detached it and published it separately as the *Great Fugue* (op. 133). Even the more modestly proportioned op. 135 (1826) concludes with a movement based on the canon *Es muß sein* ("It must be," an inside musical joke).

EXAMPLE 2.5   Opening of slow introduction from Beethoven's Sonata for Piano, op. 111, 1821–22

We cannot invariably equate elaborate counterpoint, a large number of movements, and substantial length with unrelenting earnest in the late quartets. Beethoven sometimes indulges irony in these pieces, some of it pointed, some whimsical. We can find no better example of Beethovenian irony than the String Quartet, op. 131. The composer begins with what listeners will take as a chromatic slow introduction, until it develops into a tortured fugue that places all the instruments in the extremes of their ranges. Only after spending some time on this precarious tonal footing do we realize that this is a freestanding movement. It would seem to demand an extremely weighty sonata form for the next act, but instead Beethoven gives us what usually comes as the *lieto fine* (lighthearted ending): a sonata-rondo. The main theme assumes a suitably jaunty tone, whereas the second theme (sometimes called "the couplet" in this formal type) is aggressive and bumptious (see Table 2.2). There is a minimal development after the repeat of the main theme (see Table 2.2), and in true sonata-rondo fashion Beethoven moves directly to the couplet in the recapitulation, ending with the varied main theme in the coda.

The third movement of op. 131 is no movement at all, but serves in fits and starts only as transition to the fourth movement, a glorious theme and variations. The fifth movement presents a madcap scherzo that threatens perpetual motion in the vehemence of its action. (The trio repeats twice, with hints of a third time before Beethoven restrains the hyperactive performers.) The sixth movement is another dead end, leading only to the seventh. This finale, far from a *lieto fine,* puts on the aggressive and forbidding face that should have followed the first movement: The material that ends the main theme (mm. 22–25) is a fairly obvious inversion of the first movement's fugue subject.

A slow introduction that becomes a whole movement, reversal of the usual form and weight of the outer sonata-allegro movements, an unending scherzo,

TABLE 2.2   Schematic for op. 131, mvt. 2

SECTION	*SUBSECTION*	*KEY*	*RONDO SCHEME*	*MEASURES*
Exposition				
	Mth	I	A	1–24
	transition	X		24–59
	Couplet (Sth)	V	B	60–83
Development				
	Bridge (Mth)	I	A′	84–95
	Model	X	C	96–99
	sequence			100–103
	sequence			104–107
	fragmentation (3 × 1)			108–110
	dissolution			111–113
Recapitulation				
	transition	X		114–132
	Couplet (Sth)	I	B′	133–156
Coda				
	Mth	I	A″	157–198

two pseudomovements—this is the stuff of irony. Beethoven's contemporary, Friedrich Schlegel, might have been speaking of op. 131 when he wrote, "Irony is the form paradox takes. Everything that is at once great and good is paradoxical." It is not ordinary irony, but Romantic irony, which can be wry but aims at something more than mere jest. Beethoven's late quartets often present a series of reversals and incongruities that Schlegel might regard as leading beyond the mundane to the unresolved infinite.

Beethoven certainly had the infinite and the sacred in mind when he wrote his most famous late work, the Ninth Symphony, op. 125 (1822–24). The tone of this mammoth symphony is not ironic, however, but heroic. The composer's master strategy resembles that of his Fifth Symphony. The forbidding mood of the first and second movements and the pensive mood of the third resolve in the triumphant fourth movement. Another similarity to the Fifth Symphony comes in the pronounced thematic cyclicity of op. 125, where the head motive of the first movement's main theme carries over to the head motive of the scherzo, which in turn becomes the head motive for the theme of the third movement (see Example 2.6).

When we glance back across the span of Beethoven's career, we can see him using the same basic techniques from beginning to end. The late works simply extend the scope and increase the intensity of Beethoven's tried-and-true strategies. The progression from minor to major mode increases its psychological impact because of the length of the three movements and also the dramatic conceit that begins the fourth movement. The composer opens here with a shocking doubly diminished chord. He then proceeds to replay the initial phrases from each of the previous movements, cutting them short after only a few bars. He punctuates this sequential reminiscence with an astonishing recitative, not for voice initially, but for the cellos and basses. Only later when we hear this same recitative sung by a bass soloist, do we understand explicitly that the composer is *rejecting* the relatively melancholy mood of the first three movements ("O friends, not these tones; rather let us join our voices more pleasantly, and more joyfully!").

The music that follows the sequential rejection of the previous movements consists of an elaborate theme and variations that outdoes even the last movement of the *Eroica*. As he did for the variations for the Third Symphony, Beethoven also composed a kind of preliminary study, in this case the *Choral Fantasy*, op. 80. Written for solo piano, orchestra, and chorus, this piece also begins with an amorphous instrumental introduction that coalesces into a theme, varied first in the orchestra, then in the orchestra and chorus. The theme (Example 2.7) bears striking resemblance to the hymnlike strains of the Ninth Symphony's last movement (Example 2.8).

Although Beethoven had rehearsed previously the movement from instruments to voices used in the Ninth, there was no precedent for including chorus in the context of a symphony. The sonic effect is striking, not the least because

EXAMPLE 2.6   Thematic cyclicity in themes from mvts. 1–3 of Beethoven's Ninth Symphony, op. 125, 1822–24

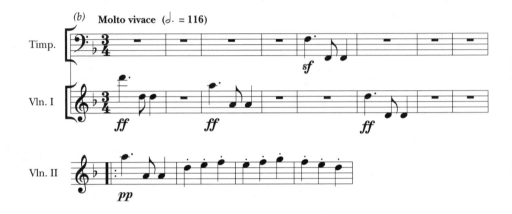

the composer often uses the voices in extreme ranges. And what begins as a seemingly normal set of ornamental variations devolves almost into a cantata (in fact, some nineteenth-century commentators label op. 125 a symphony-cantata). The progress of the variations runs its usual course (see Table 2.3) until the words "Seid umschlungen, Millionen" ("Be embraced, ye millions"), at which point Beethoven introduces a "new theme." It underscores a central point: goodwill of a "loving Father" toward his creation, the ultimate "joy" in Friedrich Schiller's hierarchical list. Of course, the "new theme" turns out to be a countermelody for another variation of the hymn (var. 12), connecting it to both the "new theme" in the first-movement development of the *Eroica* and the double theme and variations in that symphony's finale. As in the Third Symphony, the double theme and variations is linked here, now explicitly, to the sacred.

EXAMPLE 2.7   Beginning of variation theme from Beethoven's *Choral Fantasy,* op. 80, 1808

EXAMPLE 2.8   Beginning of variation theme from Beethoven's Ninth Symphony, op. 125, 1822–24

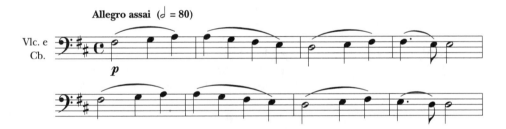

The Ninth Symphony encapsulates the intersection of Beethoven's music with the "myth of Beethoven." On the one hand it displays the composer's command of dramatic musical psychology, his proclivity for striking sonic effects, and the kind of musical insistence that replays one motivic idea through three themes and can extend variations over nine hundred measures. On the other hand we have a very public assertion of music's sacred nature and the composer's divine creativity. We stand in awe, as well we might, of a profoundly deaf composer who can write a hymn to joy. Here is the nexus of the Beethovenian myth and the source of inspiration for Klinger's statue.

However *we* regard the myth of Beethoven, later generations of nineteenth- and twentieth-century composers and writers believed it. In the arena of the

TABLE 2.3   Schematic for op. 125, mvt. IV

SECTION	CONTENT	MEASURES
Introduction		
	Dissonant fanfare	1–7
	cello-bass recit.	8–16
	Fanfare	17–25
	cello-bass recit.	25–29
	Quote of mvt. I	30–37
	cello-bass recit.	38–47
	Quote of mvt. II	48–55
	cello-bass recit.	56–62
	Quote of mvt. III	63–64
	cello-bass recit.	65–76
	Fragment of hymn	77–80
	cello-bass recit.	81–91
Theme and Variations		
Theme	Hymn tune in cello-bass	92–115
Variation 1	Hymn tune in viola, cellos; counterpoint in bassoon	116–139
Variation 2	Hymn tune in violins	140–163
Variation 3	Winds play hymn and codetta	164–207
	Fanfare returns	208–215
	"O Freunde," bass recit.	216–236
Variation 4	"Freude, schöne," hymn for bass, chorus	237–268
Variation 5	"Wem der große," hymn for soloists, chorus	269–296
Variation 6	"Freude trinken," hymn ornamented by soloists, chorus	297–320
modulation	"Und der Cherub"	321–330
Variation 7	Hymn as Turkish march for orchestra	331–374
Variation 8	Turkish march with countermelody in tenor, male chorus	331–431
Variation 9	Hymn tune as fugal subject, orchestra	432–542
Variation 10	"Freude schöne," hymn as ornamented chorale in chorus	543–594
Variation 11	"Seid umschlungen," countertheme, chorus	595–654
Variation 12	"Freude schöne" and "Seid umschlungen," hymn and countertheme in fugue, chorus	655–729
modulation	"Ihr stürzt," chorus	730–762
Variation 13	"Freude schöne," hymn ornamented by soloists	763–842
Coda	Free combination of "Seid umschlungen" and "Freude schöne" in chorus	843–940

string quartet, Beethoven's accomplishments, especially the late works, actually intimidated nineteenth-century composers. Few of his successors produced many quartets, and none of them attempted anything so audacious as op. 131. Beethoven's piano sonatas became the classical focus of several theoretical systems, including those of Adolf Bernhard Marx, Heinrich Schenker, and Arnold Schoenberg (by way of Erwin Ratz). Beethoven symphonies and overtures became touchstones of the orchestral literature. (The critic-composer Robert Schumann drew an analogy between Beethoven's importance to orchestral literature and Shakespeare's significance to drama.) The composer's insistent motivic working and repetition, his expansion of sonic color, and his manipulation of structure rippled not only through purely instrumental music but also through the realm of opera by way of Wagner. Finally, Beethoven's implicit assertions (through constant musical reference) about music as profound, even sacred thought and about the divine creativity of artists played a large role in determining the way in which music and musicians would be regarded. And so the "myth" of Beethoven became Beethoven's legacy, the reason why his life and works form the logical starting point for an introduction to nineteenth-century music.

SCHUBERT

Just as Klinger's statue of a godlike, philosophical Beethoven encapsulates long-held beliefs about the artist, so Gustav Klimt's *An die Musik* (Figure 2.2; 1899, destroyed in 1945) portrays Franz Schubert (1797–1828) in the way tradition has enshrined *him*. In this and many other depictions, we see the composer seated at or near a piano in a drawing room amid a gathering of friends (often accompanying a singer). He is the icon of what Germans call *Hausmusik*, that is, music for the home. The stereotype entails a nice set of oppositions between the two famous composers living concurrently in Vienna. On one side we have Beethoven writing a demonstrative, assertive music for a vast public enthralled by his commanding artistic persona. On the other side we have Schubert writing introspective, delicate music for an intimate, select audience entranced by his subtlety.

We would do well to remind ourselves that such oppositions are historical constructions that sometimes exaggerate the facts. Had Beethoven died at the same age as Schubert (thirty-one), we would have a group of remarkable piano pieces, two piano concerti, some chamber music, including just one set of fairly conservative string quartets, one symphony, and a number of songs. Schubert, on the other hand, found time in his short life to write seven complete symphonies, two complete operas, a number of Singspiele, a good number of string quartets, many large-scale pieces for piano, and over six hundred songs. The

Figure 2.2   *An die Musik* by Gustav Klimt, 1899 (formerly in the collection of August Lederer, destroyed 1945). Courtesy Art Resource, NY; photo: Erich Lessing.

Austrian poet Grillparzer's famous epitaph on Schubert's grave speaks only the truth: "The art of music entombed here a rich possession, but even fairer hopes." Who knows what Schubert might have composed had he lived.

The stereotype of Schubert excelling at music for more intimate settings contains, however, a grain of truth that we must take seriously. Schubert's symphonies are not performed with the same frequency as Beethoven's, nor did they exert the same influence as the older composer's. Schubert's operas appear rarely on stage, and his string quartets are not regarded as landmarks in the genre, however beautiful they might be. But Schubert's songs provided the foundation of the nineteenth-century *Lied,* and his various pieces for piano served as models for several ensuing generations of composers. Moreover, much of Schubert's music making *did* transpire in the surroundings of educated middle-class homes, whose owners aspired to cultural and political ascendancy in nineteenth-century Germany and Austria. The "judgment of history" is never *completely* unfair.

Schubert's Background

Franz Peter Schubert was a native of Vienna whose father, Franz Theodor Florian Schubert, was a schoolteacher (later headmaster) and whose mother worked before marriage in domestic service. The son demonstrated a proclivity for music early, and his talents were so exceptional that he became a choirboy in the imperial court *cappella* and enrolled in the Imperial-Royal City School (*Stadtkonvikt*) at the age of eight. There he studied conventional grammar-school subjects in addition to music; he did well in all areas and excelled in violin as well as composition. His talent was such that Salieri supervised his instruction, and it was he who encouraged the deep-seated lyricism in Schubert's compositions.

In 1812 Schubert's voice broke, and though he continued at the *Stadtkonvikt* for another year, he eventually succumbed to family persuasion and trained as an elementary teacher, signing on as a master in his father's school in 1814. All the while, Schubert continued to compose (under Salieri's guidance until 1816), and though he taught school until 1818, he came increasingly to resent the time it took away from his music. In the summer of 1818 the composer accepted a position at the Esterházy residence in Hungary as music tutor to Count Johann's two daughters, and when the family returned to Vienna in November, Schubert came with them. He continued to give them private lessons, but he never returned to teaching school, and for the remaining decade of his life he eked out a fairly slim existence on the sales of his compositions, gifts that came from various dedications, and a handful of commissions. He lived variously with friends, sometimes at home with his family, sometimes in rented rooms by himself.

In early adulthood Schubert apparently contracted syphilis (the disease that seems to have caused his death), and he spent the remainder of his years in various stages of ill health, rallying from time to time and composing all the while. During the period of the early 1820s he embarked on a large number of pieces for the theater, including two Singspiele (*Die Zwillingsbrüder* and *Die Verschworenen*) and a number of operas (two of which he completed, *Alfonso und Estrella* and *Fierabras,* neither of which was produced in the composer's lifetime). He continued to compose a very large number of songs and began to contemplate a more independent orchestral idiom in the intriguing *Unfinished* Symphony (D. 759).* Toward the end of his life, in the later 1820s, he gave a glimpse of the composer he might have become in a number of string quartets (including *Death and the Maiden,* D. 810), several piano trios, an impressive string quintet (D. 956), a large series of weighty piano sonatas, and a masterful symphony in C major (*The Great,* D. 944). Most of these pieces remained unpublished

---

*The "D" stands for Otto Erich Deutsch's catalogue of the composer's works.

during his lifetime and took years to become known. For the pieces he did publish while alive, such as the song cycles *Schöne Müllerin* (D. 795) and *Winterreise* (D. 911), Schubert enjoyed good notices and recognition in German-speaking countries. His reputation was beginning to extend more widely when he died.

Schubert led a somewhat gypsy existence during his later years, socializing and making music in a circle of close friends, including the poet Johann Mayerhofer, the singer Johann Vogl, the painter Moritz von Schwind, Josef von Spaun, and Franz von Schober. There may have been a homoerotic component to Schubert's acquaintances: He lived for a time with both Mayerhofer and Schober, some have suggested as a lover. But whatever the exact nature of the friends' physical relationships, they surrounded the composer with an intimate intellectual climate in which literature and music were valued highly. Mayerhofer initiated Schubert into this cultural circle dedicated to the combined pursuit of the arts, education, and self-improvement. Among their readings of literature and aesthetic debates, the friends organized a series of "Schubertiads" devoted to the playing and singing of Schubert's compositions. In this atmosphere chamber music, music for piano, and songs particularly flourished.

Schubert's Songs

Today we hear German songs performed by professional singers in concert halls, but this practice developed relatively late in the nineteenth century. Although public concerts might include a few isolated numbers mixed in with orchestral music, recitals consisting exclusively of songs did not appear regularly until the 1870s or 1880s. Composers fashioned their songs, instead, for talented amateurs who sang them in the home for the entertainment of family and friends. The performers and the listeners usually came from the educated middle classes whose members were, like the members of Schubert's circle, well read in the literature of their day. Just about this time German literature underwent a remarkable efflorescence in the works of Goethe, the Schlegels, Tieck, Wackenroder, Novalis, Hoffmann, the brothers Grimm, Heine, and Rückert, among countless others. Influential translations of writers such as Shakespeare, Sir Walter Scott, and Robert Burns also appeared during Schubert's lifetime. Much of the poetry set by Schubert would already have been familiar to the purchasers of his songs, and this was part of their appeal.

With the new wealth of distinguished German literature came a change in the style of song. During the late eighteenth and very early nineteenth centuries, composers such as Zelter and Reichardt had cultivated a deliberately accessible style, with relatively narrow vocal range and very simple accompaniment meant to be played by amateurs of very modest talents. The *Lied im Volkston* ("song in popular style") constituted the aesthetic ideal; it aimed to articulate verse in accurate rhythm with a minimum of melodic embellishment or interference from the accompaniment. *Lieder* (songs) had originated as folk music, after all. The new poetry by authors such as Goethe, Schiller, and Heine, though grounded in the folkloric past of the Lied, wore a more artful face that gradually elicited more elaborate settings to bring out the subtleties of mood and meaning.

The new value placed on music added to the demands of the new poetry, eliciting what the Swiss composer and aesthetician Hans Georg Nägeli called the "polyrhythmic song" in the *Allgemeine musikalische Zeitung* (*General Musical News*), a weekly music newspaper popular with professionals and amateurs alike. By "polyrhythmic" Nägeli meant that the meter and stress of the poem, the melody, and the accompaniment all had the capability of proceeding independently. They could work to reinforce one another, or they could follow separate tracks, creating a kaleidoscope of possible interpretations. In this way each composer could provide a different "reading" of a poet's verse. Moreover, Nägeli insisted that such an interaction could form a new artistic entity transcending the poetry, melody, or accompaniment by itself.

Though Nägeli had not heard of Schubert when he wrote his article in 1817, he might have been describing the twenty-year-old composer's songs. Indeed, Schubert's "Gretchen am Spinnrade" (D. 118), written in 1814 when the composer was only seventeen, already displays some qualities of "polyrhythmic song." The text comes from Goethe's *Faust*, a tale of a scholar who makes a pact with the devil in exchange for knowledge and youth. The rejuvenated Dr. Faust attracts women, and Gretchen has fallen in love with him. Her song reveals internal thoughts and feelings to which we become privy, the classic relationship between the persona (the fictional speaker) and the reader of a Lied. The infatuated girl sits at her spinning wheel preoccupied with the handsome man:

Meine Ruh' ist hin,	My peace is gone,
Mein Herz ist schwer;	My heart is heavy,
Ich finde sie nimmer	I shall find it never,
Und nimmermehr.	Never again.
Wo ich ihn nicht hab'	When he is not here,
Ist mir das Grab,	It's like the grave,
Die ganze Welt	The whole world
Ist mir vergällt.	tastes bitter.
Mein armer Kopf	My poor mind
Ist mir verrückt,	Is deranged,
Mein armer Sinn	My poor wits
Ist mir zerstrückt.	Are distracted.
Meine Ruh' ist hin,	My peace is gone,
usw.	etc.

Nach ihm nur schau' ich	I look only for him
Zum Fenster hinaus,	Out the window,
Nach ihm nur geh' ich	Seeking only him do I
Aus dem Haus.	Leave the house.
Sein hoher Gang,	His lofty bearing,
Sein' ed'le Gestalt,	His noble form,
Sein Mundes Lächeln,	His smiling mouth,
Sein Augen Gewalt.	The force of his gaze.
Und seiner Rede	And his speech's
Zauberfluss,	Magic flow,
Sein Händedruck,	The press of his hands,
Und ach, sein Kuss!	And oh, his kiss!
Meine Ruh' ist hin,	My peace is gone,
usw.	etc.
Mein Busen drängt	My bosom yearns
Sich nach ihm hin;	For him;
Ach, dürft ich fassen	Oh, if I could but clasp
Und halten ihn,	And hold him.
Und küssen ihn,	And kiss him,
So wie ich wollt',	The way I'd like,
An seine Küssen	Of his kisses
Vergehen sollt'!	I might die.

A straightforward setting of this text would involve composing one stanza's worth of music declaiming the rhythm of the verse accurately and capturing the basic mood. This music would then repeat over and over for each successive stanza.

Schubert adopts anything but this straightforward approach to Goethe's poetry. To be sure, the composer does choose a very natural iambic declamation of the meter, and he devotes four measures of music to each couplet in accordance with the regularity of the syllable count and rhyme scheme of the verse. But although he preserves the separation of Gretchen's refrain ("Meine Ruh' ist hin"), Schubert runs the other stanzas together. And taking his cue from the refrain, the composer forms the song into three main sections. The music for the refrain returns each time, but the rest of the melody never repeats exactly, revealing Gretchen's disquiet.

Schubert interprets the young girl's litany on Faust's appearance in the second grouping as growing excitement ("his bearing, his figure, his smile, his glance, his speech"), which leads the melody and harmony into more distant chromatic realms that culminate in physical contact ("his touch, his kiss!"). At this last ecstatic thought the musical pulse ceases, giving way briefly to recitative and breaking the meter of the verse entirely.

Schubert saves the greatest intensity for the third grouping, in which Gretchen fantasizes about embracing Faust and then "dying of his kisses." The composer repeats the last stanza, then reiterates its last couplet yet again, building gradually to the melody's highest point on the word "vergehen" ("die"), the musical and erotic climax of the song. The first couplet of the refrain then trails off after the climax has passed and the dream fades.

As for Schubert's accompaniment, it follows its own "rhythm." Many commentators interpret the constant repetition and cyclicity of the right-hand figure as a musical metaphor for the motion of Gretchen's spinning wheel, and there is certainly an element of this. But more important (and less mundane) is the impression of incessant unrest left by this figure. Here we find the erotic agitation of adolescent fantasy portrayed by an adolescent composer. The combination of poetry, melody, and accompaniment does more than declaim Goethe's text, it presents one possible *reading* in shifting layers of motion and emphasis. Schubert's interpretation gained much notice in the parlors of Germany and then western Europe, where it became one of his most celebrated works.

Ellen's "Hymn to the Virgin" from Sir Walter Scott's *The Lady of the Lake* in a translation by Adam Storck, also known as "Ave Maria!" (D. 839; 1825), elicits quite a different response from Schubert. Scott may have been the most popular author of the early nineteenth century. His novels dealing with medieval English history (such as *Ivanhoe*) and his epic poems about Scottish history (such as *The Lady of the Lake*) took Europe and America by storm. Many composers wrote overtures and operas on subjects taken from Scott, and the song texts appearing in his novels and epic poems received countless settings almost as soon as the literature appeared in print. In choosing texts from the epic poem *Lady of the Lake*, Schubert took advantage of middle-class fashion not only in Germany but also in English-speaking countries: He had both the German translation and the English original published in the first edition of these songs. The publishers of songs were in business for profit, after all, and they rewarded composers handsomely for their efforts in this genre (a symphony or a string quartet would fetch nowhere near so much per page of manuscript)—Lieder sold well.

The accompanimental figure for the right hand of the piano in this song tells a tale about the cultural background expected of those who bought the sheet music. At first it seems that Schubert has simply adopted a pattern of chordal arpeggiation to sustain the piano's tone under the long vocal line, and indeed the figure does accomplish that goal (see Example 2.9). But a reader familiar with the poem would hear another reference in this figure: Ellen Douglas has fled with her father to a haunted grotto, the Goblin Cave, where her prayer is accompanied by a family bard:

> But hark! what mingles in the strain?
>   It is the harp of Allan-bane,
> That wakes its measure slow and high,
>   Attuned to sacred minstrelsy.
> What melting voice attends the strings?
>   'T is Ellen, or an angel sings.

EXAMPLE 2.9   Harplike accompaniment from "Ellen's Gesang III" by Schubert, D. 839, 1825

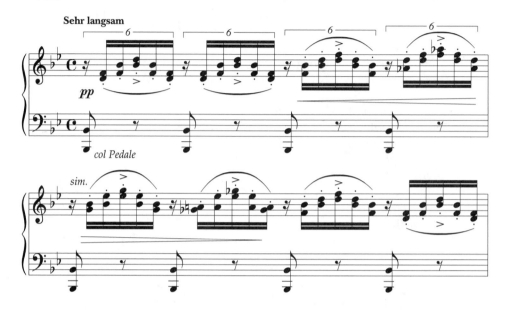

XXIX
Hymn to the Virgin

Ave Maria! maiden mild!
Listen to a maiden's prayer!
Thou canst hear though from the wild,
Thou canst save amid despair.
Safe may we sleep beneath thy care,
Though banished, outcast, and reviled—
Maiden! hear a maiden's prayer;
Mother, hear a suppliant child!
            Ave Maria!

Ave Maria! Jungfrau mild!
Erhöre einer Jungfrau flehen!
Aus diesem Felsen starr und wild,
Soll mein Gebet zu dir hin wehen.
Wir schlafen sicher bis zum Morgen,
Ob Menschen noch so grausam sind—
O Jungfrau, sieh der Jungfrau sorgen;
O Mutter, hör ein bittend Kind!
            Ave Maria!

The figuration in the piano's right hand traces a literal arpeggiation, an imitation of the harp. For good measure Schubert begins with a reminder of the harper's folkish caste, a pedal note (common symbol for *Volkston* in western European music).

To establish the "sacred" nature of Ellen's "angel" voice, Schubert floats her melody like a cantus firmus over the harp's accompaniment. The slow melodic motion also helps to smooth out irregularities in the German translation (mostly iambic) and accommodates the even more irregular English verse (predominantly trochaic). Responding to the word "Hymn" in the title, Schubert sets the poem strophically, at the same time marking the separate sentences formed by each quatrain with a break. In a particularly graceful gesture, he carries the accompanimental "harp" figure over into the voice for the climax of the first quatrain (see Example 2.10). The various elements of poetry, melody, and accompaniment can run in harmony with one another as well as in counterpoint. In "Ave Maria!" the composer paints a backdrop for Scott's verse that provides an intertextual experience for the knowledgeable reader.

Lieder contain the *internal* thoughts and feelings of the persona, and as such do not tell of external events. But poets at the beginning of the nineteenth century discovered that if they placed several Lieder in a grouping, they could imply a narrative. In this way they created song plays (*Liederspiele*) or song cycles (*Liederzyklen* or *Liederkreise*). In 1815–16 Beethoven tried his hand at a very simple one of these, *An die ferne Geliebte* (op. 98), which records the thoughts of a

EXAMPLE 2.10   Vocal imitation of arpeggiation from "Ellen's Gesang III" by Schubert, D. 839, 1825

man yearning for his beloved far away. The group of six songs implies no narrative, but it does feature thematic cyclicity à la Beethoven and a good deal of very lovely melody in *Volkston*. Schubert's cycles are both more elaborate in narrative structure and sophisticated in dramatic contrast. They include *Die schöne Müllerin* (D. 795; 1823) and *Winterreise* (D. 911; 1827).

Die schöne Müllerin (*The Beautiful Maid of the Mill*) has a stock plot about a young man who sets out into the world to find his fortune. The story unfolds in a series of twenty-three Lieder plus an epilogue and a prologue, all appearing in Wilhelm Müller's *Gedichte aus dem hinterlassenen Papieren eines Waldhornisten* ("Poems from the posthumous papers of a horn-player"). Schubert omitted both epilogue and prologue, plus three poems, to tighten the "action" of the implied narrative. The outcome of this "Wanderer" song cycle is tragic: The young man follows a brook, comes upon a mill where he is apprenticed, and falls in love with the miller's daughter, who jilts him in favor of a hunter. The apprentice then drowns himself in sorrow. Of course, we see only glimpses of various internal feelings elicited from the young man by these events. For instance, the text does not narrate the apprentice's drowning, merely expresses his yearning for "the cool peace down there" (no. 19), which is answered by "The Brook's Lullaby," singing the young man "to sleep" (no. 20).

In setting the songs, Schubert uses musical devices to increase the coherence of the implied narrative. Consistency of texture provides one kind of connection: A restless, sixteenth-note figuration pervades many of the numbers, implying the incessant motion of the brook that winds as a thread through the story (to the point that it becomes an actual player in it). A loose tonal organization also provides coherence and a sense of progression—most of the songs revolve around B-flat major, G minor (relative minor), G major (parallel), C major (with G as dominant), C minor (parallel), A minor (relative of C), A major (parallel), and D (A as dominant, dominant of G). The two large departures from this net of relationships come in no. 6 ("The Curious Man," B major), in which the apprentice asks the brook to reveal his beloved's feelings, and in no. 20 ("The Brook's Lullaby," E major) where the brook soothes his final repose. Schubert means to emphasize these by separating them tonally from their surrounding, and also highlights their underlying connection through a dominant-tonic relationship. Nature, represented by the brook, proves the best confidant and comforter, a common idea in the Romantic literature of Schubert's day. Schubert also links the disparate, internal episodes of *Die schöne Müllerin* by maintaining a constant *Volkston* throughout. He casts most of the songs in strictly strophic form, provides simple tunes, and fits them with hurdy-gurdy accompaniments. Here again the addition of music to poetry creates a new artistic whole that is more than and different from the poetry or the music by itself.

Whereas cycles of Lieder could suggest a narrative, a different variety of song, the ballad, actually tells a story. Nineteenth-century composers generally distinguished strictly between the Lied, which records the internal thoughts and feelings of a single individual, and the ballad, which involves at least two or more personae. Because ballads usually feature characters speaking lines as well as a narrator, composers of the "polyrhythmic" song often treated this genre dramatically.

Schubert's most famous ballad, "Der Erlkönig" ("The Elven King," D. 328, version d; 1815), takes its text from an actual theatrical work, *Die Fischerin,* a Singspiel by Goethe. The playwright encapsulates a tenet of Romanticism in this text, namely, that the spiritual world is every bit as real as, perhaps superior to, the physical world. The child sees and hears the evil spirit who has come to abduct him, but the father explains away each of his son's anxieties by means of some natural, physical phenomenon. Only toward the end does the father comprehend vaguely what clearly terrifies his son; but he recognizes the reality of the supernatural danger too late.

"Der Erlkönig"

Wer reitet so spät durch Nacht und Wind?	Who rides so late through night and wind?
Es ist der Vater mit seinem Kind;	It is a father with his child.
Er hat den Knaben wohl in dem Arm.	He has the child right in his arms.
Er fasst ihn sicher, er hält ihn warm.	He holds him fast, he keeps him warm.
Mein Sohn, was birgst du so bang dein Gesicht?	My son, why do you hide your face so anxiously?
Siehst, Vater, du den Erlkönig nicht?	Do you not see, Father, the Erlking?
Den Erlenkönig mit Kron' und Schweif?	The Erlking with crown and train?
Mein Sohn, es ist ein Nebelstreif.	My son, it's just a patch of fog.
"Du liebes Kind, komm, geh mit mir!	"You lovely child, come away with me!
Gar schöne Speile spiel' ich mit dir;	Quite lovely games will I play with you;
Manch bunte Blumen sind an dem Strand,	Many-hued flowers are on that shore,
Meine Mutter hat manch gülden Gewand."	My mother has many golden robes."
Mein Vater, mein Vater, und hörest du nicht,	My father, my father, do you not hear,
Was Erlenkönig mir leise verspricht?	What the Erlking softly promises me?
Sei ruhig, bleibe ruhig, mein Kind,	Be quiet, stay quiet, my child,
In dürren Blätter säuselt der Wind.	It is the wind rustling in the dry leaves.
"Willst, feiner Knabe, du mit mir gehn?	"Will you go, fine lad, with me?
Meine Töchter sollen dich warten schon;	My daughters will await you eagerly;
Meine Töchter führen den nächtlichen Reih'n,	My daughters lead the nightly reel,
Und wiegen und tanzen und singen dich ein."	And will sway and dance and sing when you come."

Mein Vater, mein Vater, und siehst du nicht dort	My father, my father, do you not see there
Erlkönigs Töchter am düstern Ort?	Erlking's daughters in that dark place?
Mein Sohn, mein Sohn, ich seh' es genau:	My son, my son, I see it exactly:
Es scheinen die alten Weiden so grau.	Those old willows seem so gray.
"Ich liebe dich, mich reizt deine schöne Gestalt;	"I love you, I'm charmed by your lovely figure;
Und bist du nicht willig, so brauch' ich Gewalt";	And if you're unwilling, then I'll use force";
Mein Vater, mein Vater, jetzt fasst er mich an!	My father, my father, now he's grabbed me!
Erlkönig hat mir ein Leids gethan!	Erlking has hurt me!
Dem Vater grauset's, er reitet geschwind,	The father is horrified, he rides swiftly,
Er hält in den Armen das ächzende Kind,	He holds in his arms the groaning child,
Erreicht den Hof mit Müh' und Noth;	And reaches the courtyard with effort in need;
In seinem Armen das Kind war todt.	In his arms the child lay dead.

Some commentators in Schubert's day labeled this ballad a "cantata," and the composer himself accompanied a performance where several singers took various "parts." In fact, each character has a different set of melodic motives. The composer smoothes the irregular scansion of the poem by setting it in long note values over a moving accompaniment, but this is hardly the "cantus firmus" approach of "Ave Maria!" The vocal lines for the narrator are not tuneful, but more declamatory, like measured recitative. The child's cries, ever higher in pitch, as well as the replies of the father in much lower register, also take a declamatory shape. Only the Erlking's lines, demarcated by quotations in Goethe's poem, appear in cantabile style. The supernatural figure "sings" in token of his superior status and power. In short, the composer ignores the strophic nature of the poetry and disguises its meter, choosing instead to bring out its dramatic qualities.

Many writers also comment on the reiterative pattern in the right hand of the accompaniment, suggesting that it sounds like a horse galloping. Whether or not we believe this (in the event, the hoofbeats of a gallop are not even) the right-hand piano figuration communicates extreme speed, even when it lightens to emphasize the aria-like passages sung by the Erlking. This rapid-fire figuration requires more dexterity than a highly talented amateur can generally muster, just as the range required of the voice for the various "roles" tends more toward the operatic. "Erlkönig" almost demands professional performers who can show it to very good advantage. Of all Schubert's songs, this ballad appeared most frequently on public concert programs before the advent of the song recital toward the end of the nineteenth century.

To this point we have considered songs in their manifestation for solo voice and piano, but Schubert also excelled at the part-song, a particularly delightful manifestation of Hausmusik. The drawing room formed the prime location for this kind of song at the beginning of the century, probably sung one on a part. But as the century progressed, various kinds of groups organized for singing (*Singvereine,* or singing clubs, and *Liedertafeln,* roughly "song banquets") took up this repertory, sometimes with several voices to a part.

Although Schubert writes for both mixed voices and women's voices, part-songs for men represent the largest part of his output, perhaps because of the company he kept. And one of the most striking songs is his setting of "Nur wer die Sehnsucht kennt," entitled "Sehnsucht" (D. 656; 1819), for five male voices. For one thing, this text, from Goethe's novel *Wilhelm Meister,* is sung by a female character, Mignon. Even though she dresses like a boy for most of the novel, it seems odd for men to sing these lines (though they contain no overtly gender-specific references). Even more remarkable, however, is Schubert's harmonic language. The composer arrays the parts for the first stanza mostly in chorale- or hymn-like style, ending the first couplet on a half cadence (see Example 2.11). But the second couplet ("Alone and separated from all joy") occasions a modulation through the parallel minor (E→e) to G, dominant of C, with many chromatic detours on the way. The chromaticism serves as an emblem of tortured loneliness, and the twists and turns through diminished chords must have provided quite a chase for drawing-room singers. Schubert had a highly developed sense of harmonic color, and his penchant for rapid tonal motion around the circle of thirds would be much emulated by later composers. Not all Schubert part-songs take the ultraexpressive road followed by "Sehnsucht," but even the more mundane ones make enjoyable additions to the choral repertory and complete the picture of Schubert's "polyrhythmic" Lieder.

Schubert's Instrumental Music

Much of Schubert's music for piano also suited the intimacy of the parlor well. Large numbers of dances—waltzes, German dances, *Ländler,* and *ecossaises*—answered the demands of light entertainment and provided the model for the short, characteristic piano pieces of the next generation. There are also some charming sets of Impromptus (D. 899, 935; 1827) and *Momens Musicals* [sic] (D. 780; 1823–28) that run in the vein of Hausmusik.

Schubert's larger works include twenty-odd sonatas for piano (the grandest of which are the last three in four movements, D. 958–960) and a group of works meant especially for virtuosic performance. Most notable among these is the Fantasy in C, also known as the *Wanderer Fantasy* (D. 760; 1822), published by Schubert as op. 15 in 1823. It receives its sobriquet from the fact that its

EXAMPLE 2.11   "Sehnsucht" for five-part male chorus by Schubert, D. 656, 1819

second section, marked *Adagio,* seems to borrow material from Schubert's song "Der Wanderer" (D. 489; 1816). We can view this same material as developing out of the beginning of the *Fantasy,* for fantasies often assume the guise of extended, far-flung improvisations on a musical subject. In this sense, the piece constitutes a prime example of "thematic transformation" (a process that would play a prominent role in the works of later composers such as Schumann, Liszt, and Franck). The four main sections of the piece incrementally change the profile of the original subject to fit the particular character desired, yet retain familial resemblance (Example 2.12).

Many writers have viewed the *Wanderer Fantasy* as a truncated sonata in one movement. The opening "sonata-allegro" has something like an exposition (mm. 1–69) and a development (mm. 70–188), but no recapitulation. The slow movement (mm. 189–244) presents a set of variations, the scherzo (mm. 245–597) in triple meter runs "presto," and the contrapuntal finale (mm. 598–720) returns to the original allegro and common time. Although the form of the "grand" sonata in four movements certainly lurks here, it intersects with the bravura character of the fantasy. The piece displays Schubert's compositional prowess in drawing one theme from another, it follows a stunning succession of far-flung keys (C major→c-sharp minor→A-flat major→C major), and it demands virtuoso execution. The *Wanderer Fantasy* reminds us that Schubert could also produce a tour de force for the soloist in the concert hall.

Schubert's ensemble chamber music also runs the gamut from simpler quartets played by members of his family to the more formidable later quartets in A minor (D. 804), D minor (D. 810), and G major (D. 887). The most quintessentially Schubertian of the chamber works may be his late Quintet in C major for two violins, viola, and two cellos (D. 956; 1828). Schubert uses the "extra" instrument (cello added to the traditional string quartet) to create a rich texture. The opening of the first movement highlights the potential of this lush sonority, with chords grouped first in the traditional quartet, then in a lower quartet (formed by omitting the first violin).

The first movement of the quintet (see Table 2.4) unfolds in a way typical of late Schubert. The main theme might at first be construed as a slow introduction, so deliberate is its harmonic rhythm. And it assumes the initial form of a period (two equal, reciprocating phrases) that sets a leisurely pace for the rest of the movement. This first theme contains a good deal of modal ambiguity, with several harmonies borrowed from the parallel minor. Reference to C minor in the main theme in turn prepares the modulatory second theme, which unfolds in three lyrical "strophes." The first two of these begin in the flat mediant and slide repeatedly into the dominant. (In the recapitulation they move analogously from the flat submediant to the tonic.) This broad and harmonically excursive treatment of the second theme in a sonata form would influence many later composers, Schumann, Brahms, Tchaikovsky, and Gustav Mahler among them. The expansive, relaxed first movement sets the tone for the

EXAMPLE 2.12   Thematic cyclicity from main sections of Schubert's *Wanderer Fantasy,* D. 760, 1822

TABLE 2.4   Schematic for D. 956, mvt. I

SECTION	SUBSECTION	KEY	MEASURES
Exposition			
	Mth	C:I	1–32
	trans.	X	33–59
	Sth		
	strophe 1	♭III→V	60–80
	strophe 2	♭III→V	81–99
	strophe 3 (varied)	V	100–116
	Closing		
	section 1	V	117–137
	section 2	V	138–154
Development			
	Bridge	X	155–166
	Core		
	Model 1		167–203
	sequence		204–239
	fragmentation (6 × 2)		240–251
	Retransition	G pedal	252–267
Recapitulation			
	Mth (shortened)	I	268–290
	trans.	X	291–322
	Sth		
	strophe 1	♭VI→I	323–343
	strophe 2	♭VI→I	344–362
	strophe 3 (varied)	I	363–379
	Closing		
	section 1	I	380–400
	section 2	I	401–415
Coda		I	416–446

remaining movements of the quintet, which never seem as neurotically driven as those in Beethoven's late chamber music.

Schubert's early symphonies also declare their independence of the Beethovenian manner. The Fifth in B-flat (D. 485; 1816) is the most popular of his youthful symphonies, much more in the style of Mozart than of Beethoven. The *Unfinished* Symphony in B minor (D. 759; 1822) begins mysteriously with a hushed main theme that poses an intriguing contrast to the lyrical second theme in the first movement. After a lovely *andante con moto*, Schubert broke off orchestration, leaving only the piano sketch of a scherzo. Given the restrained rhetoric of this symphony, so unlike Beethoven, it would be interesting to know how Schubert planned to complete it.

The *Great* C Major Symphony (D. 944; 1825–28), Schubert's crowning orchestral achievement, attains the monumental proportions so lauded by Schumann, using some Beethovenian devices. For instance, the initial phrases of the main themes for the first and last movements are "Sätze" in the sense of Beethoven's musical "sentences." And we do find in this symphony some of the drive that characterizes the older composer's work. Still, Schubert uses reiterated patterns (rather than fragmented motives) progressively orchestrated to build many of his climaxes—in the second theme of the last movement, for instance. And he also uses the harmonic device of approaching the dominant key-area through the mediant in the second theme of the first movement. Schumann would later exult in the orchestration of the *Great* C Major Symphony, "quite independent of Beethoven," as well as in Schubert's avoidance of "the grotesque forms we find in Beethoven's later works."

In the end it is remarkable that Schubert maintained his distinctive voice in the overwhelming presence of Beethoven. But then, the establishment and maintenance of a unique personal style became a central theme of composition in the late eighteenth century and would remain so in the nineteenth. This impulse springs from the diversitarian principle that formed another tenet of Romanticism (in addition to its Neo-Platonic Idealism). The trick lay in creating the personal style out of common building blocks, proceeding in accordance with the universal rules of harmonic progression and voice-leading that represented the "classic" side of a "Classic-Romantic synthesis." Schubert did this so effectively that his "polyrhythmic" Lieder and ballads built a foundation for the whole practice of art song in the nineteenth century, just as his harmonic practice in instrumental works would serve as a model for ensuing generations of composers. For that reason he takes his place beside Beethoven among the handful of Viennese composers who exercised inordinate influence on the course of western European art music.

FURTHER READING

Background

A summary of Idealism in music around the turn of the nineteenth century appeared recently in Evan Bonds's "Idealism and the Aesthetics of Instrumental Music at the Turn of the Century," *Journal of the American Musicological Society* 50 (1997), 387–20.

Beethoven

Maynard Solomon has offered a fine, short, psychobiography in his *Beethoven*, 2nd ed. (New York, 1998). The classic longer biography remains Alexander Wheelock Thayer's *Life of Beethoven*, rev. ed., ed. Elliot Forbes (Princeton, 1967). An overview of Beethoven's compositional process is found in Douglas Johnson, Alan Tyson, and Robert Winter's *The Beethoven Sketchbooks: History, Reconstruction and Inventory* (Berkeley and Los Angeles, 1985). Beethoven's formal procedures are outlined by William Caplin in *Classical Form* (New York, 1998), and issues of *The Beethoven Forum,* an annual collection of articles, present the most recent research in the composer's life and music. The website of the Ira F. Brilliant Beethoven Center (www.sjsulib1.sjsu.edu) offers an unparalleled resource for bibliography.

Schubert

Brian Newbould has written lately a fine assessment of Schubert in *Schubert: The Music and the Man* (Berkeley and Los Angeles, 1997). The classic biography by Otto Erich Deutsch appears as *Schubert: A Documentary Biography,* trans. Eric Blom (London, 1946). For questions surrounding Schubert's sexuality, readers will want to view Maynard Solomon's article "Franz Schubert and the Peacocks of Benvenuto Cellini," *19th Century Music* 12 (1989), 193–206; an issue of *19th Century Music* 17 (1993) was devoted to a contrary view and the implications. A very fine discussion of selected Schubert songs appears in Richard Kramer's *Distant Cycles: Franz Schubert and the Conceiving of Song* (Chicago, 1994). A good look at Schubert's harmonic practice in instrumental music appears in James Webster's "Schubert's Sonata Form and Brahms's First Maturity," *19th Century Music,* Part 1, 2 (1978), 18–35; Part 2, 3 (1979), 52–71.

CHAPTER 3

Operatic Premises: Musical Drama in the First Part of the Nineteenth Century

The sheet music in Figure 3.1 for Rossini's most famous aria, "Di tanti palpiti" from *Tancredi,* and the subsequent sheet music for various operas throughout this chapter reminds us of a central fact in early-nineteenth-century music reception. However much composers of the first Viennese school predominate in "modern" music history, they did not hold center stage during their time as far as middle-class consumers outside Germany were concerned. In France, Italy, and England opera was all the rage. Whether freely adapted and retexted, as in the version here by T. B. Phipps (ca. 1824), or arranged for instruments alone, a broad, steady stream of opera excerpts flooded printing presses and reached even into the recesses of the provincial United States. A collection of nineteenth-century sheet music from small-town America (Frederick, Maryland, in this case) *might* contain a few simple Beethoven piano pieces, but it would surely include a large number of selections from operas by Rossini, Bellini, and Donizetti, along with some by Weber and Meyerbeer.

Opera disclosed a world of fame and fashion to the collectors of sheet music (mostly young women). Excerpts often appeared under the banner "As sung by the famous soprano Mrs. X at Covent Garden." In the cities where theaters mounted opera, its fashionable audiences made the best composers wealthy. German aestheticians may have labored to establish the claims of instrumental music, but opera reigned supreme in the musical life of major

Figure 3.1   American sheet music (ca. 1824) for a British contrafact by T. B. Phipps of Rossini's aria "Di tanti palpiti" from *Tancredi* (1813). Music Library, University of North Carolina at Chapel Hill.

urban centers through the first half of the nineteenth century and remained important, though not paramount, in the second half. The styles and devices of opera must play a substantial role in any history of this era's music.

ITALIAN OPERA

Italy during the first part of the nineteenth century was not a national state, but a geographic and linguistic area. Three powers dominated Italy after the collapse of Napoleon's empire: Spain in the south (including Sicily and Naples), Austria in the north (including Lombardy and Venice), and the papacy in the country around Rome and in a strip running through the middle of the peninsula. Only Sardinia and Savoy fell under the rule of a native prince.

What *unified* Italy during this period, however, was its culture, and opera played a central role in that culture. After all, the Italians had invented opera. And throughout much of the eighteenth century and into the first part of the nineteenth, their opera either predominated or maintained a strong presence in much of Europe. Italian opera exerted its cultural influence because it was cultivated so widely on its native soil. Every small town in Italy had an opera house, and larger cities had several. Major centers in the north included Milan (Teatro alla Scala, Teatro Carcano, Teatro della Conobbiana) and Venice (Teatro La Fenice, Teatro San Benedetto, Teatro San Moisè). The south had Naples (Teatro San Carlo, Teatro del Fondo, Teatro dei Fiorentini). And Rome stood in the middle (Teatro Apollo, Teatro Argentina, Teatro Valle), though most creative activity centered in Naples and Milan.

Composers and singers circulated among these and many other, smaller cities with an ease surprising in the age before rail travel. Success in one city led to commissions in another, and notable achievement throughout Italy would eventually lead to international fame. The most prominent composers were invited to oversee production of their operas in London, and they usually lived in Paris for a time, writing works for the Théâtre-Italien, the Opéra, and sometimes the Opéra-Comique.

The composers of Italian opera not only circulated widely, they also created prodigiously. The repertory of the nineteenth-century Italian opera house had not yet hardened into a select group of oft-repeated classics. Instead, every season demanded new operas, and the rate of production was sometimes breakneck. Donizetti is said to have written *Elisir d'amore* in two weeks; Rossini created *Il barbiere di Siviglia* in about three. Since operas were commissioned for specific houses, the composer often knew exactly which singers would perform, and he could therefore tailor an aria to fit a particular voice, displaying it to its best advantage.

The composer could not take sole responsibility for the authorship of an opera, we should remember. The libretto came first ("with music by" second), and although composers exerted influence on librettists and could suggest changes, they depended on poets to produce suitable verse. Perhaps the most famous and influential was Felice Romani (1788–1865), who fashioned important libretti for Mayr, Rossini, Bellini, and Donizetti. He and the many other Italian poets of this period usually derived plots from other plays, operas, novels, or short stories. For that reason, nineteenth-century Italian opera came quite naturally under the sway of late-eighteenth- and early-nineteenth-century literary trends. The plays of Schiller and later Hugo served as sources, as did those of Shakespeare. Fairy tales enjoyed a certain vogue. And the Italians came to love fictional accounts of modern history, including, most notably, dramatizations of novels by Sir Walter Scott. Often set in exotic Scotland amid historic political unrest not unlike Italy's, these plots were quintessentially Romantic in nature. They evoked the Scottish highlands (mountains and mountaineering became a nineteenth-century passion), the Scottish quest for independence from England, old feuds between clans, and doomed lovers trapped in the politics of despair. In general, love enmeshed in political strife became a salient theme in *opera seria* of the nineteenth century, whether set in Egypt (another fashionable locale) or in England.

To deal with these colorful subjects, librettists and composers developed a set of formal conventions intended to integrate vocal display more fully into the dramatic action. Where eighteenth-century *opera seria* had emphasized a series of solo arias interspersed with narration of the plot in recitatives, nineteenth-century Italian opera, taking its cue in part from *opera buffa,* tended to integrate sections of more declamatory style into arias. Increased use of chorus, their intrusion along with other characters into solo segments, and continuous use of orchestra began to erode the traditional differentiation between external action in reciting style and internal action in lyrical style. Although vocal prowess still played a very important role in Italian opera, composers and librettists fashioned sectional arias, duets, introductions, and finales that provided dramatic justification for the singers' pyrotechnics.

Rossini

It is hard to imagine from our vantage point the centrality of Gioachino Rossini (1792–1868) to the history of opera in the nineteenth century. Today he is represented mainly by one comic masterpiece, *The Barber of Seville* (originally entitled *Almaviva, ossia L'inultile precauzione,* Rome, 1816), though *L'italiana in Algeri* (Venice, 1813), *Il turco in Italia* (Milan, 1814), *Cinderella* (*La Cenerentola, ossia La bontà in trionfo,* Rome, 1817), and an occasional serious opera appear from time to time. But Rossini's thirty-nine operas were ubiquitous on the Continent beginning in the teens and twenties, and he was arguably the most celebrated composer of his day. More important for us, his pieces codified both the form and the style against which all subsequent nineteenth-century opera measured itself, either by creatively adapting his practices (Bellini, Donizetti, Meyerbeer) or by professing rebellion against them (Weber and Wagner).

Rossini was born into an operatic family in Pesaro, Italy, on the Adriatic coast. His father played horn in pit orchestras, his mother took small soprano roles on stage, and the young Rossini spent much time with his grandmother while his parents toured. When his mother retired from the stage, the family settled in Bologna, where Gioachino studied privately until he entered the distinguished Liceo Musicale, taking voice, cello, and piano (his father had already tutored him in horn) as well as the usual counterpoint. As a boy, Rossini possessed a voice good enough to land him a role in Paer's *Adolfo* at the Bolognese Teatro del Corso in 1805, and he often played keyboard in local theaters. By 1806 (at the age of fourteen) he had been inducted into the prestigious Academia Filarmonica. About 1807 the tenor Domenico Mombelli offered the young man a commission for an opera, *Demetrio e Polibio,* which was not performed until 1812.

Rossini embarked seriously on his career as operatic composer in 1810 with a one-act farce, *La cambiale di matrimonio,* for the Teatro San Moisè in Venice. An astonishing stream of operas for Venice, Bologna, and Milan followed over the next several years—to name just a few: *L'inganno infelice, La scala di seta, L'occasione fa il ladro, Il Signor Bruschino, L'italiana in Algeri, Il turco in Italia,* and what Stendhal regarded as the composer's crowning early achievement, *Tancredi,* a "heroic melodrama" written for Teatro La Fenice in Venice (1813).

From 1815 to 1823 Rossini made southern Italy his base of operation, writing most of his works for Naples and Rome. These operas, many with serious libretti influenced by Romantic literature, prompted the composer to solidify formal conventions that accommodated greater dramatic expressiveness and established a foundation for later artists such as Bellini, Donizetti, and eventually Verdi. The operas from this period include the *opere serie Elisabetta, regina d'Inghilterra* (Naples, Teatro San Carlo, 1815), *Otello* (after Shakespeare; Naples, Teatro del Fondo, 1816), *La donna del lago* (after Scott; Naples, Teatro San Carlo, 1819), *Maometto II* (Naples, Teatro San Carlo, 1820), and *Semiramide* (after Voltaire, Venice, Teatro La Fenice, 1823). The two famous comedies, *Il barbiere di Siviglia* and *La Cenerentola,* both written for Roman houses, also date from this period. For both serious and comic operas, the composer created large-scale structures that increasingly lent a sense of continuity to the succession of musical "numbers."

In the fall of 1823, having achieved international fame at the age of thirty-one, Rossini embarked on a tour of France and England. A season of Rossini operas in London (1823–24) was largely unsuccessful, and in 1824, after a vacation in Bologna, he returned to Paris. There he became director of the Théâtre-Italien, producing his operas and the operas of other composers. (He introduced Meyerbeer to Paris with *Il crociato in Egitto,* 1825.) Though he was involved in the Théâtre-Italien until 1836, he negotiated a new contract in 1826 permitting him to turn his attention mostly to composing for the Opéra. At this juncture the government designated Rossini *premier compositeur du roi* and *inspecteur général du chant en France,* and in this capacity he composed his last operas, including *Le Comte Ory* (1828) and *Guillaume Tell* (1829). These works joined Italian structure and melodic style with the French love of spectacle to prepare the new style of French grand opera for composers such as Meyerbeer.

Although Rossini's most significant contributions to the opera of his day proceeded from his serious works, we can gain a good idea of his approach by examining various parts of his most frequently performed opera today, the comic *Barber of Seville.* It begins with a suitable "Rossinian" overture, though not one originally composed for *Barber.* Rather, the composer adopted one he had written for *Aureliano in Palmira* (Milan, La Scala, 1813). Rossini's overtures consist basically of a sonata form without development. They include a slow introduction, a main theme, a transition, a secondary theme, and a closing, but a simple modulation back to the recapitulation replaces a formal development section (see Table 3.1).

One of the most striking features of this overture derives from an effect called the "Rossinian crescendo," heard prominently in the closing section of both exposition and recapitulation. Here the composer repeats an agile figure while progressively adding more instruments at ever louder volumes until he breaks a fragment off and increases the pace of repetition even more. By this means Rossini builds a powerful climax to end the exposition and, ultimately, the overture as a whole. He also uses this device for creating a sense of forward motion in arias and larger ensembles where it is dramatically appropriate.

TABLE 3.1   Schematic of "Rossinian" Overture for *The Barber of Seville*

SECTION	*SUBSECTION*	*KEY*	*REHEARSAL*
Introduction		I (E maj.)	1–2
Exposition			
	Mth	i	3–4
	trans.	i-III	5–7
	Sth	III	8
	Closing	III	9–11
modulation		x	12, mm.1–4
Recapitulation			
	Mth	i	12–13
	Sth	I	14
	Closing	I	15–16
Coda		I	17–19

Although Rossinian opera still preserves the distinction between outer action (the plot exposed mostly in recitative) and inner action (characters' reaction to situations as expressed mostly in arias), the composer increasingly attempted to subvert the artificiality of the separation by creating large musico-dramatic units combining the two kinds of action. One such large-scale structure appears in the *introduzione* (introduction), which usually consists of interwoven choruses, recitative-like passages, and extended lyrical solos. The *introduzione* in *The Barber of Seville* provides a good example of the typical Rossinian plan (see Table 3.2). It begins with a group of musicians assembled by Count Almaviva's henchman, Fiorello, to serenade the object of the count's desire, Rosina. When Almaviva arrives, a parlando exchange between him and Fiorello interrupts this choral section briefly, which then repeats with the count giving further instructions to the band. To this point outer action has held the stage, but now inner action takes over with a *cavatina* (or "entrance aria") expressing Almaviva's feelings for Rosina. Rossini arranges even this aria to lend a sense of dramatic motion by starting with a slower cantabile, in which the count calls on his lady to awaken, and ending with a faster cabaletta declaring Almaviva's undying love. Of course, this aria, with its paired, repeated phrases and passagework in the cabaletta, also shows off the tenor's voice. A brief interlude of recitative ensues in which Fiorello and Almaviva determine that Rosina has not answered the count's pleading. The *introduzione* concludes by repeating a section of the opening chorus and appending a *stretta,* a faster coda with Rossinian crescendo in which Almaviva and Fiorello try to quiet the musicians' increasingly boisterous gratitude.

Many scores of this opera divide the *introduzione* into several separate "numbers," but in Rossini's autograph the various sections all constitute a single unit. Its tonal closure and musical "rounding" unite the various textures and types of dramatic action to create a satisfying whole that propels the audience into the drama.

TABLE 3.2 Schematic of the *Introduzione* for *The Barber of Seville*

SECTION	*MATERIAL*	*KEY*	*DRAMATIC FUNCTION*
Chorus	A	I (G maj.)	Fiorello sets up serenade
rec.		x	Almaviva enters
Chorus	A	I	Almaviva's instructions
Cavatina			
cantabile	B	IV	Almaviva summons Rosina
cabaletta	C	IV	Almaviva declares love
rec.		x	Rosina fails to appear
Chorus	A	I	Fiorello pays musicians
stretta	D	I	Chorus thanks count

What critics often portray as threadbare formulae in Rossini's music are in fact clever strategies that serve multiple constituencies. The famous two-part aria (slower cantabile—faster cabaletta) established a universal convention that allowed the librettist and the composer to expedite their writing. At the same time, it served the drama by lending a sense of forward motion to an essentially static act (the expression of a character's inner feelings). And it provided the singers a chance to maximize their display of dramatic and vocal prowess.

We can find the perfect example of the advantages of this arrangement in Rosina's cavatina (entrance aria), "Una voce poco fa."

Cantabile

Una voce poco fa	A voice a little while ago
qui nel cor mi risuonò;	resounded in my heart;
il mio cor ferito è già,	my heart is already pierced,
e Lindor fu che il piagò.	and it was Lindoro who wounded it.
Sì, Lindoro mio sarà;	Yes, Lindoro shall be mine;
lo giurai, la vincerò.	I swear I shall triumph.
Il tutor ricuserà,	My guardian may refuse,
io l'ingegno aguzzerò.	I'll sharpen my wits.
Alla fin s'accheterà	In the end he'll be appeased
e contenta io resterò.	And I'll be left satisfied.

Cabaletta

Io sono docile—son rispettosa,	I am docile—I am respectful,
sono ubbidiente—dolce, amorosa;	I am obedient—sweet, loving;
mi lascio reggere—mi fo guidar.	I can be ruled—I can be led
Ma se mi toccano—dov'è il mio debole,	But if you touch me—on my soft spot,
sarò una vipera—e cento trappole	I become a viper—and a hundred tricks
prima di cedere—farò giocar.	before yielding—I'll play.

Rossini's librettist, Cesare Sterbini, separated the aria into two parts, each with its own poetic structure, which I will outline just this once as an example of technique. The cantabile has ten eight-syllable lines forming couplets with alternating end rhyme, and the cabaletta features a sestet (six lines) of two five-syllable groupings (*doppio quinario*) with the rhyme scheme *aabccb*. This structural distinction highlights a dramatic distinction: The cantabile outlines the situation as Rosina sees it, whereas the cabaletta lists the personality traits that will enable her to accomplish her stated goal. Both sections reveal internal sentiments, but the progression from the first to the second yields a sense of dramatic motion.

Rossini reinforces Sterbini's intimation of inner action by setting the cantabile in a slower, slightly more punctuated and rhythmically uneven style (see Example 3.1). The tempo quickens slightly for the cabaletta, the accompaniment becomes more regular in its rhythm, and new melodic material appears

EXAMPLE 3.1   Beginning of the cantabile from Rosina's cavatina in Rossini's *Barber of Seville,* Act I

(see Example 3.2). In both sections the composer provides the singer with a series of parallel, arched phrases that move up and down gradually, combining scales or graceful arpeggiations with some coloratura (fast, intricate passage-work) inserted for display. This writing permits the singer to maintain an even vocal color throughout her scale while showing off her agility. Display is particularly evident in the cabaletta, which usually features some repetition in a scheme *AA'* plus coda with cadenza ad libitum.

One last type of number appearing in *Barber of Seville* deserves mention, though we will view the formal norms later: the finale. Like the *introduzione,* the finale to Act I presents a multipartite structure that uses key to unite inner and outer action through a wide variety of textures. In the finale, Almaviva plots to meet Rosina in person by posing as an officer to be quartered in her guardian's home. Rossini chooses C major for the overarching key, with excursions to E-flat and A-flat, ending finally with a stretta not unlike the cabaletta of an aria. After preliminaries, it begins *sotto voce* with a dotted theme (*Mi par d'esser con la testa*)

EXAMPLE 3.2   Beginning of the cabaletta from Rosina's cavatina in Rossini's *Barber of Seville,* Act I

that gradually builds to a section of rapid patter and cadences for soloists and chorus (playing the police who have entered to break up the fracas). This process then repeats in classic *AA'* form (with a brief diversion to the key of E-flat major) and concludes with a coda. The succession of textures in the finale, ranging from solo cantilena to fughetta, emphasizes the incremental hilarity of cascading events (Almaviva's assault, Bartolo's discomfiture, Rosina's collusion, the principals' melee, and the arrival of the police). Rossini's brilliant music makes for superb theater.

Bellini

Vincenzo Bellini (1801–35), born a scant nine years after Rossini, nonetheless numbers among the heirs of an operatic tradition established by his older colleague. Their relative historical position stems in part from Rossini's precocity (first commission at the age of fifteen) and in part from the length of Bellini's apprenticeship (first student opera at the age of twenty-four). Bellini's role as "follower," however, did not obscure his international fame, cut short only by death just before his thirty-fourth birthday. Sheet music of selections from his *Norma* (see Figure 3.2) and *La sonnambula* seems to appear more frequently in nineteenth-century collections than numbers by any other composer.

Bellini's biography offers many parallels to that of Rossini. In pursuing music as a profession, Bellini also followed in a family tradition that extended back in his case to his grandfather, who served as *maestro di cappella* in Catania. Young Vincenzo played piano brilliantly by the age of five and started composing under his grandfather's tutelage at age six. Not surprisingly in light of his grandfather's occupation, Bellini's first compositions centered on church music.

After he learned all he could from his grandfather, Bellini enrolled at the Naples Conservatory in 1819, supported by a scholarship from the municipal government of Catania. Eventually he was taken into the composition class of Nicolò Zingarelli, director of the conservatory. There Bellini studied the instrumental works of Haydn and Mozart, producing a series of instrumental and sacred works as exercises. In 1824 he attended a Naples performance of Rossini's *Semiramide,* and this proved to be the most influential encounter of his student years.

Early in 1825 Bellini composed an *opera semiseria, Adelson e Salvini,* for an all-male cast of his fellow students at the conservatory. Its success resulted in a commission for *Bianca e Gernando,* performed at Teatro San Carlo (Naples) in 1826, and the triumph of this piece established Bellini's career. He wrote his next eight operas in collaboration with Felice Romani: *Il pirata* (La Scala, 1827), *La straniera* (La Scala, 1829), *Zaira* (Ducale, Parma, 1829), *I Capuleti e i Montecchi* (La Fenice, Venice, 1830), *La sonnambula* (Carcano, Milan, 1831), *Norma* (La Scala, 1831), and *Beatrice di Tenda* (La Fenice, 1833).

By 1833 Bellini had won international fame, and he contracted for a spring season of opera at the King's Theatre in London. After London, following a pattern reminiscent of Rossini almost a decade earlier, Bellini gravitated to Paris, where he became involved with productions of *Il pirata* and *I Capuleti e i Montecchi* at the Théâtre-Italien. In Paris he became more closely acquainted with Rossini, Chopin, Paer, and also Heinrich Heine. He received a commission from the Théâtre-Italien for an opera entitled *I puritani,* with libretto by Carlo Pepoli, an Italian émigré. Bellini celebrated a great success with the new piece and was elevated to the Legion d'honneur before dying abruptly in August 1835.

Bellini's output was relatively small, even considering his short life span, and it was also marked by the lack of comic operas. Aside from *Adelson e Salvini* and *La sonnambula,* both *opere semiserie* (dramas with mixed endings), the composer pursued only *opere serie.* It is no wonder, then, that he is known today mainly for two operas, *sonnambula* and *Norma,* the latter of which even Wagner conducted and admired.

Norma (1831), the story of a love triangle between a Gallic Druid priestess, her friend the temple virgin Adalgisa, and a Roman military governor, Pollione, has subject matter fashionable for the times. Romance and infidelity are unremarkable in themselves until they appear against the backdrop of political insurgency. Norma's Gauls want to overthrow their Roman oppressors, and Norma is torn between her duty to her people, her love for Pollione, and her despair over his infidelity. Bellini and Romani give much attention to Gallic unrest, the counterpart of Italian political unhappiness in the early nineteenth century. Norma does the correct "political" thing when she destroys herself at the end, but she is not a weak, pathetic figure. Her suicide is a courageous act, and she dies as one of many women in the nineteenth century beside whom men are weak, duplicitous creatures.

Norma embodies many structural features of Rossinian *opera seria*. Though Bellini invented none of the techniques, he used them to great advantage through his scrupulous declamation of text and talent for long-breathed melody. All the innovations in Italian nineteenth-century opera aimed at increasing dramatic plausibility and continuity, as we can see clearly in the scene surrounding Norma's famous cavatina, "Casta Diva." The first thing immediately apparent in listening is the absence of *secco* (dry) recitative played by a keyboard preceding the aria, a development that marks most Italian opera from the late teens on. The orchestra accompanies all recitations, further eroding the distinction between outer and inner action. "Casta Diva" follows a *scena* in which Norma invokes the Druid gods' aid against the Romans (with whom she has secret personal sympathies). She is surrounded by her priests and by Gallic warriors, whose choral interjections punctuate her recitative and accompany her aria.

To accommodate the interweaving of personal and political motivation, the simple two-part aria has expanded here to three parts. In the highly decorated and slower cantabile ("Casta Diva"; see Table 3.3 and Example 3.3),

TABLE 3.3   Schematic for "Rossinian" Three-Part Aria from Bellini's *Norma*: "Casta Diva"

SECTION	*TEMPO*	*KEY*	*INCIPIT/CONTENT*
Cantabile	Andante sostenuto assai	F major	"Casta Diva"/ Norma invokes the goddess and counsels patience
Tempo di mezzo	Allegro/Allegro assai maestoso	E-flat major/x	"Fine al rito";/ Norma ends invocation and promises ultimate victory over Romans
Cabaletta			
A	Allegro	F major	"(Ah! bello a me ritorna . . .)"/ Norma discloses love for Roman governor/Druids swear revenge
A′	1mo tempo	F major	repeat text/content
Coda		F major	orchestral exit march

EXAMPLE 3.3 Beginning of the cantabile from Norma's cavatina in Bellini's *Norma,* Act I

Norma invokes the Druid goddess to the chanting of the Gauls, admonishing them to strike the Romans only when the time is right. The second section of the aria presents a *tempo di mezzo* (intermediate tempo), with more declamatory writing for the soprano answered by bloodthirsty cries for vengeance by the chorus. This section modulates briefly to E-flat major, providing a sense of tonal as well as dramatic motion and recalling the initial recitative and preceding chorus. In the faster third part of the aria, a concluding cabaletta, Norma sings an aside confessing that she still loves her Roman governor, Pollione, while the Druids continue to dream of vengeance. Sadly, many performances and recordings truncate the cabaletta, omitting repetition of the lines that allow the soloist to display her skill at vocal ornamentation. A long orchestral postlude, its material recapitulated from an earlier entry march, affords a coda to accompany the exit of the Druids and their priestess. Taken as a whole, the scene runs more than twenty minutes. Although its three-part aria still centers on internal action, it yields a very strong impression of dramatic progress, shifting as it does between Norma's external proclamations, her internal doubts, and the chorus's demands for revenge. The returning march music binds the whole to the larger action of the opera.

Nowhere is the fluidity of later Rossinian *opera seria* more evident than in the highly developed duet, of which Bellini's *Norma* has a classical example in the second act. Here Norma and Adalgisa argue about the latter's affair with Norma's Roman lover. The abandoned Norma intends to commit suicide while her children are sleeping, and she summons Adalgisa to take charge of them. After Bellini exposes this situation in a recitative, he devotes the first section of his four-part duet (see Table 3.4) to establishing the conflict between the two characters: Norma commends her children to Adalgisa's care ("Deh! con te"), but Adalgisa insists that she will send Pollione back to Norma ("Vado al campo"). In the second part ("Mira, Norma") both characters probe their feelings about the situation, Adalgisa imploring Norma to think of her children and Norma weakening in the face of her friend's pleas. This reflection unfolds over a classic Bellinian melody (see Figure 3.2), rising and falling gently in long, parallel arched phrases that became a perennial favorite of the nineteenth century. This kind of writing, so grateful for the voice, came to be known as *bel canto* (literally, "beautiful song"), applying equally to the music and the style of singing it fostered. At the end of this lyrical interlude the musical texture changes to one punctuated by chords in the full orchestra. The declamatory setting of the text accompanies verse "broken" between the two characters, that is to say, poetic lines divided in dialogue. Norma responds to Adalgisa's cries to yield, and having resolved the conflict, both celebrate Norma's decision to live in a joyous cabaletta.

TABLE 3.4   Schematic for "Rossinian" Duet from Bellini's *Norma*: "Deh! con te"

SECTION	*KEY*	*MUSICO-POETIC FEATURES*
I. Tempo di primo initial confrontation "Deh! con te"	C major	Characters lay out initial positions in parallel stanzas separated by broken verse divided between the two. During the course of their concluding exchange in broken verse the music modulates.
II. Cantabile "Mira, Norma"	F major	Characters reflect on the situation, each repeating one stanza, then singing together, either in simple counterpoint or in parallel thirds or sixths.
III. Tempo di mezzo "Cedi, deh cedi!"	x	Characters decide on a course of action, trading lines back back and forth in broken verse set in declamatory style.
IV. Cabaletta "Si, fino all'ore"	F major	Characters reflect on resolution of conflict, singing together either in parallel thirds or simple counterpoint; the tempo is usually faster if the resolution is a happy one.

Figure 3.2   Cantabile ("Mira, Norma") from the second-act duet of Bellini's *Norma* (1831) in an American sheet music edition with English translation (ca. 1839). Music Library, University of North Carolina at Chapel Hill.

Of course Romani, Bellini's librettist, cast his verse in this conventional form before the music was ever written. But in adopting the convention, he never intended to place a straitjacket on the drama—quite the reverse. Like the three-part aria, the four-part duet created a large, fluid dramatic unit that negotiated the movement between the characters' outward conflict, their internal reflection, and their joint resolve. It also provided for a variety of textures, tempi, keys, and melody that reinforced the drama with colorful music and beautiful singing. In a Rossinian duet the boundaries between inner and outer action begin to blur, and all benefit—the singer, the audience, and dramatic effect. By means of the new Rossinian conventions in Italian opera, Bellini and Romani were able to fill the turbulent dramatic canvas of *Norma* and their other *opere serie* with convincing and sympathetic figures.

Donizetti

Unlike either Bellini or Rossini, Gaetano Donizetti (1797–1848) did not come from a musical background, nor did he win fame easily. Born in Bergamo to a very poor family, he had the good fortune to be taken in hand by the local *maestro di cappella,* Johann Simon Mayr, a translocated German who had quite a reputation as a composer of Italian opera in his own right. Mayr undertook Donizetti's basic musical education at the local school of music from 1806 to 1814, helped him gain entry (and partially supported him) at the Liceo Filarmonico Musicale in Bologna (where Rossini had studied), and arranged for opera contracts when the young composer returned to Bergamo in 1817. Early in 1822, as a result of a successful performance of *Zoraida di Granata* at the Teatro Argentina in Rome, Donizetti was offered a contract to write a piece for the Teatro Nuovo in Naples. He composed and conducted a large number of operas there, as well as a few for Milan, Rome, Palermo, and Genoa, but none achieved extraordinary fame.

Donizetti had composed thirty operas before he celebrated a triumph with *Anna Bolena* in Milan (1830). Performances of this opera in London and Paris secured him an international reputation, and he eventually broke his Naples contract to take advantage of his wider fame. In subsequent years he composed operas for Rome, Milan, Florence, Venice, and finally, at Rossini's invitation, for the Parisian Théâtre-Italien in 1835. Eventually in 1838 Donizetti, like Rossini and Bellini before him, took up residence in Paris and had stunning success in composing operas for the Opéra and the Opéra-Comique. His Parisian operas are some of his best known, including *La fille du régiment* (Opéra-Comique, 1840) and *Don Pasquale* (Théâtre-Italien, 1843). During his residence in Paris Donizetti's health deteriorated, and by the end of 1843 his behavior had become erratic. Eventually he was diagnosed with tertiary syphilis, returning to Bergamo in October of 1847 to spend his few remaining months before dying in 1848.

Donizetti was far more prolific than Bellini, and his output encompasses both comic and serious operas. Although his comic operas are often performed, his greatest contribution came in his serious operas, especially those dealing with fictionalization of British history: *Anna Bolena* (Milan, 1830), *Maria Stuarda* (Milan, 1835), and *Roberto Devereaux* (Naples, 1837). They take full advantage of the new dramatic flexibility in Italian opera, adding powerful deployment of the orchestra, especially the woodwinds and brass, to create striking colors. Verdi took much of his inspiration from Donizetti's full and evocative orchestrations for *opere serie*.

A good example of an evocative Donizetti opera with fictionalized historical plot appears in *Lucia di Lammermoor* (1835), a work widely acclaimed in its day (as we can see in Figure 3.3) and still part of the standard repertory. The story for the opera originated in Sir Walter Scott's quintessentially Gothic-Romantic novel *The Bride of Lammermoor*, based on real events in far-off Scotland at the end of the seventeenth century. Adapted by Salvatore Cammarano from earlier dramatizations, the plot involves a brother, Enrico Ashton (Henry), who wishes his sister, Lucia (Lucy), to marry a political ally, Arturo (Arthur) Bucklaw, to preserve the family fortune and hold onto the castle of Ravenswood. Enrico does this by deceiving Lucia into thinking that the man she truly loves, Edgardo Ravenswood (Edgar, of the family whose estate the Ashtons have seized), has forgotten her. Unfortunately, Edgardo shows up at the sealing of the marriage contract *after* Lucia has signed her name. His consequent denunciation of Lucia deranges her mind, leading her to murder Arturo in the bridal chamber. She dies of a broken psyche and spirit, and Edgardo commits suicide in remorse for having wrongly accused her. Again we have the theme of political oppression paired with a woman far more noble than the scheming, vain, and impetuous men around her.

The opera offers its share of three-part arias, of course, the most famous being Lucia's "mad" scene. The *scena* in Act III begins not with recitative but with chorus, yet a further step in interweaving external action with the internal sentiments expressed by soloists. Lucia then enters singing in broken, disjunct arioso ("Il dolce suono"; E-flat major). The soprano erupts from time to time irrationally into coloratura, now used as the sign of her madness. And when the cantabile finally arrives ("Ardon gl'incensi"; E-flat major), the flutes carry the melody at first while the soprano continues on declamatory repeated pitches. The long *tempo di mezzo* ("S'avanza Enrico") in an unstable C-flat major features dialogue between Lucia, Enrico, their minister, Raimondo, and the courtiers. The cabaletta ("Spargi d'amàro pianto" featured in Figure 3.3 with English contrafact; E-flat major) proceeds at a moderate tempo because joyous celebration would be inappropriate in this tragic situation. The abrupt melodic leaps mirror Lucia's instability, as do her more florid embellishments in the standard *A'* repetition of the opening section. Together with the unearthly piping of the flutes and the shocked interjections of the onlookers, this standard cabaletta is not just

Figure 3.3   American sheet music (ca. 1841) for "Spargi d'amàro pianto" from Donizetti's *Lucia di Lammermoor* (1835). Music Library, University of North Carolina at Chapel Hill.

a little horrific, proving that librettists and composers of Donizetti and Cammarano's talents could use the conventional forms to stunning dramatic advantage.

Nowhere is Donizetti's artful manipulation of convention so clearly displayed as in the finale to Act II of *Lucia di Lammermoor*. In this climactic scene, sometimes called "The Contract Scene," Edgardo bursts in unexpectedly on Lucia reluctantly signing her marriage agreement with Arturo. The Rossinian finale builds on the basic form of the four-part duet by adding an opening chorus. In this case the chorus provides dramatic contrast by lauding the happy day of betrothal (see Table 3.5). Enrico and Arturo then begin with what seem to be conventional paired stanzas for a *tempo primo* (compare with Table 3.4), which Donizetti underlays with a repeated figuration that builds tension (a device much imitated later by Verdi). Unlike a duet, however, the continuation must include Lucia, who enters to her own accompaniment in minor mode. Throughout this section the orchestra evokes the proper mood with its melody while the singers declaim their lines in parlando style over the rich orchestral tapestry.

After Edgardo's unexpected appearance halts the proceedings, Donizetti freezes time with one of the most ravishing sextets ever penned (see Example 3.4). Its translucent accompaniment serves as more than just the conventional "sixty-piece guitar." The pizzicato prickles like the hair on the back of the neck

TABLE 3.5   Schematic for "Rossinian" Finale from Act II of Donizetti's *Lucia di Lammermoor*

SECTION	*KEY*	*FEATURES*
I. Chorus "Per te d'immenso"	G major	Dramatic irony prepared by chorus setting "happy" scene.
II. Initial exchange "Se in lei"	D major–C minor	Enrico and Arturo lay out initial positions in stanzas, then in broken-verse dialogue.
"Ecco il tuo sposo"		Minor key reflects Lucia's unhappy mood at entrance. Followed by modulation at the appearance of Edgardo.
III. Cantabile (sextet) "Chi mi frena"	D-flat major	Characters reflect on the complication, foes Enrico and Edgardo in the first stanza, then all joining in counterpoint with chorus added at the end.
IV. Tempo di mezzo "T'allontana"	D major	Characters take positions on the turn of events, trading lines back and forth in declamatory style, interspersed with sections of arioso.
V. Stretta "Esci, fuggi"	D major	Characters state their final positions, singing together and with chorus; the tempo quickens, reflecting tension.

EXAMPLE 3.4   Beginning of the cantabile (sextet) from the finale of Act II in Donizetti's *Lucia di Lammermoor*

in fright. Its melodic loveliness, contrasting starkly with the terror and shock of the characters, underlines the import of the moment with Romantic irony.

The librettist and the composer extend the *tempo di mezzo* to accommodate the dramatic situation: Enrico and Edgardo battle each other, only to be interrupted by the minister, Raimondo, in a pompous display of arioso. Edgardo, shown the signed marriage contract, then denounces Lucia and crushes her engagement ring underfoot. The conclusion of the finale is a "stretta" that functions as cabaletta, quickening in tempo here to reflect the accumulated tension of the dismaying events.

Through all of this extended "number" Donizetti, aided by Cammarano, mediates brilliantly between the need for bel canto, orchestral coloring, scenic spectacle, and dramatic interaction. To this end he employs all the resources offered by the Rossinian forms. The drama and cohesion of this and the other *scene* in *Lucia di Lammermoor* undermine the description of Italian opera from this period as a mere succession of "numbers." The fluidity of events, textures, players, and orchestral commentary yield something much more moving than a mere glance at the table of contents at the beginning of the score suggests. Vocal melody still predominates in nineteenth-century Italian opera, while the orchestra accompanies, of course. But the later works of Rossini, Bellini, and Donizetti are a far cry from the *opere serie* of the eighteenth century.

GERMAN OPERA

The German-speaking regions of Europe at first glance seem to resemble the Italian peninsula, both politically and culturally, during the first part of the nineteenth century. They were divided into a number of smaller or larger states, ranging from the ever-growing Kingdom of Prussia to smaller duchies such as Weimar. Even the German-speaking portions of the Hapsburg Empire divided technically into smaller principalities. Many courts and almost all cities supported musical activity, and many had theaters for their own opera companies or for touring companies. These conditions would seem to augur well for a flourishing native practice of opera.

From the last decades of the eighteenth century there had been a concerted effort to establish German-language opera. And yet for all the works presented to a potentially large audience, few gained a lasting foothold in the repertory, even in their own time. Mozart's two outstanding contributions, *Die Entführung aus dem Serail* (*The Abduction from the Seraglio*) and *Die Zauberflöte* (*The Magic Flute*), held their own. These are both Singspiele: a conglomeration of songs, arias, and choruses interspersed with spoken dialogue. Beethoven's *Fidelio* seems also to fall in this tradition, but it actually proceeds from another, that of the opéra comique. (The libretto for *Fidelio* was based directly on J. N. Bouilly's *Léonore* as set by Pierre Gaveaux.) Opéras comiques at the turn of the century often featured serious political themes amid the admixture of songs, arias, choruses, and "reminiscence motives," melodic ideas that returned through the course of the work. In a sense, then, *Fidelio* emphasizes the fact that opéras comiques in translation vied with the native tradition. Together with Italian opera (also in translation), they formed a large part of the German repertory.

Many early-nineteenth-century composers tried their hand at works for the German musical theater. Meyerbeer encountered singular failure (though his works for the French Opéra later triumphed in Germany). Schubert contributed *Die Zauberharfe* (a melodrama premiered in 1820), *Die Zwillingsbrüder* (Singspiel; 1820), and a host of works unperformed in his time. E. T. A. Hoffmann took up a fairy-tale subject in *Undine* (1816), and Ludwig (Louis) Spohr explored the legend of *Faust* (opera after Goethe, 1813), orientalism in *Jessonda* (opera; 1823), and medieval religion in *Der Kreuzfahrer* (*The Crusader*, 1845).

German composers tended toward "Romantic" themes in the literal sense of the word, as in old tales or "romances." These involved the folkloric and supernatural, the medieval and chivalric, or sometimes all of these combined. Many of the operas cited above address such themes, and the operas of Heinrich Marschner, to take just one nineteenth-century German example, provide a kind of *catalogue raisonné. Der Vampyr* (1827) came from Byron's *Lord Ruthwen* (the supernatural), *Der Templer und die Jüdin* (1829) originated in Scott's *Ivanhoe* (the chivalric and medieval), and *Hans Heiling* (1833) came from an old tale (folkloric and chivalric). The only composer, however, from this generation to combine the themes with any lasting success in Germany was Carl Maria von Weber.

Weber

Carl Maria von Weber (1786–1826) came from a family with a long and distinguished history in the practice of music. Not only did his father, Franz Anton Weber, work as a Kapellmeister and composer, but so did his uncle, Fridolin. Carl Maria counted a number of singers among his older cousins, including Mozart's wife, Constanze. Weber himself started music lessons at an understandably early age, surrounded by a music-making family as he was, and he soon took up studies with Michael Haydn in Salzburg. He composed his first Singspiel at the age of twelve in Munich, after being exposed there to the eclectic mixture of Singspiele and opéras comiques at the Munich theater. By the age of fourteen he had composed *Das Waldmärchen,* a "romantic comic opera" in Freiburg, where he had gone to help his father open a lithography business for the printing of music. For a short time from 1803 to 1804, Carl studied in Vienna with Abbé Vogler before taking up a post as Kapellmeister in Breslau during the summer of 1804. There followed a series of short appointments in Carlsruhe and Stuttgart, and then stints as a freelance soloist in Heidelberg and Darmstadt (again in the company of Vogler and his students). Weber toured Germany as piano virtuoso during the ensuing years until he reached Prague in early 1813, where he was asked to fill a sudden vacancy as director of the Prague Opera (a private company) at the age of twenty-seven.

In Prague, a large and cultured city, Weber immediately set about trying to improve the standard of performance and scheduled a large number of new works, most of them opéras comiques, by composers such as Isouard and Boieldieu. These works, combining everyday characters with folkish musical color and spoken dialogue, would influence greatly Weber's own "Romantic operas." While in Prague, Weber also championed the cause of German opera, including his own *Silvana,* Beethoven's *Fidelio,* and his friend Meyerbeer's *Wirt und Gast.* Weber remained in Prague only three years, however, and he set off again in 1816 on tour. During a stop in Carlsbad to take "the cure," he met Vitzhum, the new intendant of the Dresden Opera. Vitzhum wanted to create a German company in the royal Saxon capital, and he engaged Weber as its music director. Weber arrived in Dresden early in 1817 to assume his post.

What Weber found in Dresden was a substantial court opera dominated by the Italians, with whom internecine strife continued intermittently until the end of his tenure. The appointment lasted, with interruptions for various excursions, until the end of the composer's brief life. During the Dresden years Weber wrote his most famous operas, though none of them specifically for his own company. *Der Freischütz* (1821) was commissioned by Berlin, *Euryanthe* (1823) by the Kärtnertor Theater in Vienna, and *Oberon* (1826) for Covent Garden in London. During this period Weber's health went into serious decline. He had long suffered from tuberculosis, widespread in Europe during the nineteenth century, and he died of it in London while conducting performances of *Oberon* there in 1826.

Weber was active not only as a performer and composer but also as a music critic. His reviews of operas by French and German composers established a set of principles that he sought to realize in his own operas and that influenced subsequent German composers, most importantly Wagner. For instance, he observes in a review of Spohr's *Faust* how successfully

> . . . a few melodies run through the whole [work] like delicate threads that hold it together in spirit. In this respect the effective overture, in which the composer found it necessary to provide a foreword about what was to follow as in a printed book, is not entirely comprehensible until the entire opera has been heard.

This is a description of operatic overtures that establish "leitmotifs" and provide a microcosm of the dramatic action. In another influential review of Hoffmann's *Undine,* Weber characterizes the ideal German opera as "a self-contained work of art, in which all the elements and contributions of the employed and related arts merge into one another until they disappear, and in a certain sense submerge, to create a new world." This is nothing less than an early description of a "Gesamtkunstwerk" (total work of art) such as Wagner promoted later in the century.

We can understand the extent to which Weber realized his ideals by examining briefly *Der Freischütz,* the only one of his operas performed with any regularity today, and then only in Germany. In its day it was widely acclaimed in Paris (under the title *Robin des Bois*) and also in London (whence the music in Figure 3.4 made its way to an American publisher). The action is set in "olden times": Bohemia after the Thirty Years' War (the seventeenth century). The main characters are simple folk—huntsmen and farmers—with a benign prince putting in a brief, nonsinging appearance in the last act (quite unlike the Italian and French grand operas, in which the nobility or gentry provide the main characters). The plot concerns an assistant gamekeeper, Max, who must win his bride, Agathe, in a shooting contest. He is seduced into cheating by using "Freikügeln" (magic bullets) cast by means of witchcraft. These will hit anything the marksman desires until the seventh shot, which belongs to the Black Huntsman (Samiel), a demon who will take a soul with it. Of course, Agathe is the intended victim, but at the last minute a pious hermit intervenes to save the innocent girl and bring forgiveness to the repentant Max. The presence of demons, magic bullets, and devout hermits are all intrusions of Gothic romanticism into a rural setting that comes straight out of the opéra comique.

Just as the plot derives from a pastiche of musico-theatrical traditions, so Weber's music combines the traditions of the Singspiel, opéra comique, and even Italian opera. Weber's overture for *Der Freischütz* provides a good example of the synthesis. Weber was a fine instrumental composer who learned much from Beethoven and Mozart. The substantial orchestration and full-fledged sonata form of this overture follow in the Viennese tradition of *Zauberflöte* and *Fidelio.* But Weber combines the German practice with the opéra comique's penchant for the "reminiscence motive" to make of this prelude a hybrid of sonata-form and "potpourri" overture, the latter incorporating motives that appear in various arias or scenes. The overture really does resemble "the foreword of a book," a feature the composer had praised in Spohr's overture to *Faust.*

The sheet music in Figure 3.4 represents *Freischütz*'s heavy investment in what Dahlhaus calls the "characteristic"—that is, local color (as opposed to the cosmopolitan). This chorus of hunters invokes the folkloric to create a rustic atmosphere that is another central feature in opéra comique, though here it connotes German, not French, culture. The interludes played by a trio of horns, the close part-writing, the overly simplified harmonies, and the nonsense syllables of yodeling (not shown in Figure 3.4) after each verse all establish the folkish cast. This sheet music reminds us that part-songs also enjoyed a public.

To the local color of the opéra comique Weber added elements from the Italian opera. Both Agathe and her friend Ännchen receive three-part arias. Agathe's comes in the second act as no. 8 (two-verse cantabile, andante *tempo di*

Figure 3.4 "Hunter's Chorus," no. 15, from Weber's *Der Freischütz* (1821) in an American edition (ca. 1825) with parallel English and French translation. Music Library, University of North Carolina at Chapel Hill.

mezzo, and vivace con fuoco cabaletta), with the soprano melody of the vivace (see Example 3.5) formed from a reminiscence motive that appears as closing material in the overture. Weber places Ännchen's three-part aria in the third act, constructing it as an intriguing hybrid. The initial cantabile consists of a *romanze,* the tale of a "ghost," in this case with a comic ending (the evil spirit turns out to be the family dog). The *tempo di mezzo* features dialogue between Ännchen and Agathe, and Ännchen's admonishment for Agathe to cheer up makes a logically faster cabaletta with something like coloratura in the vocal writing. Here we have the folkish supernatural tale (*romanze*) paired with Italianate vocal writing in a number with Italianate structure overall.

The most famous part of the opera, the one invariably discussed by music historians, is the "Wolf's Glen Scene," where Max and the evil Kaspar cast the magic bullets of the story. Scholars will often cite its "through-composed" features and its fluidity of writing (spoken dialogue, arioso, recitative, with mood set by the orchestral background). In fact, the Wolf's Glen Scene comes straight out of the opéra comique tradition of the melodrama. In this case the term refers not to overacted drama but to a specific technique in which a composer writes orchestral music to create mood under spoken dialogue. Weber's only extension here is to begin with a long accompanied recitative, interspersed with declamatory choral writing and sections of arioso. He punctuates this with evocative orchestral motifs, many returning from the overture. The scene is a wonderful bit of theater, full of spine-chilling special effects. But in the end it explores little new operatic territory: Like all finales, it moves freely between inner and outer action, combining the techniques of reminiscence melodies and melodrama from the tradition of the opéra comique. The attraction to contemporary audiences must have stemmed in part from the staging, which calls for all sorts of ghostly apparitions, off-stage noises, thunder, and the like. Such scenic effects were something like special effects in film: They provided their own reason for going to see a production, independent of other operatic features.

American audiences may find a performance of *Der Freischütz* disappointing. The short, folkish choruses and relatively modest arias are no match for Italian or French operas of the same period. Germans, however, revere this piece as the prime example of early "Romantic Opera," the genre that Wagner would later cultivate, ultimately transforming it into his peculiar brand of musical theater.

FRENCH OPERA

Unlike both Italy and Germany, France had long been united, the very model of the European national state. Its strong central government in Paris resulted in a cultural establishment that orbited around that city's gravitational pull. Paris set

EXAMPLE 3.5   Beginning of the cabaletta from Agathe's aria in Weber's *Der Freischütz,* Act II

the fashion, and as one of Europe's largest cities, it offered both the financial resources and the talent necessary to maintain a flourishing artistic life. The tides of nineteenth-century Parisian musical life responded in part to a succession of national regimes, beginning with the First Empire of Napoleon from 1804 to 1814. His downfall led to a restoration of the dispossessed Bourbon monarchy during the period from 1815 to 1830. In 1830 the Bourbons were overthrown again, this time in favor of a constitutional monarchy under Louis Philippe (the "citizen king"), who ruled until the 1848 revolution.

Within this political framework, three main companies, all supported and regulated in some measure by the government, dominated opera in Paris during the first part of the nineteenth century. The most prestigious of these in the Napoleonic era (1804–14) and beginning again around the reign of Louis Philippe (1830–48) was the Opéra. It featured lavish productions usually of fictionalized historical themes such as *La vestale* (1807) and *Fernand Cortez* (1809) by Gaspare Spontini, and later *La muette de Portici* (1828) by Daniel-François-Esprit Auber, *Guillaume Tell* (1829) by Rossini, *Les Huguenots* (1835) by Giacomo Meyerbeer, *La juive* (1835) by Fromental Halévy, and *Benvenuto Cellini* (1838) by Hector Berlioz. There was also the Opéra-Comique, which featured spoken dialogue between a variety of musical numbers (arias, songs, choruses, melodramas, and so forth). The word "comique" in the title does not translate directly into comic plots: The subject matter was often serious, with political overtones. But everyday characters peopled opéra comique with plenty of local color in works with titles such as *Les rendezvous bourgeois* (1807) and *Cendrillon* (1810) by Nicolas Isouard or *Le nouveau seigneur de village* (1813) and *La dame blanche* (after Sir Walter Scott's *Guy Mannering*, 1825) by Adrien Boieldieu. Finally, the Théâtre-Italien, founded in 1801, made for a prominent foreign presence in Paris, particularly with the arrival of Rossini's *L'italiana in Algeri* in 1817. As we saw earlier, the maestro himself took up residence in 1824, followed by Bellini and Donizetti. Famous Italian singers rounded out a distinguished expatriate company.

For some reason that has not been fully analyzed, only the opera fashioned by Italian composers for Paris during the early part of the nineteenth century survives in the active repertory. We can hear Rossini's *Guillaume Tell* occasionally, as well as Bellini's *I puritani di Scozia* (distantly inspired by Scott's *Old Mortality*) or Donizetti's *La fille du règiment* and *Don Pasquale*. But the acclaimed French operas or opéras comiques by Boieldieu or Auber or Meyerbeer remain virtually unknown today. Still, there is some point in familiarizing ourselves with at least some features of opera by Meyerbeer to see how this most lionized and successful figure fits into the operatic history of the nineteenth century.

Meyerbeer

Like many of the composers prominent in French opera of the early nineteenth century, Giacomo Meyerbeer (1791–1864) was not French by a long shot. He had grown up the scion of a wealthy Jewish family in Berlin. Although his father and mother had no particular musical talents of their own, they maintained a flourishing salon frequented by musicians, intellectuals, and the Prussian nobility, including the crown prince himself. Meyerbeer evinced early talent as a pianist and studied composition with Zelter (later Mendelssohn's teacher) from 1805 to 1807. He continued his studies with Abbé Vogler in 1810, a distinguished theory teacher in Darmstadt, where he enjoyed the company of Vogler's other talented students, among them Carl Maria von Weber.

By 1812 Meyerbeer had embarked on a career as a composer of German operas, gaining an appointment to the Hessian court in early 1813. But the string of German operas he wrote for various cities all proved unsuccessful, and there was some question whether he would pursue a career as a piano virtuoso. He was diverted from this ambition by a brief trip to Italy in 1816 that lengthened into a stay of nine years with some interruptions. In Italy he came to know and gained the respect of the leading impresarios, librettists, and singers, and he commenced a very successful career in Italian opera with six ambitious works. These eventually earned him a reputation on a par with that of Rossini.

Rossini himself brought Meyerbeer to Paris for a production of *Il crociato in Egitto* (Venice, La Fenice, 1824) at the Théâtre-Italien in 1825. It made a sensation, establishing Meyerbeer as a major operatic composer. He capitalized on this success by enlisting the French playwright Thomas Sauvage to rework *Margharita d'Anjou* (libretto by Romani; Milan, La Scala, 1820) for the Odéon Theater in 1826. On the heels of this success, Meyerbeer was persuaded by the director of the Opéra-Comique to embark on an entirely new work with a French libretto in 1827. To that end the composer enlisted one of the most talented and prolific playwrights in Paris, Eugène Scribe. The two eventually reworked their first collaboration, *Robert le diable,* as an *opéra,* which had its Paris premiere in 1831 to unprecedented acclaim. Not just a little of the success must be credited to Louis Véron, who had made his fortune in patent medicine and was licensed to take over the Opéra in 1831. He had a talent for showmanship that translated into theatrical spectacle. *Robert* went on to triumph all over Europe.

Meyerbeer remained very much the international figure during his later years. He never became a resident of Paris, though he spent some months there every year. After his success with *Robert,* he fashioned a series of French operas, usually with Scribe, including *Les Huguenots* (Opéra, 1836), *Le prophète* (Opéra, 1849), *L'étoile du nord* (Opéra-Comique, 1854), *Le pardon de Ploërmel* (Opéra-Comique, 1859), and finally the posthumously produced *L'africaine* (Opéra, 1865). In 1842 Meyerbeer was appointed *Generalmusikdirektor* at the Prussian court opera in Berlin, holding that post until 1848. He then returned to work on operas in Paris, dying while *L'africaine* was still in rehearsal.

The fame of such Meyerbeer operas as *Robert le diable* (1831) can be gauged from the excerpt printed as American sheet music in Figure 3.5. *Robert* in particular mined the popularity of medieval subjects. The plot is set in the eleventh century, when Robert, Duke of Normandy, is cast out by his subjects for his dissolute behavior. Making his way to Sicily, he falls in love with the Princess Isabelle and makes the acquaintance of Bertram, a demon disguised as a knight. Bertram turns out to be none other than Robert's father, and he vies for Robert's soul with the duke's pious sister, Alice, with his mother's memory, and with his love of Isabelle. In the end the demon father loses the battle, but not before the spectator is treated to all manner of unearthly occurrences. Meyerbeer and Scribe's opera has many favorite nineteenth-century elements, including feudal chivalry, the supernatural, minstrelsy, and sacred redeeming love, an admixture of Bram Stoker and Sir Walter Scott, as it were. Even Wagner conceded that "*Robert le diable* has a wonderful, almost sinister atmosphere . . . ," and took a page out of Scribe's book for *Flying Dutchman*. Scribe and Meyerbeer, in their turn, had taken lessons in atmosphere from Meyerbeer's friend, Carl Maria von Weber.

Meyerbeer learned *musically* from his friend Rossini, and also from the traditions of the opéra comique where *Robert* had its birth. This latter fact, together with the subject matter itself, may account for the abundance of strophic arias with folkish cast. For instance, as part of his Rossinian *introduzione* (in the customary three parts) Meyerbeer includes a ballad ("Jadis règnait en Normandie") by the minstrel Raimbaut. Cast in the traditional compound meter for such narrative arias, the unusual feature of this supernatural tale is its "reflexive" function. Unaware of his audience, Raimbaut tells Robert's own story in the duke's presence. The first act also features a "romance" (*romanza*, "Va, dit-elle, va, mon enfant") by Alice reminding Robert of his mother's love, and later we find a "siciliene" ("Le Duc de Normandie") sung by Robert as part of a finale in which he gambles all his wealth away.

While Robert and his French compatriots take on the folkish accents of medieval Normandy in their strophic arias, the cultured Princess of Sicily, Isabelle, understandably sings in Italianate forms. Her cavatina at the beginning of the second act ("Il me délaisse trompant") falls in the standard three-part form, with interjections by the chorus and dialogue with Alice providing the *tempo di mezzo*. The cabaletta ("écoute, jeune amie"; Example 3.6) displays all the vocal fireworks that any lover of intricate passagework could desire, as well as the standard *AA'* form. Indeed, the vocal writing throughout the opera is more Italianate than anything else. Even Alice's third-act "couplets et scène" ("Quand je quittai la Normandie"; Figure 3.5) features an increasingly elaborate series of roulades, trills, and cadenzas over the course of three stanzas. Meyerbeer punctuates the simple, strophic form, moreover, with various interjections from Alice and Bertram in recitative, and even from the chorus. The composer seeks in every way possible to smooth the boundaries between outer and inner action in the interest of seamless drama.

The peculiarly French elements of *Robert* come in the lavish number of scene changes spread over five acts (the canonic number for a French grand

EXAMPLE 3.6   Beginning of the cabaletta from Isabelle's aria in Meyerbeer's *Robert le diable,* Act II

opera) and in the deference paid to the dance. The finale of the third act is given over entirely to a ballet in which Bertram summons the spirits of dead nuns who did not maintain their vows. The fallen sisters dance a bacchanal attempting to lure Robert to his damnation. It is tempting to deride this scene, but in fact it takes on a spooky cast, set as it is amid the ruins of a convent, with music both sinister and eerie. In the end the spirit of Robert's departed mother triumphs: The last act takes place at the Cathedral of Palermo, first outside and then inside, where the duke's soul is redeemed through his marriage to Isabelle. The struggle between good and evil provides for an elaborate contrast of settings (ruined monastery at night, large cathedral in ceremonious garb) that yields splendid pageantry.

Wagner would criticize French grand opera for its "effects without causes," but at its best in Meyerbeer the grand scenes result from dramatic situations that meld perfectly with the exotic plots. Not just a few Italian composers, especially Verdi, took cues from Meyerbeer's command of orchestral recitative and ability

Figure 3.5 "Quand je quittai la Normandie" from Meyerbeer's *Robert le diable* (1831) in an American sheet music edition with parallel English and French texts (ca. 1835). Music Library, University of North Carolina at Chapel Hill.

to move effortlessly between soloist and chorus. And Wagner's own orchestrations owe much to Meyerbeer's large, adroitly manipulated instrumental ensemble as well as the older composer's way with operatic pomp. The later developments in nineteenth-century opera involve evolution more than revolution. Verdi and Wagner later in the century followed a logical course plotted by composers such as Rossini, Bellini, Donizetti, Weber, and Meyerbeer.

FURTHER READING

At present no general history of opera reflecting current scholarship exists, though readers might wish to consult *The New Grove Masters of Italian Opera* (New York, 1983) for that region.

Rossini

For Gioachino Rossini, readers can do no better than Philip Gossett's article in the *New Grove Dictionary of Music and Musicians,* 2nd ed., augmented by his articles "Gioachino Rossini and the Conventions of Composition" (*Acta Musicologica,* 1970) and "The Overtures of Rossini" (*19th Century Music,* 1979). Stendhal's *Life of Rossini,* trans. Richard Coe (Seattle, 1972), still makes for interesting reading.

Bellini

Vincenzo Bellini is also represented in an article for *The New Grove Masters* by Friedrich Lippmann, though the most current information will appear in John Rosselli's recent biography, *The Life of Bellini* (Cambridge, 1996).

Donizetti

William Ashbrook's standard biography, *Donizetti* (Kassell, 1965), is dated but still useful. More insightful criticism appears in Philip Gossett's *Anna Bolena and the Artistic Maturity of Gaetano Donizetti* (Oxford, 1985).

Weber

The excellent standard biography comes from John Warrack, *Carl Maria von Weber* (Cambridge, 1976). Because Weber was a voluble and exceptionally perceptive critic, readers may also want to consult his *Writings on Music,* ed. Warrack, trans. Martin Cooper (Cambridge, 1981).

Meyerbeer

The English language offers little on Meyerbeer, the best being *Giacomo Meyerbeer, A Life in Letters,* trans. Mark Violette (Portland, OR, 1989). There are, however, a number of studies on nineteenth-century French opera, including Patrick Barbier's *Opera in Paris, 1800–1850: A Lively History* (Portland, OR, 1995) and, most recently, Anselm Gerhard's *The Urbanization of Opera: Music Theater in Paris in the Nineteenth Century* (Chicago, 1998).

CHAPTER 4

The Styling of the Avant-Garde

The front page of the first issue for Robert Schumann's *Neue Leipziger Zeitschrift für Musik* (*The New Leipzig Journal for Music;* Figure 4.1) embodies an essence of European classical music during the decades of the 1830s and 1840s. The "new" in its title reaches beyond the simple fact of its inauguration to embrace connotations of artistic "progress." That progress involved first and foremost notions of superior taste informed by a discerning intellect (rather than mere technical prowess). And that intellect proceeded in turn from an acculturation in the musical past, without which the notion of "progress" had no meaning. It was no coincidence, then, that this period saw the rise of a concept called "classical music"—that is, music of an ideal type that would remain eternally valid to the educated listener. For the avant-garde aimed at much more than mere novelty: Composers intended their singular pieces to become part of a museum that included exceptional specimens of past and present music in its collection. And thus what seem to be conflicting currents—the performance of long-forgotten music versus the demand for an increasingly original musical idiom; the codification of traditional musical forms versus the avoidance of fixed forms; the fixation of a musical canon versus the determined promotion of stylistic plurality—actually form a larger, dialectical synthesis.

The generation of the *New Journal* did not invent the aesthetic trends that formed the synthesis, but it did intensify them. Increased interest in music history had originated in the late eighteenth century, as had the increased emphasis on

Neue Leipziger
Zeitschrift für Musik.

Herausgegeben
durch einen Verein von Künstlern und Kunstfreunden.

Erster Jahrgang.   № **1.**   **Den 3. April 1834.**

Die allein,
Die nur ein lustig Spiel, Geräusch der Tartschen
Zu hören kommen, oder einen Mann
Im bunten Rock, mit Gelb verbrämt, zu sehen,
Die irren sich.   Shakspeare.

Diese Zeitschrift liefert:

Theoretische und historische Aufsätze; kunstästhetische, grammatische, pädagogische, biographische, akustische u. a. Nekrologe, Beiträge zur Bildungsgeschichte berühmter Künstler, Berichte über neue Erfindungen oder Verbesserungen, Beurtheilungen ausgezeichneter Virtuosenleistungen, Operndarstellungen; unter der Aufschrift: Zeitgenossen, Skizzen mehr oder weniger berühmter Künstler, unter der Rubrik: Journalschau, Nachrichten über das Wirken anderer kritischen Blätter, Bemerkungen über Recensionen in ihnen, Zusammenstellung verschiedener Beurtheilungen über dieselbe Sache, eigne Resultate darüber, auch Antikritiken der Künstler selbst, sodann Auszüge aus ausländischen, Interessantes aus älteren musikalischen Zeitungen.

Belletristisches, kürzere musikalische Erzählungen, Phantasiestücke, Scenen aus dem Leben, Humoristisches, Gedichte, die sich vorzugsweise zur Composition eignen.

Kritiken über Geisteserzeugnisse der Gegenwart mit vorzüglicher Berücksichtigung der Compositionen für das Pianoforte. Auf frühere schätzbare, übergangene oder vergessene Werke wird aufmerksam gemacht, wie auch auf eingesandte Manuscripte talentvoller unbekannter Componisten, die Aufmunterung verdienen. Zu derselben Gattung gehörige Compositionen werden öfter zusammengestellt, gegen einander verglichen, besonders interessante doppelt beurtheilt. Zur Beurtheilung eingesandte Werke werden durch eine vorläufige Anzeige bekannt gemacht; doch bestimmt nicht das Alter der Einsendung die frühere Besprechung, sondern die Vorzüglichkeit der Leistung.

Miscellen, kurzes Musikbezügliches, Anekdotisches, Kunstbemerkungen, literarische Notizen, Musikalisches aus Goethe, Jean Paul, Heinse, Hoffmann, Novalis, Rochlitz u. A. m.

Correspondenzartikel nur dann, wenn sie eigentliches Musikleben abschildern. Wir stehen in Verbindung mit Paris, London, Wien, Berlin, Petersburg, Neapel, Frankfurt, Hamburg, Riga, München, Dresden, Stuttgart, Cassel u. a. — Referirende Artikel fallen in die folgende Abtheilung.

Chronik, Musikaufführungen, Concertanzeigen, Reisen, Aufenthalt der Künstler, Beförderungen, Vorfälle im Leben. Es wird keine Mühe gescheut, diese Chronik vollständig zu machen, um die Namen der Künstler so oft, wie möglich, in Erinnerung zu bringen.

Noch machen wir vorläufig bekannt, daß, wenn sich die Zeitschrift bald einer allgemeinen Theilnahme erfreuen sollte, der Verleger sich erboten hat, einen Preis auf die beste eingesandte Composition, für's erste auf die vorzüglichste Pianofortesonate, zu setzen, worüber das Nähere seiner Zeit berichtet wird.

Ueber die Stellung, die diese neue Zeitschrift unter den schon erscheinenden einzunehmen gedenkt, werden sich diese ersten Blätter thatsächlich am deutlichsten aussprechen.

Wer den Künstler erforschen will, besuche ihn in seiner Werkstatt. Es schien nothwendig, auch ihm ein Organ zu verschaffen, das ihn anregte, außer durch seinen directen Einfluß, noch durch Wort und Schrift zu wirken, einen öffentlichen Ort, in dem er das Beste von dem, was er selbst gesehen im eigenen Auge, selbst erfahren im eigenen Geist, niederlegen, eben eine Zeitschrift, in der er sich gegen einseitige oder unwahre Kritik vertheidigen könne, so weit sich das mit Gerechtigkeit und Unparteilichkeit überhaupt verträgt.

Figure 4.1   First page of the first issue of Robert Schumann's *New Journal for Music*, which began publication in Leipzig, 1834. Music Library, University of North Carolina at Chapel Hill.

individual originality fostered by the diversitarian premises of early Romanticism. The composers and critics (they were often one and the same) of the 1830s focused these tendencies and articulated them so clearly that by the end of the 1840s something very like a modern canon of enduring "classics" had been established. Schumann and his fellow travelers added Schubert to the First Viennese School (Mozart and Haydn as precursors to Beethoven were already well established) and went on to name Mendelssohn, Chopin, Liszt, and Berlioz to the roster of "great composers."

Much avant-garde music before 1848 was instrumental, as a result again of amplifying German aestheticians from the turn of the century. But this instrumental music lay far from the later concept of "absolute music," that is, music "absolved" from external influence. Quite the contrary, the new generation took over musical Idealism lock, stock, and barrel. If anything, they reemphasized the notion that music reflected ideas in the spiritual realm or that pieces *had* spirit. According to this point of view, works with programs did not represent the written word or paint a natural object. They manifested in music the spirit of literary works, programs, or natural phenomena. Following the lead of Beethoven, the new generation intensified their standing as "tone poets" able to express a spiritual essence in the superior language of music. This explains their delight in musical portraiture, songs without words, programs, and programmatic titles, all of which they regarded unparadoxically as dispensable. "The main thing remains," Schumann wrote of Berlioz's *Symphonie fantastique* in his *New Journal*, "whether the music without text or explanation is something in itself, and above all whether it is imbued with spirit."

"Imbued with spirit" might constitute the best description of the music by the avant-garde of the 1830s and 1840s. Its colorful idiosyncrasy and poetic expressivity led twentieth-century composers of film music to quote it copiously, granting many present-day listeners instant familiarity with pieces such as Mendelssohn's "Spring Song" (from his *Songs without Words,* op. 62), Schumann's "Happy Farmer" (from his *Album for the Young,* op. 68), Liszt's *Les préludes* (from his *Symphonic Poems*), Chopin's "Funeral March" (second movement of his Piano Sonata, op. 35), or Berlioz's "Sylphs' Ballet" (from *The Damnation of Faust,* op. 24). If there is a commonly held symbolism in Western music, these composers were instrumental in supplying its vocabulary. Of course, their contribution lies in much more than cinematic commonplaces. But their intrusion into the popular consciousness gives some idea just how well they succeeded in endowing their music with character.

LEIPZIG

Viewing German musical life in the 1830s and 1840s as centering on Leipzig has an artificial air about it, and yet the construct of a "Leipzig school" has its uses. Though smaller than Berlin and Vienna, this Saxon town of about 40,000 inhabitants influenced nineteenth-century musical life out of all proportion to its size. Because it had a long history as a "free city," run without the interference of a local aristocracy, it possessed a number of middle-class musical institutions that served as models for other German cities. For instance, Leipzig sported the oldest permanent orchestral subscription concerts in Europe. They took place in what had been the assembly room of the local weaver's guild (the Gewandhaus), and the ensemble is still known today as the Leipzig Gewandhaus Orchestra. Leipzig also had an inordinate number of music publishers, including the houses of C. F. Whistling, C. F. Peters, Friedrich Hofmeister, and Breitkopf and Härtel (which published the influential *Allgemeine musikalische Zeitung*). Finally, Leipzig founded a highly influential conservatory under Mendelssohn's guidance in 1843, becoming an international mecca for aspiring student performers and composers (including many Americans later in the century).

Musical culture in Leipzig was distinguished above all by the total domination of the middle classes. The musical life of Berlin, Vienna, and Dresden revolved around opera houses that enjoyed the prestige of royal support. But Leipzig provided the model for the new order in which a larger, middle-class audience supported the institutions and types of music that lent prestige to its cultural and political pretensions. If it did not possess patent or pedigree, the bourgeoisie could ennoble itself by demonstrating superior taste, not only in contemporary music, but also in select music from the past. Here, too, Leipzig could lay claim to an extraordinary chapter in the history of music by invoking the spirit of J. S. Bach, who had resided in the city for twenty-seven years. Even Wagner, who later repudiated the musical values of his native city, incorporated some of its Protestant reforming zeal and its penchant for orchestral music into the operatic tradition. But that is a story for another chapter. Here we concentrate on the leaders of Leipzig's musical society, the critic-composer Robert Schumann, the piano virtuosa Clara Wieck, and the conductor-composer Felix Mendelssohn.

Robert Schumann

It seems odd that Robert Schumann (1810–56), the most provincial of all his contemporaries, should have become the aesthetic spokesman for his age. Perhaps his relatively narrow geographical acquaintance (he would travel in adulthood mostly as the consort of his more famous, virtuosic wife) prompted him to develop unusually wide-ranging critical tastes. Whatever the reasons, Schumann became the artistic conscience of his generation through his *Neue Zeitschrift für Musik,* and he also established himself in later years as one of the most important German composers between Schubert and Brahms.

Schumann was born in Zwickau, a little town south of Leipzig in what was then the kingdom of Saxony. His father owned a small publishing firm specializing in pocket editions of Sir Walter Scott and other foreign literature in translation. Robert received a far more thorough education in literature than in music. As a child he took lessons in piano and dabbled in musical composition from an early age, and though he evinced talent, he was not a prodigy. Schumann's father briefly entertained a notion of sending him to study composition with Weber, but the master died before the idea was broached. And when August Schumann himself died in 1826, his will placed a goodly sum in trust for Robert with the stipulation that he complete at least three years of university education in some unspecified subject. That subject turned out to be the law at the insistence of his mother and guardian, after Robert had completed his classical training at a *Gymnasium* in 1828.

Schumann used his study of law at the University of Leipzig as an excuse to sample the city's rich cultural life and to take piano lessons with Friedrich Wieck. He spent his time improvising, playing any Schubert he could find, reading the novelist Jean Paul, and composing assorted songs, duets for piano, and even a little chamber music. In May of 1829 he moved to Heidelberg, ostensibly to study law with Anton Justus Thibaut, who just happened to have written a famous treatise advocating the notion of a "classical music." Thibaut maintained a private salon (in addition to lecturing in law) where choral masterpieces by Handel, Palestrina, and Bach were performed. Though Schumann found Thibaut dogmatic and limited, he was greatly influenced by the older man's notion of a music with lasting value akin to the literature of classical antiquity. Schumann returned to Leipzig in 1830 and finally persuaded Wieck to intercede with his mother in order to pursue the career of a piano virtuoso.

Schumann proved a rather wayward student both of keyboard and of music theory, and an injury to his hand rendered him incapable of becoming a piano virtuoso. This turned out to be providential, for he discovered a perfect outlet combining his musical and literary interests in the *Neue Zeitschrift*. He founded this "New Journal" in 1834 with a group of Leipzig friends, but as they dropped away one by one for various reasons, Schumann was left in sole possession. During his editorship (1834–44), the *New Journal* provided a model of independent music criticism (it accepted no advertising from music publishers), championing music of "better" quality by Beethoven, Schubert, Chopin, Berlioz, and Mendelssohn, among many others.

All the while Schumann wrote music criticism, he composed, at first exclusively for the piano in the 1830s, turning to Lieder in 1840, symphonic music in 1841, chamber music in 1842, and the oratorio in 1843. In the meantime he married Clara Wieck over her father's strenuous public objections. Clara was much more famous than Robert at the beginning of their marriage, and she campaigned vigorously for his music. Not only did she program his piano pieces, but she also took her husband on tour with her, often coupling her performance of concerti to renditions of her husband's symphonies.

In 1844 Schumann sold the *New Journal* to Franz Brendel and put aside his teaching position at Mendelssohn's newly founded conservatory to devote more time to composition and a career as a conductor. In the last decade of his life he increased his output enormously and with it his reputation as a composer, but he failed to establish himself as a performer. He began in Dresden conducting choral groups, made an unsuccessful bid for the Gewandhaus orchestra after Mendelssohn's death in 1847, and wound up in Düsseldorf (1850), where mental collapse eventually rendered him unfit. His compositions from the last decade ran the gamut from chamber music, Lieder, part-songs, and short piano pieces to concerti for piano, violin, and cello, three symphonies, assorted works for chorus and orchestra, and the opera *Genoveva*. He even found time to pen one last important piece of criticism heralding the arrival of Johannes Brahms on the German musical scene. All this constituted a last brilliant incandescence: In 1854 Schumann was committed to an asylum in Bonn, where he died in 1856, probably of tertiary syphilis.

Schumann's first impact on the musical world came as critic. He not only edited the *Neue Zeitschrift* but also contributed many of its important articles. He applied the aesthetic of a "classical" music (which required intellectual content coupled with superior craftsmanship to produce pieces of timeless value) to modern composition. In doing so he rejected the "philistine" taste of virtuoso-composers such as Herz and Hünten in favor of more substantial composers who shunned display for its own sake, such as Schubert, Chopin, and Mendelssohn. Schumann clothed his opinions, moreover, in a highly stylized literary prose modeled on the criticism of E. T. A. Hoffmann, whom he greatly admired. Schumann's writing is often ironic, and it indulges conceits such as the invention of characters (the most famous being Floristan and Eusebius) to debate the merits of music from different points of view. All this rendered his criticism especially rich in wit and metaphor. He could award laurels:

> When a German speaks of symphonies, he speaks of Beethoven: he considers the two words one and indivisible; they are his pride and joy. Just as the Italian has Naples, the Frenchman has his Revolution, and the Englishman his navy, so the German has his Beethoven symphonies.

He could also shy brickbats:

> . . . Haydn's music has always been much played here, and one can learn nothing new from him. He is like a familiar household friend who is always greeted with pleasure and respect but no longer holds great interest for the present day.

He hailed Chopin with the line, "Hats off, gentlemen! A genius!" Schumann was often right and always entertaining. Above all, his criticism was infused with the notion of artistic progress that we find, for instance, at the end of his *Symphonie fantastique* review:

If these lines . . . should gain recognition for [Berlioz's] symphony, not as the art-work of a master but as a work distinguished from all others by its intellectual power and originality, if, finally, they should incite German youth . . . to renewed activity, then in truth they will have fulfilled their purpose.

Schumann sought artistic progress in his own composing as well as in that of his fellow artists. For piano music this translated into a shift away from the fixed-form sonata of Beethoven's generation to free-form pieces made from a patchwork of smaller, often undeveloped episodes. The inspiration for such pieces often derived from extramusical sources of a literary or at least a poetic nature. *Papillons* (op. 2; 1831) presents an example of a work that drew its inspi-ration from a novel: the scene of a masked ball in Jean Paul's *Flegeljahre*. (The symbolism in the novel of the butterfly is interwoven with metamorphosis—the change wrought by "masks," or *Larvae* in German.) The composer actually annotated a copy of the Jean Paul episode with numbers of the various dances in op. 2. Though Schumann suppressed this literary connection, the piece clearly presents a collection of eccentric waltzes juxtaposed in a succession of quickly changing moods "imbued with the spirit" of a ball. There are bizarre episodes (the contrapuntal one in no. 3, for instance), some limpid parlor music, and quotations from popular tunes (the "Grandfather's dance" that begins no. 12). The poetic quality of the piece is most evident in the "Finale," where the strains of the "Grandfather's Dance," fragments of the opening waltz, and a bell tolling an early-morning hour intimate the ball's dissolution (see Example 4.1). This summation reminds us that the impressionistic whole is more than the sum of its miniature parts. The epigrammatic coda also stands as an example of the wit and irony that are mainstays of Schumann's style.

Many of Schumann's piano works from his first maturity consist of col-lected miniatures, and a fair number draw inspiration from extramusical conceits, including the *Davidsbündlertänze* (op. 6; 1837), *Phantasiestücke* (op. 12; 1838), *Kinderszenen* (op. 15; 1839), and *Kreisleriana* (after Hoffmann; op. 16; 1838). One of the most revealing of these is *Carnaval: scènes mignonnes sur quatre notes* (op. 9; 1837). The "four notes" of the title refer to a motto woven through-out the piece (A, E-flat, C, B-natural, or A [E]S C H in German). Asch is the name of a town in which one of Schumann's girlfriends lived, and the motto rearranged as SCHA also stands for Sch[umann], [Robert] A[lexander]. Each piece bears the title of a carnival masker: Some come from the commedia del'arte (Pierrot, Arlequin, Pantelon, Colombine), some come from Schu-mann's fanciful criticism (Florestan, Eusebius), some refer to other musicians (Chiarina [Clara], Chopin, Paganini), and there is even a silent group of "Sphinxes" (riddles that spell SCHA and ASCH in the German system). The irony of this last gesture repeats elsewhere in pieces such as "Pause" ("Intermis-sion"), which races like the wind. And in a miniature such as "Chopin" (Example 4.2), Schumann features his wit as a mimic. The elegant Chopinesque

EXAMPLE 4.1   Excerpt from "Finale" of Robert Schumann's *Papillons,* op. 2, 1831

EXAMPLE 4.2 Beginning of "Chopin" from Robert Schumann's *Carnaval,* op. 9, 1837

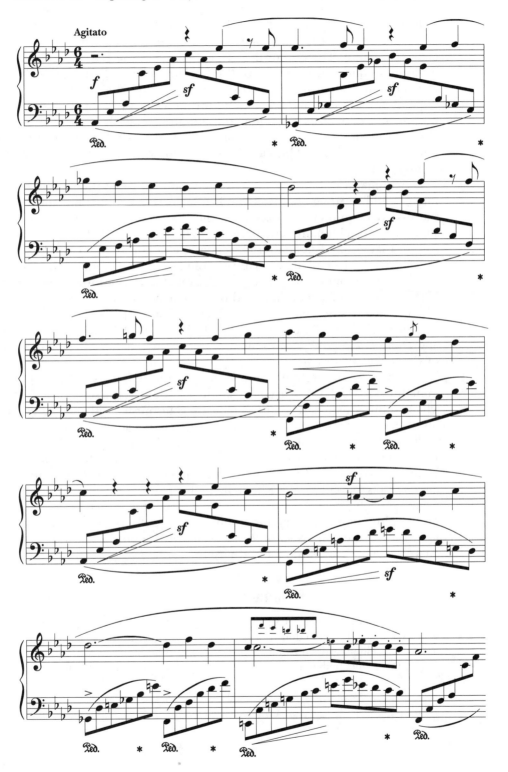

arpeggiations, the progression in the second measure to the flatted subtonic, and especially the chromatic filigree in measure 10 all display a talent for poetic characterization. The end of the piece, "March of the Davidsbund against the Philistines," quotes the "Finale" of *Papillons* and suggests that the mosaic of characters in *Carnaval* forms a composite artistic entity. The notion that groups of piquant miniatures could combine to form serious works of art drew both supporters and detractors. As Schumann admitted ruefully, "Much of [*Carnaval*] may charm this or that [individual], but the musical mood changes more quickly than the general public, which does not wish to be startled at every turn, could follow."

Schumann's ability to invest musical miniatures with rapidly changing, intense, and startling characterizations was precisely the talent that led to his success as a composer of Lieder. After the eleven songs he composed during his student years, Schumann did not return to the Lied until 1840, the year his court suit for Clara's hand came to trial. Schumann discovered that, unlike his collections of avant-garde piano miniatures, volumes of songs found immediate favor with audiences and therefore drew relatively high honoraria from publishers. He dashed off well over a hundred before the couple's wedding in September. The list includes notable cycles: the Heine Lieder, op. 24; *Myrthen,* op. 25; the Kerner Lieder, op. 37; the Eichendorff Lieder, op. 39 ("my most romantic"); and *Dichterliebe,* op. 48, not to mention many miscellaneous volumes of Lieder or *Romanzen und Balladen.*

Schumann brought his refined literary sensibilities as well as his talents as miniaturist to the Lied. The combination is evident in the song cycle *Dichterliebe,* which returns us again to the milieu of Hausmusik, with its highly literate, middle-class audience. The composer created a plot similar to his earlier Heine cycle, op. 24, by selecting poems from the *Lyrisches Intermezzo* in Heine's *Buch der Lieder.* He assumed that his audience would know the subtext spelled out in Heine's prologue, which tells of an oafish poet-knight whose quest for love will always be disappointed. "Im Rhein, im heiligen Strome" (no. 6) presents a good example of the odd undertone engendered by this Romantic irony. The text begins with sacred imagery and seems at first to concern the "holy" nature of love. But the persona is so obsessed by his girlfriend that he sees her worldly charms in a portrait of the Blessed Virgin.

"Im Rhein, im heiligen Strome"

Im Rhein, im heiligen Strome,	In the Rhine, the holy stream,
Da spiegelt sich in den Well'n	There in the waves is reflected
Mit seinem großen Dome,	With its great cathedral,
Das große, heilige Köln.	Great, holy Cologne.

Im Dom, da steht ein Bildnis,	In the cathedral hangs a picture
Auf goldenem Leder gemalt;	Painted on gilded leather;
In meinem Lebens Wildnis	Into my life's wilderness
Hat's freundlich hinein gestrahlt.	It has beamed amiably.
Es schweben Blumen und Englein	Flowers and cherubs hover
Um uns're Liebe Frau;	Around Our Dear Lady;
Die Augen, die Lippen, die Wänglein,	Her eyes, her lips, her cheeks
Die gleichen der Liebsten genau.	Are like my beloved's exactly.

Schumann's setting, in the tradition of the "polyrhythmic" Lied inherited from Schubert, responds to the "sacred" backdrop of the poem with a melody proceeding like a cantus firmus in uncommonly long note values, surrounded by a filigree of faster, dotted rhythms in the piano (see Example 4.3). The effect is appropriately solemn, but Schumann does not stop with mere reinforcement of the poetry: His accompaniment also offers a commentary. Its minor mode and heavily dotted rhythms recall a funeral march. The speaker is doomed, even as his lust causes him to violate the distinction between the sacred and the profane. The same accompanimental device appears in the last song of *Dichterliebe,* where the persona "buries" his love in a gigantic coffin sunk into the sea. Schumann creates coherence in his song cycles by alluding to earlier patterns, by repeating material, and sometimes by related keys. Each song in *Dichterliebe* has its own distinct character, and the progression of numbers forms a larger whole in much the same way as Schumann's collections of piano miniatures do.

Schumann had a gift for the lyrical as well as the ironic, as one of his most famous songs, "Widmung," demonstrates. It opens *Myrthen,* op. 25, which was intended explicitly for Clara as a wedding present. Its text by Rückert runs appropriately:

"Widmung"
("Dedication")

Du meine Seele, du mein Herz,	You my soul, you my heart,
Du meine Wonn', o du mein Schmerz,	You my bliss, oh you my pain,
Du meine Welt, in der ich lebe,	You are the world in which I live,
Mein Himmel du, darein ich schwebe,	You the heaven in which I soar,
O du mein Grab, in das hinab	You the grave in which
Ich ewig meinen Kummer gab.	I have forever laid my sorrow.
Du bist die Ruh', du bist der Frieden,	You are rest, you are peace,
Du bist vom Himmel mir beschieden,	You have been bestowed on me by heaven,

EXAMPLE 4.3   Beginning of "Im Rhein, im heiligen Strome" from Robert Schumann's *Dichterliebe,* op. 48, composed 1840

Daß du mich liebst, macht mich mir wert,
Dein Blick hat mich vor mir verklärt,
Du hebst mich liebend über mich,
Mein guter Geist, mein beßres Ich!

That you love me makes me worthy,
Your gaze has transfigured me,
You raise me lovingly above myself,
My good spirit, my better self!

Schumann handles the two stanzas quite differently. The first receives a frenetic accompaniment and active melody (see Example 4.4). The second stanza, however, not only modulates to the mediant key but also begins in a subdued declamatory tone that grows in lyric intensity beginning with the words "That you love me. . . ." Schumann gains a great deal of expressive range by intermixing the declamatory with the lyrical in his songs and by varying the piano accompaniment from moment to moment to suit his reading of the poetry.

EXAMPLE 4.4   Beginning of "Widmung" from Robert Schumann's *Myrthen,* op. 25, 1840

Though Schumann's fame today stems more from his piano music and songs, in his own time he gained his reputation mainly from his works in the larger genres, including choral, chamber, and orchestral music. The choral works, such as *Das Paradies und die Peri* (after Thomas Moore's *Lalla Rookh;* op. 50; 1845), seem less compelling today, and only a few chamber works, such as the Piano Quintet, op. 44, and the Piano Quartet, op. 47, have any currency. Schumann's Piano Concerto, op. 54, and his symphonies still hold a steady place in the repertory. Here, too, Schumann sought "progress" in the genre, something especially evident in his Third Symphony (op. 97; 1851), often called the *Rhenish*. Its intentionally strong folkish and nationalistic tone resulted in part from sentiments stirred up by the failed 1848–49 revolution. Its formal and harmonic structure advances along the "new" (that is, newly discovered) Schubertian lines. The exposition of the first movement (see Table 4.1), for instance, takes Schubert's proclivity for "strophic" themes a step further, and Schubertian harmonic progress through the mediant to the dominant becomes evident in Schumann's second theme. Of course, combined with the "new" Schubertian style was the old Beethovenian symphonic imperative for cyclicity. There is a strong resemblance between themes in the trio of the scherzo and the solemn fourth movement, between parts of the third movement and the main theme of the fifth movement, between the fourth movement and the development of the fifth. The last two movements stand in relationship of slow introduction to allegro. These were some of the "new paths" and old traditions that Johannes Brahms would later adopt for his own symphonic output. Schumann hailed Brahms's arrival using just these terms ("Neue Bahnen") in his last influential review for the *Neue Zeitschrift* in 1853. The concept of an avant-garde (and its antithesis of enduring tradition) animated Schumann's thought to the very end.

TABLE 4.1   Schematic for Schumann, Op. 97, Exposition

SUBSECTION	KEY	MEASURES
Main theme	I	1–20
and trans., strophe 1	I→vi→I	21–56
Main theme	I	57–76
and trans., strophe 2	x→iii	77–94
Second theme	iii	95–110
and codetta, strophe 1	V→iii	111–126
Second theme	iii	127–142
and codetta, strophe 2	V	143–165
Closing	V	166–184

Clara Wieck Schumann

Music in the nineteenth century was dominated, as we might expect, by men. Women had previously played an important role as singers on the public stage, but they seldom became prominent instrumentalists and rarely composers. The nineteenth century offers some pioneers in breaking these gender barriers, however, and one of the most prominent was Clara Wieck (1819–96), daughter of Schumann's piano teacher and later the composer's wife. She participated directly in the life of the Leipzig "school," and her career as both composer and performer illuminates something of a woman's place in the musical scene.

Clara Wieck's father, Friedrich, decided from the beginning that she would be a virtuoso pianist and, not incidentally, the shining exemplar of his genius as a teacher. The genius turned out to be all hers: Wieck produced no other players of her rank. But he did have a proprietary sense of responsibility for Clara's career, and he pressed her early to appear at the Gewandhaus (1828) and to give her first solo recital (1830). He arranged for and accompanied her on an international concert tour from 1831 to 1832, and this established her fame as virtuosa. She was acclaimed by figures such as Mendelssohn, Paganini, and Chopin. By 1838 her fame had reached such proportions that the Austrian court bestowed the title Imperial–Royal Chamber Virtuosa on her, and she was also elected a member of the Gesellschaft der Musikfreunde in Vienna.

If Friedrich Wieck, to his credit, encouraged his daughter to perform and compose, it must be said that it redounded to his financial benefit. It was the support provided by his daughter as well as his pedagogical investment in her playing that prompted her father to shield her from the attentions of his former piano student Robert Schumann.

Schumann was nine years Clara's senior, and she fell in love with him as an impressionable adolescent (at the age of sixteen). Because she had not yet attained the age of consent, Schumann was obliged to ask Wieck's permission for their marriage. Wieck refused, and Schumann sued in court for Clara's hand. The two married one day before her majority deliberately to spite her father, but she escaped his rule only to encounter another domineering figure in Robert. Though he encouraged her composing, he initially discouraged her career as a performer. He needed quiet around the house for his own work, she reported in their common marriage diary, and this prevented her from practicing. Schumann was also, we may guess, jealous of her fame (which far exceeded his early in their marriage), especially in a career foreclosed to him.

Schumann soon discovered that he could not live without the income Clara's appearances generated, and what was more, she built his reputation by playing his music and even linked performances of his orchestral works to her concert appearances. He joined her for common tours, enduring her renown with an ill grace. (He returned home pouting from one tour to take care of the children, in part because he was denied admittance to her recital before the king of Denmark.) When Robert's fame as a composer grew, Clara helped to copy his music, made piano reductions of his orchestral works, served as an accompanist for choir rehearsals, and lent a hand in general. During this time Clara managed to bear Schumann eight children in addition to her other activities.

When Robert collapsed mentally in early 1854, the burden of supporting a large family fell on Clara. To augment the small income from the family trust, she went on tour, leaving her children and household accounts for a time in the hands of Johannes Brahms. The extent of their intimacy is not known, but they remained devoted friends for the rest of their lives. After Robert Schumann died in 1856, Clara moved to Berlin in 1857, then to Baden-Baden in 1863, and back to Berlin in 1873. She settled finally in Frankfurt in 1878, taking a position as the head of piano instruction at the conservatory there. All the while she continued to tour, she edited the first complete edition of her late husband's works, and played a role as the doyenne of the conservative German party in musical life. To the end of her life Brahms sent her his compositions for her appraisal.

In spite of her critical acumen, Clara lacked confidence in her ability as a composer. Almost all her compositions date before her husband's death, many before her marriage. The latter usually present brilliant concert pieces for piano, as would be expected from a virtuosa of her time. Schumann shifted her away from showy concert fare to more substantial keyboard music (*Three Preludes and Fugues,* op. 16, 1846, for instance), chamber music (such as the Piano Trio, op. 17; 1847), and serious Lieder. In fact, at the beginning of their marriage, Schumann persuaded his wife to embark on a joint composition, *Twelve Poems from F. Rückert's Liebesfrühling.* Clara's style in a song such as "Er ist gekommen" (Example 4.5) reflects her musical background: The piano arpeggiations are much more elaborate and accomplished than those her husband would write for such an accompaniment. The voice recedes slightly, and the harmonic palette is more limited than what we find in a typical Schumann song. But we need make no apologies for this Lied, with its stormy motion ("He is come in wind and rain . . .") and chorale writing in its final stanza ("Now Spring's blessing is come . . ."). It would not be so easy to sort Robert's contributions to *Liebesfrühling* from Clara's if we did not already know which was which.

Why, then, did Clara stop composing after her husband's death? Her concertizing and teaching to support her family must have left little time for writing music. And she may have been motivated by some sort of piety toward his memory not to overshadow his name in any way. But we must also remember that a woman composer had a hard time making her way in an almost exclusively male profession.

EXAMPLE 4.5   Beginning of "Er ist gekommen" by Clara Schumann from her joint opus with her husband, *Liebesfrühling,* 1841

Mendelssohn

The most renowned of the figures in the Leipzig orbit during his lifetime was Felix Mendelssohn (1809–47), scion of a wealthy and distinguished family. His grandfather, Moses Mendelssohn, was the leading Jewish figure of the Enlightenment in Germany. His father, Abraham Mendelssohn, was a Hamburg banker who fled the French in 1811, settling in Berlin. Abraham used his substantial private means to help defeat Napoleon and handled French reparations after the war. Felix's mother, Lea Salomon Mendelssohn, came from a family moving among the upper circles of the Prussian government, and she maintained a glittering salon attended by artists, university professors, and even the crown prince.

The young Felix had all the educational benefits of his parents' wide acquaintance. As a boy he studied basic subjects with Carl Wilhelm Heyse (a philologist), theory and composition with Carl Friedrich Zelter (a distinguished conductor and composer), and painting with Johann Gottlob Rösel. Regular guests in the family circle during Felix's adolescent years included the natural scientist Alexander von Humboldt, the philosopher Hegel, the theorist and critic Adolf Bernhard Marx, the violinists Ferdinand David and Eduard Rietz, and theologian Julius Schubring. In his travels with his family Mendelssohn encountered Goethe, Spohr, Thibaut, Cherubini, Hummel, Meyerbeer, and Rossini. He became a talented pianist, conductor, composer, and painter, with a commanding technique in each of the fields to which he put his hand.

Mendelssohn began composing by the age of thirteen, and some of his most striking works came from his teens, including the Octet, op. 20 (1825), and his overture to *A Midsummer Night's Dream,* op. 27 (1826). At the age of twenty he helped to organize and directed the first nineteenth-century performance of Bach's *St. Matthew Passion,* which led to the revival of Bach's works. By the age of twenty-one he had been offered (but declined) a chair in music at the University of Berlin. He toured widely in Europe during this period, conducting and playing the piano. When he lost an election to the directorship of the Berlin Singakadamie after Zelter's death, he took a position as the director of city music in Düsseldorf, also conducting famous performances of Handel at the Lower Rhenish Music Festival. He composed an oratorio of his own during this period, *St. Paul,* and also many *Lieder ohne Worte* for piano, performed in the middle-class salons of Düsseldorf.

As a result of his success in Düsseldorf Mendelssohn was appointed director of the Leipzig Gewandhaus Orchestra in 1835. His conducting brought the orchestra to a level of unparalleled excellence (though his use of a baton initially stirred some controversy), and he championed the music of Bach, Mozart, and Beethoven, and even conducted the first public performance of Schubert's Ninth Symphony (Schumann sent him the manuscript from Vienna). During this period he continued to concertize (his Leipzig contract allowed him six months away) and became a particular favorite in England, where his music and conducting were esteemed by Queen Victoria herself. Among his lasting gifts to Leipzig was the formation of a conservatory, for which he petitioned the Saxon government tirelessly and which he largely organized.

After the death of Friedrich Wilhelm III, the Prussian king, in 1840, Mendelssohn was induced by the new monarch to undertake a complete reworking of the royal musical establishment. The composer retained his nominal position in Leipzig, but Ferdinand David deputized for him at many performances, and he moved his household to Berlin. His Berlin duties were never clearly defined, however, and aside from composing notable incidental music for a series of plays (Sophocles' *Antigone* and *Oedipus at Colonos*, Shakespeare's *Midsummer Night's Dream*, and Racine's *Athalie*), his dealings with the Prussian king eventually dropped off. He resumed his full-time Leipzig duties in August 1845, this time with the aid of the Danish composer and conductor Niels Gade as deputy. He made concert tours to England, Frankfurt, Düsseldorf, Aachen, and Cologne. But when he returned to Leipzig in September of 1847 after a month of concerts in England, his health was broken by a series of strokes, perhaps brought on by his distress at the death of his sister Fanny (who also evinced talent as a composer). He died of a cerebral hemorrhage in November 1847.

Writers often portray Mendelssohn as a "classicist"—a holdover from the previous age. But Mendelssohn's music does not support such a casual generalization. It is true that his symmetrical phrase structure, regularity of form, and clarity of texture occasionally remind us of Mozart. But Mendelssohn's harmonic palette, his ability to imbue his music with pronounced character, and his insistence on extramusical inspiration place him firmly among Schumann's "progressives," even though he may be the most controlled of the group.

A good example of Mendelssohn's "progressive" side appears in his cultivation of a new genre called the "concert overture." Although Carl Maria von Weber had written one overture entirely independent of any opera, the *Jubel-Ouvertüre* of 1818, Mendelssohn could claim to be the first composer to cultivate the genre systematically. His first, Overture to *A Midsummer Night's Dream,* was not inspired by any particular performance of Shakespeare's play, nor was it meant as incidental music (though he would compose some in 1843 for a performance directed by Ludwig Tieck). The idea for a freestanding overture occurred to the composer as a youth of sixteen in 1826, and he carried it to Adolf Bernhard Marx, who gave some suggestions for finishing the project.

The genre of the overture was perfectly suited for extramusical inspiration. As the habitual preface to an opera, the overture frequently took up themes from the dramatic action. (Weber's overture to *Freischütz* provides just one prominent example.) But in Schumann's words, "one would not want to draw out a crude narrative thread from [the concert overture]. Mendelssohn conceives in such a poetic and magnificent way, that he indicates only the characters. . . ." In *A Midsummer Night's Dream* after the magic of the slow introduction's shifting mode (see Example 4.6*a*), we hear first what Mendelssohn in a communication to Breitkopf confirms as "elven music" in the main theme (*b*). The forceful codetta of the main theme (*c*) embodies the character of "Prince Theseus of Athens," whose music is commingled with that of the forest elves in the transition. The second theme (*d*) is inspired by "the tender lovers, who lose and find themselves" in the wandering chromatic phrase at measure 138. And "finally [comes] the troop of clumsy, coarse tradesmen, who ply their ponderous amusements" in the closing material at measure 194. In the braying of Bottom here we find the only imitative sounds in the overture, as Mendelssohn's incidental music for this character later confirmed. Mendelssohn's music intimates the spirit of these characters, but it rarely "represents" them or the story. It takes instead the traditional form of the overture—a three-part sonata form. The music is both "something in itself" and "imbued with spirit."

EXAMPLE 4.6   Themes from the exposition of Mendelssohn's *A Midsummer Night's Dream*, op. 27, 1826, including (*a*) introduction, (*b*) "elven music," (*c*) theme of Prince Theseus, and (*d*) the lovers' theme

After this initial, brilliant foray into the character-laden realm of the concert overture, Mendelssohn would go on to compose *The Hebrides* (op. 26; inspired by the seascape of the Scottish island of Staffa), *Calm Sea and Prosperous Voyage* (op. 27; inspired by two Goethe poems), and *The Tale of the Beautiful Melusina* (op. 32; a reaction against Conradin Kreutzer's opera of the same name), which main theme Wagner covertly plundered for the beginning of *Das Rheingold.* Schumann accurately described these pieces as "poetic"; they form the aesthetic and musical basis on which all subsequent concert overtures and "tone poems" were built.

Songs without Words (*Lieder ohne Worte*) represent another avant-garde genre cultivated by Mendelssohn. Today these pieces often seem to us the essence of stolid, middle-class parlor music—what the Germans call Biedermeier art. It is easy to forget that middle-class parlor music *was* progressive in nineteenth-century Germany and that Mendelssohn could use its clichés in unconventional fashion. A good example appears in the form of the "Venetian Gondola Song" from op. 62 (no. 5; 1842), a genre cultivated by a number of composers during this time, Chopin and Liszt included. In this particular example Mendelssohn supplies many of the features expected in the type: the 6/8 accompaniment is standard in barcaroles (boat songs) of all kinds, as is the obvious cantilena in the right hand. But when we examine the accompanimental pattern more closely (see Example 4.7), we can see that the composer has displaced the

EXAMPLE 4.7   Beginning of Mendelssohn's "Venetian Gondola Song," op. 62, no. 5, 1842

typical arpeggiation by an eighth note (the bass A would usually fall on the downbeat). In addition, Mendelssohn leaves us unclear about the downbeat of the measure by placing the initial "cry" of the boatman on the first beat, but later on the fourth beat an octave lower. The tune itself enters on beat 4 in the fourth measure but seems to double back on itself in measure 7. In short, we float in the shifting rhythmic currents of the piece, a marvelous play on the programmatic title. There are also ingenious harmonic touches, such as a return to the second "stanza" of the song through chromatic motion that moves directly from the secondary dominant of E (the dominant) to a second-inversion A chord (the tonic). Mendelssohn could be prosaic in his *Songs without Words*, but there are many more truly inspired moments amid their pages.

The composer was equally at home in the larger genres. These include an Octet for strings (op. 20; 1825) as an inspired piece of writing from his youth, some moving piano trios from his adulthood (opp. 49 and 66), five symphonies, the most striking of which are the *Scottish* (op. 56; 1842) and the *Italian* (published posthumously as op. 90; 1833), and a highly popular Violin Concerto (op. 64; 1845). The violin concerto appeared so frequently in nineteenth-century performance that the Germans coined a phrase for its beginning theme, "Schon wieder, schon wieder, das Mendelssohn Konzert" ("Again and again, the Mendelssohn concerto"). The popularity of the composer's works during his lifetime and just after led to overexposure and a reaction at the end of the century. These were the works of cultivated regularity against which later composers rebelled.

Mendelssohn's oratorios have encountered just such resistance, and yet they deserve better. The oratorio in the nineteenth century embodied both the thesis of "progress" and the antithesis of "historicism." This was not a new phenomenon: We find it several generations earlier in Haydn's *Creation* and *Seasons,* as well as in Beethoven's *Christ on the Mount of Olives.* But the contrast between the two antithetical poles of the synthesis intensifies in Mendelssohn's generation. The composer championed the performance of passions and oratorios in his role as conductor. He followed the famous Berlin performance of Bach's *St. Matthew Passion* with an almost systematic exploration of the Handel oratorios in Düsseldorf and at the yearly convocations at the Lower Rhenish Musical Festivals. Elements of both Bach's and Handel's choral works with orchestra surface in Mendelssohn's *St. Paul* (op. 36; 1836), *Elijah* (op. 70; 1847), and the incomplete *Christus.*

At first *Elijah* seems to be modeled after Handel oratorios such as *Solomon.* After the opening prologue (an accompanied recitative), we have something like the Baroque's fugal overture (see Example 4.8). But the fugue turns out to be the dramatic prelude to an opening chorus ("Help, Lord!"), which in turn flows into a "choral recitative" ("The deeps afford no water"). And this "number" moves seamlessly into a duet with chorus ("Lord, bow thine ear to our pray'r!"). In short, what we find at the beginning of *Elijah* is a thoroughly mod-

EXAMPLE 4.8   Fugal opening from the overture to Mendelssohn's *Elijah,* op. 70, 1847

ern *introduzione* with all the continuity valued in the newest Italian and German operatic dramaturgy of the time. The whole of the first part progresses this way, with accompanied recitatives used more to connect the numbers than to separate them. The finale presents the dramatic action of Elijah ending the drought he has proclaimed at the outset. Thus we have the invocation of Handel in the "overture," in fugal choruses, in the subject matter, and in the genre itself, all serving as a foil to display the modernity of the work. For in the end history *was* progress; its "scientific" (*wissenschaftlich*) study of the past made it the property of the learned middle classes in Germany. They hoped to assert their right to dominion through their professional command of knowledge, whether of the human or the natural world. *Elijah,* like the other music of the Leipzig school, bears a quintessentially bourgeois stamp. And in turn, its historical allusions represent yet another way in which a composer of the avant-garde could imbue a piece with "character," here the classically sacred and monumental.

PARIS

To insist unreflectively on a "Parisian school" of avant-garde composers would be as big a distortion as a simplistic notion of a "Leipzig school." But again, the abstract idea proves a useful tool in understanding some of the things composers who gathered in Paris seem to have held in common. We have already seen that Paris attracted almost every significant composer of opera in the first half of the nineteenth century. The prestige of this genre elicited a competitively flamboyant concert life, mainly supplied in salons and recital halls by virtuosi. Orchestral music took third place. The excellent large orchestra of faculty, students, and former students at the Conservatoire organized by François Antoine Habeneck into the Société des Concerts du Conservatoire in 1828 gave only a handful of concerts annually.

Concert life was dominated above all by the piano, which became the quintessentially nineteenth-century instrument. Like much in nineteenth-century music, the piano was hardly new. But developments in its construction prepared it for a central role in the musical scene. Following the lead of the English manufacturer Broadwood, many builders in the first half of the century began to construct their frames from iron components with two salutary results. The iron frame allowed heavier stringing, and this in turn gave the piano more power in increasingly large halls. At the same time the metal frame expanded and contracted less than a wooden frame, rendering the piano a more reliable instrument in the home. Increased demand for pianos (which remained fairly pricey items before midcentury) resulted in more capacity for production. For example, the Parisian firm of Erard, which produced about 160 instruments annually at the end of the Napoleonic wars, made 600 a year by the end of the 1820s, and 1,500 a year at midcentury. By applying the techniques of mass production, manufacturers supplied over 200,000 pianos annually worldwide by the end of the century.

The sale of pianos became big business, organized at first in vertically integrated firms. Pleyel in Paris, or Breitkopf in Leipzig, or Dubois and Stodart in New York published music, sold music at retail, manufactured instruments, sold instruments, and offered lessons, all out of the same establishment. They enlisted talented pianist-composers to help market their wares, and in Paris each of the prominent avant-garde players associated himself with a firm. Chopin made his Parisian debut and played his last public concert in the Salle Pleyel on one of Pleyel's instruments. (He used one at home to give lessons as well.) Liszt, on the other hand, allied himself initially with Erard, a firm that prided itself on patenting a double-escapement action allowing faster repetition of notes. The piano and the literature written for it merged the notions of technological and artistic progress to form an important partnership in the creation of the Parisian avant-garde.

The musical style created by Parisian composers combined the requirements of piano writing with an operatic flair for the dramatic. To sustain tone on an essentially percussive instrument, composers developed ornate, rapidly moving patterns of figuration that often employed intense chromatic motion. Musical gestures tended toward the extravagant, not only to display the brilliance of the player, but also to demonstrate the range of the instrument from the most delicate cantabile to the most massive "tutti." When Berlioz translated this dramatic, virtuosic style for a technically progressive orchestra, vividly contrasting textures, chromatic motion, and extroverted display persisted.

Joseph Danhauser's famous *Liszt at the Piano* (1840; see Figure 4.2) reminds us, however, that even the Parisian avant-garde viewed its activity against a backdrop of tradition. From left to right the painter depicts the literary figures Alexandre Dumas, Victor Hugo, George Sand (Chopin's mistress), and the violinist Paganini embraced by Rossini, all watching the master play (adored by *his* mistress, the Countess Marie d'Agoult). But the pianist gazes not at the authors of modern literary inspiration, not at his fellow musicians symbolizing the conjoined cultures of musical virtuosity and drama, nor at his lover, but at a classicized bust of Beethoven. Liszt draws his artistic strength from a musical past that weaves its way even through the fashionable musical milieu of Paris.

Figure 4.2   Joseph Danhauser's *Liszt at the Piano* (1840, oil), featuring (from left to right) Alexandre Dumas (seated), Victor Hugo, George Sand (seated), Paganini, Rossini, Liszt, and the Countess Marie d'Agoult. Bildarchiv Preussischer Kulturbesitz, Berlin, Germany.

Chopin

Fryderyk Chopin (1810–49) enjoyed one of the most placid and orderly careers of the Parisian virtuosi. He was born to French émigré parents in Poland, where his father served first as a clerk, then briefly as an army officer, and subsequently as a French teacher for children of the nobility and at a secondary school. Fryderyk demonstrated early an astonishing talent on the piano and in his childhood was largely self-taught. (Lessons from Wojciech Żywny served mostly to acquaint his pupil with literature rather than to mold his technique.) As the son of a teacher, he also received a fine general education that prepared him well for the elevated circles in which he later moved. His youthful improvisation at the piano eventually resulted in composing at the age of seven, and he performed a concerto by Gyrowetz in his first public concert at the age of eight.

Chopin continued his musical education at the Warsaw Conservatory while he was in secondary school. After finishing his general examinations in 1826, he enrolled for a three-year course in composition with Jósef Elsner at the conservatory. He wrote student exercises under Elsner's tutelage, such as the First Sonata, op. 4, and also more advanced works, such as his *Variations on "Là ci darem la mano"* (on a theme from Mozart's *Don Giovanni*), op. 2, for which Schumann hailed him in 1831. During his study with Elsner, Chopin also began exploring Polish folk music as a source of inspiration for his pieces.

After he passed his final examinations with distinction at the Warsaw Conservatory in 1829, Chopin sought a wider career. Initially this quest took him to Berlin for exposure to its musical culture and to Vienna, where his concerts created a sensation. He returned to Warsaw in 1830 to play concerts that included much music with a nationalistic flavor, and then he departed for extended touring. He traveled to Breslau, Dresden, and Prague before an extended stay in Vienna during the first part of 1831. He went on to Munich and Stuttgart, where he learned that the Russians had overrun Warsaw to put down an attempted nationalist insurgency there. Unable to return to his native city, he made his way to Paris in 1831, where he would remain for the rest of his life.

When Chopin arrived in Paris during September 1831, he was not sure how to establish himself, and he considered taking lessons from Frédéric Kalkbrenner, an established virtuoso of the old school. But the young pianist soon determined to follow his own path, and his first concert in February of 1832 was greeted by an ecstatic review from François-Joseph Fétis. The critic hailed Chopin's compositions as containing "an abundance of original ideas of a kind not found elsewhere." This reception established him on the musical scene. He was befriended by the likes of Meyerbeer, Berlioz, Liszt, Heine, Balzac, and Mickiewicz and guaranteed entry into the drawing rooms of the Rothschilds, the Stockhausens, and the aristocracy.

Chopin's initial success secured financial support for the rest of his life. He earned most of his income from giving piano lessons for considerable fees to the wealthy and aristocratic. He appeared only sporadically in Parisian concert halls after his first recital and played no public concerts between 1838 and 1848. He played often, however, in the salons of his important patrons, occupying a unique place as both guest and artist. Chopin's independence of the concert stage and his concentration on a select group of patrons and artistic friends allowed him the freedom to explore novel musical ideas.

Between 1838 and 1847, Chopin's muse was stimulated by a famous affair with the novelist known as George Sand (the pen name of Aurore Dudevant). He passed most summers in the rarefied artistic atmosphere of Nohant, her home near Châteauroux, where he did most of his composing. Winters he spent in Paris, where he socialized a great deal but composed less. Eventually he broke with Sand over a protracted family quarrel involving her children in 1847. His health declined quickly after this, and he barely found the strength to undertake a concert tour of England during 1848. He returned to Paris broken, unable to compose or give lessons, and he died there of tuberculosis in October of 1849.

Chopin devoted his output largely to solo piano, and even his little chamber and orchestral music features the piano prominently. In addition to being conceived in a highly original and pianistic idiom, his works extended the limits of harmonic practice and also featured a good deal of nationalistic color.

Chopin, like his avant-garde contemporaries, cast the piano in one of several modes, the first of which involved instrumental dance rhythms. Pieces in this style included whole series of waltzes, marches, mazurkas, and polonaises, the last two possessing a distinctly Polish flavor. Polonaises in particular, with their heavy stamping on the first beat in triple meter, display both nationalistic style and the ability of the newer pianos to generate large volumes of sound. We can see a good example in Chopin's Polonaise, op. 53, in A-flat major (1843), which bears the sobriquet *Heroic*. The composer first offers a grand introduction that embellishes a dominant harmony (see Example 4.9a) with chromatic motion. This chromaticism is evident not only in the parallel motion of the sixteenth-note chords in first inversion but also in the larger harmonic progress upward every four measures until the accelerated movement around the circle of fifths begins in measure 9. This kind of chromatic motion, if sustained long enough, becomes structural rather than merely decorative. In this case the second chord of the introduction, F-flat major, respelled as an E major chord, prepares the surprising key of the polonaise's thundering trio (m. 81). It was this variety of short- and long-range harmonic experimentation, as well as the strongly accented rhythms of the dance (see Example 4.9b), that so attracted performers of Chopin's music and showed the piano to such great advantage.

The other popular mode of piano composition imitated vocal models (as we have seen in Mendelssohn's *Songs without Words*). In this style Chopin provided many nocturnes patterned after the serenades so popular in Romantic literature and in nineteenth-century song. And there is a counterpart to

EXAMPLE 4.9a   Chromatic beginning of Chopin's Polonaise, op. 53, 1843

EXAMPLE 4.9b   Theme of Chopin's Polonaise, op. 53, 1843

Mendelssohn's "Gondola Song" in the extended Barcarole, op. 60. But perhaps the most elaborate of Chopin's vocally modeled compositions are his four ballades, which trade on allusions to several layers of genre. Schumann (to whom the Second Ballade is dedicated) claimed that Chopin had the literary ballads of the Polish nationalist poet Mickiewicz in mind when he composed his pieces. Poetic ballads in turn were often set to music—for instance, Schubert's "Erlkönig," discussed earlier. In Chopin's First Ballade (op. 23; 1836) the introduction and the coda act to frame the action as a narrator in a poetic or vocal ballad might. The "action" played out in the body of the piece unfolds as an improvisation on two themes, one brooding in minor mode (Example 4.10a), the other in major mode (Example 4.10b). The cantabile melodies are so distinctive that they seem to present musical characterizations (just like Mendelssohn's themes in his concert overtures). Chopin presents fragments of the themes in various "situations" and juxtapositions until they repeat at the end for a "denouement," the resolution of a dramatic narrative. Lurking beneath all of this is a third layer of genre, the familiar sonata form (see Table 4.2). Such a structural reading of the First Ballade reminds us again that in so many avant-garde compositions with literary titles "traditional" musical and extramusical allusions coexist and play against one another to create a kaleidoscope of shifting meanings.

EXAMPLE 4.10a   First theme from Chopin's First Ballade, op. 23, 1836

EXAMPLE 4.10b   Second theme from Chopin's First Ballade, op. 23, 1836

Chopin also contributed a host of compositions intended to display or develop pianistic technique. There are a number of etudes (studies), a famous group of *24 Preludes* (op. 28; 1839), and a series of extraordinary recorded improvisations or "impromptus," including the magnificent *Fantasie-impromptu* (op. 66, 1855). Amid all these miniatures and longer pieces compiled from disparate episodes, sonatas play a distinctly lesser role, as they did in Schumann's output for piano. This does not mean that Chopin's sonatas are unworthy pieces, just that he invested less time in this genre as a group than in more "avant-garde" varieties of piece. Freedom of form and novelty of idiom would be the qualities most valued by Chopin's generation. As Liszt puts it in his famous biography of the composer:

TABLE 4.2   Schematic for a "Sonata-Form" Reading of Chopin's First Ballade, op. 23

SECTION	SUBSECTION	KEY	MEASURES
Introduction		$g{:}(N^6{-}i{-}$	1–3
		$V{-}i^{6/4}{-}$	4–6
		$V^{9/6/4})$	7
"Exposition"			
	First theme	i	8–35
	codetta	i	36–57
	trans.	i→III	58–67
	Second theme	III	68–81
	codetta	VI	82–90
"Development"			
	bridge	x	91–93
	mth	$\sharp$vi	94–105
	sth	II	106–125
	episode	x	126–165
"Recapitulation"			
	Second theme	III	166–179
	codetta	VI	180–193
	First theme	i	194–207
Coda		i	208–264

One cannot study and analyze Chopin's efforts closely without finding beauties of a highly elevated kind, sentiments of a completely new character, a harmonic fabric as original as it is learned. His boldness is always justified; richness, even exuberance never exclude clarity, idiosyncrasy never degenerates into the bizarre, form is never disordered, the wealth of ornamentation never overcomes the elegance of the principal lines.

Liszt

Franz Liszt (1811–86) also developed a novel, colorful approach to the piano and extended the bounds of harmonic practice. But where Chopin was intensely private and his music often introspective, Liszt sought a very public celebrity and wrote a great deal of extroverted music (though there is much variety in his extensive output). Liszt's father occupied a minor position at the court of Prince Nikolaus Ersterházy, whose family was renowned in the history of Viennese music. Adam Liszt was an amateur cellist and pianist of some accomplishment, and Liszt's initial fascination with the piano came from listening to his father (just as the composer's later decision to take minor Roman Catholic orders stemmed in part from his father's brief vocation as a Franciscan novice). Young Franz began lessons with his father at age seven, began composing at age eight, and began giving concerts the year afterward. A group of wealthy Hungarians, realizing the boy's talent, decided to support his musical education. In 1821 the Liszt family moved to Vienna so that Franz could take piano lessons from Carl Czerny and composition from Antonio Salieri. Though Liszt would make much of his Hungarian nationality, his early training was more Viennese than anything else. As a child he made the acquaintance of Beethoven and Schubert, and in 1823, at the age of twelve, he was invited by Diabelli to contribute a variation on a theme for a symposium of fifty Austrian composers.

In fall of 1823 Liszt moved with his family to Paris, where he studied theory with Anton Reicha and composition with Ferdinando Paer. He gained fame in Paris as a prodigy on the piano and toured England, Switzerland, and the French provinces. But the death of his father in 1827 brought a hiatus in his concert career. He established a household in Paris for his mother and himself, taught private lessons, and acquainted himself with the artistic life of Paris (see Figure 4.2). He made the acquaintance of the writer Victor Hugo, the poets Lamartine and Heine, and the composer Berlioz. Liszt was especially influenced by the violinist Nicolò Paganini, whose virtuoso style he transferred to the piano, and by the harmonic and pianistic innovations of Chopin. Among Liszt's artistic accomplishments during these years were sets of brilliant variations on well-known French operas of the time and transcriptions of orchestral works by Berlioz. He also began to publish a series of essays on music and musicians, some of which may have been ghostwritten by the Countess Marie d'Agoult, with whom he lived in Switzerland and Italy between 1835 and 1839. Liszt's extensive music criticism, including books on Chopin and Wagner, ranks in importance just behind that of Schumann, Berlioz, and Wagner in its influence on the course of nineteenth-century music.

After he broke with the Countess d'Agoult in 1839, Liszt resumed the life of the touring virtuoso, gaining the kind of fame that we associate today with major celebrities. He had numerous affairs with women who swarmed his concerts, and he eventually fell in love with the Princess Carolyne Sayn-Wittgenstein, wife of a Russian nobleman. The princess persuaded Liszt to give up touring, and they settled in the German town of Weimar, where Liszt became director of music at the ducal court. There he composed a great deal of music, championed the cause of musical progress (eventually as a leader of the "New German school") by conducting pieces ranging from Schumann's *Genoveva* to Berlioz's *Benvenuto Cellini,* and taught a number of piano students, Hans von Bülow among them. With an orchestra at his disposal during the Weimar period, Liszt turned his attention to a genre he called the "tone poem," and he devoted much time to mastering the art of instrumentation.

As the music of the "New German school" became more and more politically charged, and as the public increasingly disapproved of his cohabitation with a married woman, pressure mounted on Liszt to resign his position in

Weimar, which he did in 1858. After some years of travel that took him to Berlin and Paris, he finally settled in Rome in 1861, turning his attention to religious music. Inspired by the renewed interest in the history of chant, he composed a *Missa choralis* (1865), and he also completed two oratorios, *Die Legende von der heiligen Elisabeth* (1857–62) and *Christus* (1862–67). At the same time he embraced historical genres, he also wrote a series of highly experimental piano pieces that explored what would become "impressionistic" idiom. (Debussy visited Liszt in 1885 and was considerably influenced by some of his late piano music.) In 1886 he embarked on a final tour of Europe, attending concerts of his music as he went and performing selectively. He died on tour while sojourning in Bayreuth.

Liszt was certainly the most cosmopolitan of the avant-garde composers, and it may seem capricious to label him "Parisian" when he seems to have spent as much of his life in German-speaking lands. But he passed the crucial formative years of adolescence and young adulthood in Paris, and his contact with Chopin, Berlioz, and the keyboard virtuosi of that city such as Sigismond Thalberg determined many of his stylistic affinities. The intricate chromatic figuration of his writing, especially for piano, and its overt flamboyance all point toward the flashier style of the big city and away from the more prosaic intellectualism of Germany's intimate circles. Liszt's residence in Weimar does not stand as a complete exception in view of the long tradition of French music at that court. We might speak with justification of a Weimar-Paris axis, just as we could justify a Leipzig-Vienna axis. At any rate, Liszt was well aware of the camp into which he fell: He once infuriated Schumann by characterizing Mendelssohn's music as too "Leipzigerisch."

Liszt's virtuoso music for piano lies furthest from the Leipzig style, and like much of Chopin's music it sometimes invokes the exotic nationalism of the expatriate. In his series of *Hungarian Rhapsodies* Liszt draws on the dance music of Hungarian Gypsy *verbunkos* bands as the stylistic substrate that displays pianistic technique. A familiar example appears in Liszt's well-known Second Hungarian Rhapsody (C-sharp minor; 1847), which consists of two loosely joined improvisations on a slow ("Lassan") dance song and a fast ("Friska") dance song. Some of Liszt's rhapsodies include actual Gypsy melodies, and all rely on certain stereotypical traits that signal folkish style in the context of European classical music. In the Second Rhapsody they include minor mode in the slow section (see Example 4.11a), an initial drone (C♯–G♯–C♯) that becomes an ostinato, and imitation of a "gypsy" violin beginning in its lowest register. From time to time the pianist pauses for showy chromatic cadenzas. The real pianistic fireworks, however, come in the fast section, which begins delicately (Example 4.11b), imitating the Hungarian cimbalom (a variety of hammered dulcimer). This soon gives way to a vigorous dance in F-sharp major that ends in a coda displaying an accelerating series of runs. The effect of the slow, soulful beginning in minor mode yielding to the fast, exuberant ending is entirely theatrical and

EXAMPLE 4.11a   Beginning of slow section ("Lassan") from Liszt's Second Rhapsody, 1851

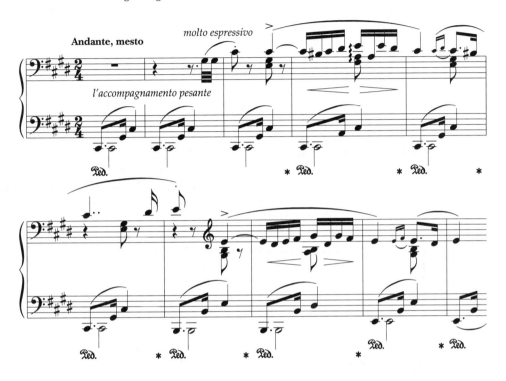

EXAMPLE 4.11b   Beginning of fast section ("Friska") from Liszt's Second Rhapsody, 1851

has rightly become a cliché of virtuosic showmanship. Schumann and the Leipzig composers disapproved of what they regarded as this charlatan aspect of Liszt's music. But in fact, as a display of the piano, the pianist, and colorful material, the Second Hungarian Rhapsody is a great deal of fun.

Liszt also explored a more intimate pianistic style in some of his *Années de Pèlerinage,* which collected descriptive miniatures from his years of touring. The first *Année* (1848–54) offers musical glimpses of Swizterland, the second (chronologically first, 1837–49) discloses glimpses of Italy, and the third (1867–77) centers on Rome. Prominent in all three collections are proverbial "songs without words," and the second collection, "Italie," offers a literal take on this genre. Liszt originally composed its three "Petrarch Sonnets" as songs. The piano versions translate strophic repetition into a series of ornamental variations.

The first "stanza" of "Sonetto 104 del Petrarca" displays the usual cantilena in the top voice of the right hand (see Example 4.12), with an unusually sparse chordal accompaniment that grows increasingly elaborate with every reprise. The most extraordinary feature of this example, however, lies in the introduction. At first glance, it appears simply to exhibit the kind of parallel harmonic chromaticism we have seen earlier in Chopin, and this Parisian tendency to abandon functional chord progression is indeed present here. But closer inspection also shows that Liszt based this introduction on an octatonic scale. This eight-note division of the octave alternates half steps and whole steps (F♯ G A B♭ C D♭ E♭ E). Because the pattern of the scale is uniformly symmetrical, it establishes no center and therefore has no place of repose, responding in all probability to the opening words of the Petrarch sonnet, "I find no peace" ("Pace non trovo . . ."). Whatever Liszt's reasons for employing it, the octatonic scale would become a favorite of later composers, especially Russians such as Rimsky-Korsakov and his pupil Stravinsky, who used it frequently in *Petrushka* and *The Rite of Spring.* Liszt was one of the most adventuresome composers of an adventuresome generation.

We can gain only the barest glimpse of Liszt's pianism from these two examples. His output was vast, and an important part consisted of adaptations of other composers' works. There were, of course, the usual series of variations on melodies taken from operatic and symphonic novelties of the day, a genre much cultivated by Parisian keyboard virtuosi. But more important were literal transcriptions of Lieder by Schubert, Mendelssohn, and the Schumanns; opera overtures and excerpts by Mozart, Rossini, Bellini, Donizetti, Meyerbeer, and Wagner; and symphonies by Beethoven and Berlioz. Schumann's famous review of Berlioz's *Symphonie fantastique* was based on Liszt's brilliant transcription for piano two hands, which remained the only version available in print for a decade.

It stands to reason that a composer so talented at transcribing other composers' scores would become an orchestral composer of standing in his own right. Liszt began this process in Paris during the 1830s with a number of works for piano and orchestra, including two concerti and a *Grande fantasie symphonique* (1834) based on themes from Berlioz's *Lélio.* When Liszt had an orchestra

EXAMPLE 4.12   Beginning of Liszt's "Sonetto 104 del Petrarca," no. 5 in *Années de Pèlerinage* II ("Italie"), 1837

at his disposal in Weimar, he came to terms with orchestral literature in earnest. Not entirely confident of his orchestrations at first, he employed copyists August Conradi and Joachim Raff to help with his scores. Eventually Liszt dispensed with this assistance and revised all his orchestral music on his own to establish its final form. His output includes a *Faust Symphony*, a *Dante Symphony,* and a number of "tone poems," a term Liszt coined to describe orchestral works in no fixed form.

Liszt originally composed many of his early tone poems as overtures, and their kinship to Mendelssohn's concert overtures is quite apparent in a work such as *Les préludes* (1848). This most-often performed of Liszt's tone poems was originally written as the preface to an unpublished, four-movement choral work, *Les quatre éléments.* Liszt detached the orchestral beginning and hit upon a long poem by Lamartine, "Les préludes," as capturing the essence of his music. To the idealist way of thinking this proved no logical contradiction: A piece and its program need share only a common spirit. Neither was a literal translation of the other.

Liszt's *Les préludes* presents us with shape and idiom that fit roughly into the genre of a concert overture in sonata form. Taking the Beethovenian symphonic ideal one step further, most of the thematic material is related by a set of "thematic transformations." The initial idea of the slow introduction (see Example 4.13*a*) forms the basis for the head motive of the "first theme" (4.13*b*),

EXAMPLE 4.13   Transformed themes from Liszt's *Les préludes,* 1848, including (a) theme from introduction, (b) main theme, (c) secondary theme

EXAMPLE 4.13 *continued*

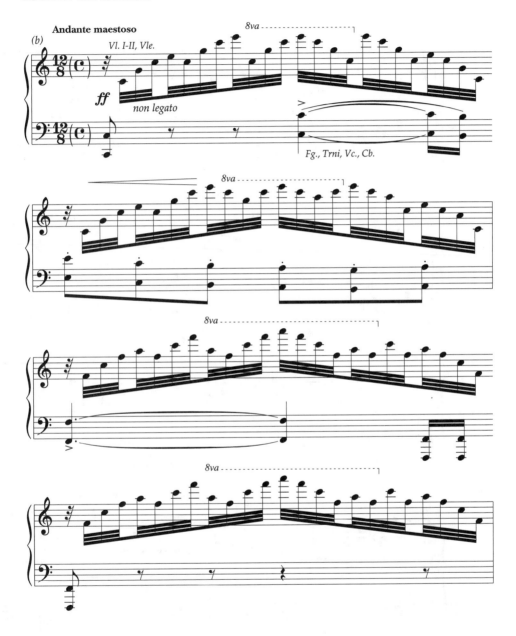

EXAMPLE 4.13 *continued*

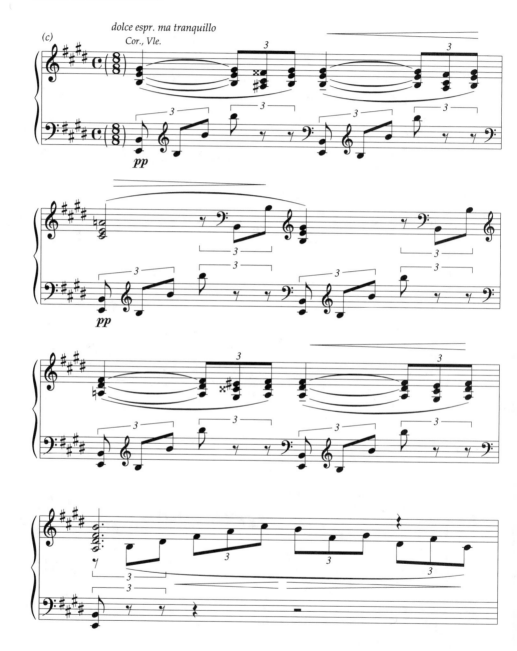

TABLE 4.3   Schematic for Liszt's *Les préludes*

SECTION	SUBSECTION	KEY	MEASURES
Introduction		C:I	1–34
Exposition			
	first theme	I	35–46
	transition	I→III	47–69
	second theme	III	70–108
Development		X	
	bridge		109–130
	core		131–181
	retransition		182–259
Recapitulation			
	second theme	VI–I	260–343
	transition	I	344–404
	first theme	I	405–419

and the "second theme" in turn borrows the prominent downward half step from both themes (compare 4.13*c*). The material then recycles in a fairly standard development section (see Table 4.3; the retransition is exceptional for its recitative-like writing). The recapitulation replays the first and second themes in reverse, an echo of Chopin's practice in his First Ballade (see previous section) and in the first movement of Berlioz's *Symphonie fantastique* (see next section). Many listeners will hear hints of Wagner in the "retransition" of this Liszt tone poem, especially of *Tannhäuser,* which Liszt conducted in Weimar about this time. But we should not conclude that Liszt was somehow unoriginal. The body of symphonic poems, from *Tasso: lamento e trionfo* (inspired by Byron; 1849) to *Hamlet* (inspired by Shakespeare; 1858) to *Von Wiege bis zum Grabe (From Cradle to Grave;* 1881–82) spans a range too wide to be derivative of any one style or composer.

Time has not been kind to Liszt's works: Much of the piano music is too difficult for lesser pianists to keep in the repertory, and his orchestral works are too idiosyncratic. Nonetheless, he was one of the most influential composers of his generation, and he remained a steadfast proponent of musical "progress" throughout his long and productive career.

Berlioz

Hector Berlioz (1803–69) had the most singular career of the Parisian avant-garde and produced arguably the most unusual body of music among this vanguard of highly idiosyncratic and original composers. Not surprisingly, he had the most unusual background, though there are some parallels in his biography to Schumann's. Berlioz was born into a well-to-do family of La Côte-St-André near Grenoble in the French Alps. His father was a prominent physician who taught his son at home until he was seventeen, with studies including the Latin classics and modern literature. Berlioz did not take up a musical instrument until the relatively advanced age of twelve, and even then he did not take up the piano but the flageolet (a small flute) and the guitar. He taught himself harmony from Rameau's *Traité de l'harmonie* and began to compose about the age of thirteen. Among his early pieces were some quintets for flute and strings, and some songs with piano accompaniment that he offered to Parisian publishers when he was fifteen.

Though Berlioz loved music, he complied with his father's wishes to follow in the family tradition of medicine when the time came to choose a career. After obtaining his baccalaureate in Grenoble in 1821, the seventeen-year-old went off to Paris to the École de Médecine, where he studied restlessly until 1824. In that year he composed a mass for the church of St. Roch, which was performed successfully in July 1825. At that point he resolved to become a "great composer," and in spite of his family's withdrawal of financial support, he pressed on, composing a cantata and parts of an opera called *Les francs-juges* (*The Secret Judges*), and also writing music criticism for the papers.

In 1826 Berlioz was admitted to the Conservatoire, where he studied theory with Anton Reicha and composition with Jean-François Le Sueur. During this period Berlioz recognized his affinity for the orchestra after hearing Beethoven for the first time at the Conservatoire concerts conducted by Habeneck. At the same time, he expanded his literary sensibilities: Acquaintance with a translation of Goethe's *Faust* prompted *Huit scènes de Faust* (1828–29), and Sir Walter Scott's *Waverley* resulted in a concert overture by the same title (1828). He developed a passion for Shakespeare that would inspire his later work and also an obsession with the Shakespearean actress Harriet Smithson. Though he would later marry her (unhappily), her initial rejection prompted him to compose the *Symphonie fantastique* (1830). In 1830 Berlioz also won the Prix de Rome, the Conservatoire's highest honor, for his cantata *La mort de Sardanapale*.

The Prix de Rome provided for a period of residence in Italy and a stipend for several years, but more important, it established a composer's reputation. This would have been splendid if Berlioz had not chosen to lavish so much of his talent on orchestral music. For, as the historian, theorist, and critic Fétis wrote in 1830:

> It is unfortunate that the lack of institutions here limits the careers of composers to dramatic music. . . . The symphony is completely neglected, because a musician who attempts to write one cannot succeed either in publishing his works or in having them heard. Nature would be laboring in vain to have a Haydn or a Beethoven born in France; such talent would be better hidden in the milieu of the capital than a diamond in the bowels of the earth.

Habeneck's marvelous, large orchestra was still coming to grips retrospectively with Beethoven. There was little room for a composer of new orchestral music, and in fact, none of Berlioz's works would appear first at the Conservatoire concerts.

Much of Berlioz's music first appeared, instead, in specially organized concerts. His *Symphonie fantastique,* possibly the most original instrumental work composed until the end of the nineteenth century, first saw the light of day at the Opéra, where it provoked consternation. When the composer returned from his Italian sojourn, another specially organized concert featuring this piece and its choral sequel, *Le retour à la vie,* received a scathing review from Fétis. (This was the article Schumann hoped to counter with his analysis in the *Neue Zeitschrift.*)

In spite of these initial setbacks, however, Berlioz began to gain public recognition at the end of the 1830s as a composer of exceptional originality and ability. On the strength of his reputation he received two governmental commissions for a *Grande messe des morts* (or Requiem; 1837) and a *Grande symphonie funèbre et triomphale* (1840). Both required vast forces that had to be specially assembled, and both made significant impressions on their audiences. *Harold en Italie,* commissioned as a concerto by Paganini to show off his Stradivarius viola, was initially rejected by the virtuoso because it featured too little solo work and technical display. But when he finally heard it in 1838, he realized *Harold's* genius and made a gift of 20,000 francs to Berlioz. Only success at the opera eluded Berlioz: *Benvenuto Cellini,* an opera based on the artist's autobiography and inspired by the composer's Italian trip, was a flop.

Aside from his compositions, Berlioz wrote a great deal of music criticism for *L'Europe littéraire, Le rénovateur,* the *Gazette musicale,* and the *Journal des débats.* He also took up conducting, at first only to ensure the competent performance of his own works. He later grew into one of the finest *chefs d'orchestre* in all of Europe, touring its length and breadth for twenty years beginning in the 1840s. His *Grande traité d'instrumentation et d'orchestration modernes* (1843) became famous in foreign lands, his orchestral music won great sympathy in Germany and Great Britain, and he made the acquaintance of figures such as Schumann and Wagner.

Berlioz's compositions from the 1840s through the 1860s include a reworking of the scenes from *Faust* as *Le damnation de Faust* (1845–46); the oratorio *L'enfance du Christ* (1850–54); the operas *Les troyens* (based on Virgil's *Aeneid,* 1856–58) and *Béatrice et Bénédict* (after Shakespeare's *Much Ado about Nothing,* 1860–62); the song cycle *Les nuits d'été* (poetry by Gautier; composed 1840–41, orchestrated 1843–56); and a series of concert overtures. Many of these pieces received good receptions in Paris, and *Les troyens* finally achieved an operatic success on the Parisian stage for its composer in 1863 (but only after he discarded the first half, which he was never to hear in his lifetime).

After 1863 Berlioz gave up both music criticism and composition, descending into an increasingly morbid and bitter old age. To read his memoirs we would think him neglected and unrecognized, though he enjoyed wide esteem as a great composer. Toward the end of his life he was still receiving and accepting invitations to conduct his works, the last taking him to St. Petersburg in 1867. The death of his son, Louis, broke his spirit, and after a long decline he died in 1869.

Among all the composers of the "avant-garde" generation, Berlioz alone came to music without the aid of a piano. Although his musical style captures the spirit of his virtuoso friends in its flair for drama and its chromatic élan, he was free to imagine sonority in a way quite unlike his contemporaries. As a result his counterpoint moved beyond the harmonically governed writing of his fellows. Berlioz thought directly in terms of ensemble sonority (rather than projecting a short score onto a larger canvas), and he also imagined spatial location as an element of composition.

These qualities surfaced early in the *Symphonie fantastique*. This work, first composed in 1830 and revised in 1831–32, bears marks of Beethoven's influence: The five-movement form and programmatic references follow in the footsteps of the *Pastoral* Symphony premiered in Paris by Habeneck in 1829. Typical of the second-generation Romantics, Berlioz was not content merely with Beethoven's programmatic titles. For the *Symphonie fantastique* he fashioned an extensive tale of a failed romance "in the life of an artist," inspired by his infatuation with Harriet Smithson. Each movement became an episode in the tale (*Harold en Italie* would use a similar device), with the image of the beloved circulating through each episode as an *idée fixe*, an obsessively returning melodic idea (see Example 4.14).

Lest we believe that the *idée fixe* "portrayed" the artist's beloved, we should remember that the melody originated in *Herminie*, a cantata Berlioz entered for the 1828 Prix de Rome competition. Similarly, the fourth movement, "Marche au supplice," originated as the "Marche des gardes" in the abandoned opera *Les francs-juges*. In short, Berlioz's program for the *Symphonie fantastique* came after certain musical ideas. But that did not matter. Music did not represent; it shared the *spirit* of the written text. As Berlioz himself put it, "The aim of the program is by no means to copy faithfully what the composer has tried to present in orchestral terms. . . . He knows very well that music can take the place neither of word nor picture. . . ."

The outline of the *Symphonie fantastique* is best viewed in light of the standard tradition. The first movement, for instance, presents us with a modified sonata form including slow introduction. In this plan (which Chopin and Liszt also employed in *their* works; see Tables 4.2 and 4.3), the first and second themes reverse order for the recapitulation, yielding an "arch" form (see Table 4.4). Repetition of the main theme in the middle of the development section, however, is quite unprecedented (and was admired by Schumann, who used the gesture in the first movement of his First Symphony, op. 38).

EXAMPLE 4.14 Main theme (*idée fixe*) from Berlioz's *Symphonie fantastique* (1830)

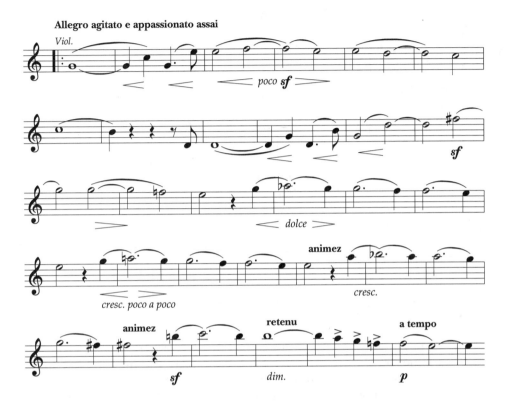

Just as the overall "form" responds to tradition in its way, Berlioz's phrase structure also finds some precedent. For instance, the main theme (*idée fixe;* Example 4.14) takes the shape of a Beethovenian "sentence," with a phrase repeated in sequence and then fragmented to form a continuation. But there are just as many passages that neither Beethoven, nor Schumann for that matter, would ever have imagined. The Parisian love of parallel chromatic motion is particularly striking, for instance in measures 200–230 or the transition from 360–411. And the orchestra, with its extra woodwinds, battalion of brass, including two ophicleides, two harps, extensive array of percussion, and fifty string players, indulges a dramatic extravagance far beyond anything in German practice.

The inner movements each have their arresting moments. We find Berlioz at his most graceful in the second movement ("A Ball"), which uses the *idée fixe* for its "trio." The third movement ("In the Country") opens with an explicitly spatial concept of sonority: The composer instructs the first oboe to play from

TABLE 4.4   Schematic for Berlioz's *Symphonie fantastique,* mvt. I

SECTION	SUBSECTION	KEY	MEASURES
Introduction		C:i	1–71
Exposition			
	Mth (*idée fixe*)	I	72–110
	transition	I→V	111–149
	Sth	V	150–167
Development			
	bridge	x	168–199
	core	x	200–233
	Mth	V	234–279
	core	x	280–312
	retransition	V/I	313–323
Recapitulation			
	Sth	I	324–359
	transition		360–411
	Mth	I	412–440
Coda		I	441–527

"behind the stage" to give the effect of one cowherd in the distance piping to another in the foreground (the English horn). The movement concludes with *four* timpanists imitating distant thunder. The "extra" fourth movement ("March to the Scaffold") is really a funeral march, the hybrid descendant of the *Eroica* and the *Pastoral* symphonies.

We can see the unusual interaction between program and music best in the audacious fifth movement. At this point in the story the artist's obsession with his beloved has led him to smoke opium, and in his drugged delirium he has murdered her and suffered execution (the fourth movement). In the fifth movement, according to Berlioz's written commentary,

> [The artist now] sees himself at the sabbath, in the midst of a frightful troop of ghosts, sorcerers, monsters of every kind, assembled for his funeral. Strange noises, groans, bursts of laughter, distant cries which other cries seem to answer. The beloved melody reappears again, but it has lost its character of nobility and shyness; it no more than an ignoble dance, trivial and grotesque; she is come to the sabbath. . . . A roar of joy at her arrival. . . . She takes part in the diabolical orgy. . . . Funeral knell, burlesque parody of the *Dies irae. Sabbath round dance.* The sabbath round dance and the *Dies irae* combine.

We can attach certain events in the program to specific musical passages. The "cries" appear in measures 4–7, repeated in measures 17–20. The *idée fixe* begins in measure 21, the roar of greeting in measure 29, and the "ignoble" dance in 40. Berlioz places the tolling bells at measure 102 "behind the stage," and he marks both the *Dies irae* (m. 127) and the "witches round dance" (m. 241) in the score. In this sense, the program provides an account of the unprecedented "music" (or "sound effects") for an audience that had never heard anything like it. The parallel chromatic harmonic motion at the beginning alone is outlandish enough to demand explanation.

At the same time as the program "explains" to the audience, it also gives the composer leave to place new sounds in a traditional framework. The bell tolling backstage, the *Dies irae* from the Catholic Mass for the Dead, and the banal "Witches Round Dance" did not form part of the ordinary musical arsenal in Berlioz's time. He uses the last two as themes in a double variation set (influenced, no doubt, by the finale of Beethoven's *Eroica*). By virtue of their distinctive qualities, the familiar chant and "popular" dance retain their identities in nonimitative contrapuntal combination ("The sabbath round dance and the *Dies irae* combine," m. 414). They also refer to an ancient cantus-firmus tradition; in short, the composer plays historicism against "progress." By alluding to the age-old tradition of chant currently being revived in nineteenth-century France, Berlioz also invokes the notion of eternal validity for his own music, as if to say that the *Symphonie fantastique* too is immortally "classical." In the long run this characterization would prove true, though Berlioz would wait some time for recognition of the piece's genius.

If the *Symphonie fantastique* did not win Berlioz immediate plaudits, his *Grande messe des morts* received instant acclaim. This piece, commissioned by the government in the spring of 1837 and performed after some delays in December of that year, falls in a long tradition of French ceremonial music. Written for performance in the vast and acoustically resonant church of Les Invalides, Berlioz had originally conceived his Requiem for five hundred performers, though the government provided funding for only three hundred in the end. Still, the array of singers, large orchestra, and four brass choirs located in different corners of the performing space proved extraordinarily impressive.

Large performing forces were nothing new in France since the time of the Revolution, but Berlioz could still produce effects that astonished his listeners. The best example comes, predictably, in the *Dies irae*. It begins quietly, exposing two of three contrapuntal lines by themselves before combining them into the layered, nonimitative overlay that marks much of Berlioz's writing (see Example 4.15). The composer then rearticulates the various themes in three segments, each higher in pitch (A minor, B-flat minor, D minor), modulating by means of parallel chromatic thirds. Each segment is also slightly faster in tempo and cast at a higher dynamic level. All this builds to the *Tuba mirum*, the traditional place for grand orchestral effects in a requiem and the juncture at which Berlioz brings in his four, spatially separated brass choirs and sixteen timpani. The Requiem contrasts such cataclysmic episodes with writing of the utmost delicacy—for

EXAMPLE 4.15   Triple counterpoint in the *Dies irae* from Berlioz's Requiem, 1837

instance in the tenor solo of the Sanctus, accompanied by one flute, four solo violins, and violas divided into parts playing *pianissimo* tremolo chords. The extreme disposition of the assembled forces prompted Alfred de Vigny to characterize the piece as "beautiful and bizarre, wild, convulsive, and searing."

It is all too easy to forget Berlioz's more lyrical side in the face of his large-scale pieces. A much gentler Berlioz, and one attuned to the historicist currents of his time, produced *L'enfance du Christ,* which he refrained from calling an oratorio (though it surely belongs to that genre). It grew in stages between 1850 and 1854, and Berlioz offered the central part, *L'adieu des bergers,* in his Société Philharmonique concerts of 1850–51 as the work of an imaginary seventeenth-century composer, Pierre Ducré. Another manifestation of Berlioz's more delicate sensibilities appears in *Les nuits d'été,* a cycle of songs relating a tale of lost love with text by the romantic French poet Théophile Gautier. The composer originally wrote the songs for piano and voices (mezzo-soprano, tenor, alto, or baritone) in 1840–41, but he returned to orchestrate the group elegantly in 1856. ("Au cimetière" was orchestrated and published by itself in 1843.) For those accustomed to the regularity of phrase structure in the German Lied, these songs come as a surprise. The voice adopts a declamatory tone in many of them, particularly in "Sur les lagunes" and "Absence." Only "Villanelle" and "L'île inconnue" offer conventionally "songlike" melodies. Yet the overall effect of this cycle is ravishing, and like so much else in Berlioz, singular.

No discussion of Berlioz's career would be complete without what he considered its crowning achievement, *Les troyens.* This grandest of all French grand operas takes its subject from Virgil's *Aeneid,* a favorite of the composer's since childhood. Berlioz himself fashioned the libretto in archaic French verse during April of 1856, and he finished composing two years later in April of 1858. Though he campaigned vigorously for performance at the Opéra, he finally settled for a performance at the Théâtre-Lyrique. The composer compromised further by eliminating the first two acts, which related the fall of Troy and the escape of Aeneas. Only the story of Dido and her encounter with the Trojans remained. Thus reduced and renamed *Les troyens à Carthage,* the work received twenty-two performances in November and December of 1863. Berlioz was gratified by the warm public reception, but he felt the piece incomplete without the first two acts, and he discouraged revivals of the shortened opera in later years.

Les troyens presents us with an amazing combination of diverse elements: story from classical antiquity, noble simplicity and stately pacing from Gluck, dramatic conception from Spontini, pageantry from Meyerbeer, operatic form from Rossini. The chorus and the ballet are much in evidence, as in all French grand opera of this period. Perhaps the best example of Berlioz's particular admixture comes in the opening of Act III, featuring Dido in the midst of her people. This scene opened the opera in its shortened version of *Les troyens à Carthage,* and it takes the form of a Rossinian *introduzione*: beginning chorus and national hymn, Dido's cavatina, and choral ending, including a repetition of the

EXAMPLE 4.16   Beginning of the hymn to Dido from Berlioz's *Les troyens,* 1858

national hymn as *stretta*. But there is no dramatic action, for this is a scenic tableau meant to create a spectacle with as many choristers and extras on stage as possible. It is grand in the way that only Berlioz can be. The hymn to Dido (excerpt in Example 4.16) consists of a carefully measured processional, with a melody moving majestically against the steady tread of the bass. The melodies of the solo arias have this same static quality, and this may account in part for the fact that *Les troyens* has not survived as a regular component of the modern operatic repertory. Its sobriety, motivated in part by the classical subject, precludes the sweet blandishments of Italian cantilena. Still, the work manifests immense creativity and a conception as impressive as that in Wagner's *Götterdämmerung*. It stands as a monument to a generation that used tradition and even the distant past as a foil for its vision of progress and as a measure of artistic worth.

FURTHER READING

Many interesting points about the piano music and the general style of this group of composers appears in Charles Rosen's *The Romantic Generation* (Cambridge, MA, 1995).

Robert Schumann

John Daverio's recent new biography, *Robert Schumann, Herald of a New Poetic Age* (New York, 1997), presents a fine overview of Schumann's life and works, as well as an entry into bibliography. The new Schumann edition in Germany is producing a great deal of new material about the composer that will eventually change some of our ideas about his activity.

Clara Schumann

Clara Schumann is served well by Nancy Reich's *Clara Schumann: The Artist and the Woman* (Ithaca, NY, 1985), though Berthold Litzmann's *Clara Schumann: An Artist's Life, Based on Material Found in Diaries and Letters* (New York, 1972), trans. Grace Hadow, still holds its own.

Mendelssohn

Finding a good biography of Felix Mendelssohn may prove difficult. Eric Werner's *Mendelssohn: A New Image of the Composer and His Age* (New York, 1963) should be approached with caution for its many biases and inaccuracies. A collection of essays such as *Mendelssohn and His World* (Princeton, 1991), ed. R. Larry Todd, or Todd's study on *Mendelssohn, the Hebrides and Other Overtures* (Cambridge, 1993), even if more narrowly focused, may prove more informative.

Chopin

Students of Chopin have an excellent new biography in the form of Jim Samson's *Chopin* (Oxford, 1996; New York and London, 1997). The more daring may wish to explore

Jeffrey Kallberg's *Chopin at the Boundaries: Sex, History, and Musical Genre* (Cambridge, MA, 1996). Liszt's biography remains an affectionate tribute, *Chopin* (Paris, 1852).

Liszt

Aficionados of Liszt's music will find a fine account of his life and works by Alan Walker in three volumes, *Franz Liszt, the Man and His Music* (New York, 1983).

Berlioz

The most recent research appears in D. Kern Holoman's *Berlioz* (Cambridge, MA, 1989). David Cairns also presents a fine study in *Berlioz, 1803–1832: The Making of an Artist* (London, 1989). Jacques Barzun's older study, *Berlioz and the Romantic Century* (Boston, 1950), may still be worth a look, though it is dated and sheds little light on the composer's music.

CHAPTER 5

The Complete Work of Art: Operatic Development from Midcentury

The towering figures of Verdi and Wagner, contemporaries on the operatic scene, tend to cast the latter part of nineteenth-century musical theater in a unique light. Their breadth of imagination, forceful creativity, and political influence, as well as the continued presence of their works on the stage, all lead justifiably to this special regard. Their operas, together with a handful by French contemporaries, touch us in a way that still seems relevant and compelling.

Although we may be tempted to view opera from midcentury as something special, we should remember that Verdi, Wagner, and the rest continued down dramatic trails blazed by Rossini, Bellini, Donizetti, Weber, and Meyerbeer. Writers tend to regard Verdi and French composers as doing little more than perpetuating tradition; Wagner and the Germans, on the other hand, are usually perceived as reformers overthrowing outworn conventions. Without denying the evidence supporting those characterizations, we can view the common roots and goals that lie beneath the composers' varying technical means. Verdi and the French did far more than merely repeat the conventions they inherited, just as Wagner and the Germans did not entirely reinvent the genre.

Some of the trends woven through nineteenth-century opera include increasingly fluid motion between various distinct textures (parlando and cantabile; solo, choral, and instrumental), an expanded harmonic palette, more orchestral color, and interconnection by motivic reminiscence. These techniques blurred the distinction between outer and inner action, smoothed the flow of dramatic time, and promoted overall cohesion. This resulted in more dramatic impact and also caused composers to think of operas increasingly as indissoluble "works." Rossini composing rapidly might shift overtures from one opera to the next and cannibalize old arias to create new ones. But composers writing slowly and deliberately in the later part of the nineteenth century made interpolation or deletion almost unthinkable. We tend to take this for granted with Wagner, but Verdi was just as strict. Contracts with his publisher attached stipulations to performance rights forbidding cuts, transpositions, or changes in instrumentation under the threat of substantial fines. All these developments emerged gradually over the course of the 1840s and matured in the 1850s and beyond. Once achieved, they left opera firmly ensconced in the canon of "classical music."

VERDI

Background and "First Period"

Giuseppe Verdi (1813–1901) inherited the mantel of the Italian operatic tradition during a period of political unrest and change. Born of lower-middle-class parents whose families had been small landowners, tavern keepers, and tradesmen around Busseto, he evinced musical talent at the very young age of three, when he began music lessons with the local organist. At eleven he entered the local *ginasio* for an education in classical letters, taking instruction at the same time with Ferdinando Provesi, the director of Busseto's municipal music school. In 1831 he went to live in the house of the merchant and musical patron Antonio Barezzi, who financed his first year of professional education in 1832–33. Verdi failed to gain admission to the Milan Conservatory and so studied composition privately with Vincenzo Lavigna, who had been a mildly successful opera composer early in the century. As a student, Verdi showed particular promise in counterpoint, and after three years of study he won accolades at the state musical exams held in Parma in 1836.

In April of 1836 Verdi returned to his hometown under contract as its municipal music director. His duties included giving lessons in voice, keyboard, composition, and counterpoint, and conducting concerts of the philharmonic society. He married Barezzi's daughter and composed instrumental pieces for concerts, sacred music for church, and songs for publication in Milan. All the while, he was impatient to break out of his small-town surroundings. To that end he worked on various operatic plans, which finally coalesced in *Oberto, Conte di San Bonifacio*. In 1838 he spent his two-month leave in Milan, and he moved his family there in February 1839. *Oberto* made its first appearance at La Scala in

November, and its success prompted the director of the theater to commission three more operas. Verdi had found his calling.

Although the first commissioned opera, a comedy titled *Un giorno di regno,* failed miserably amid family tragedy (his wife and children died), Verdi had success with his other two works for La Scala. Both had libretti by Temistocle Solera, who was under suspicion by the Austrians ruling northern Italy for his strong patriotic leanings. In *Nabucco* (*Nebuchadnezzar;* 1842) and *I lombardi alla prima crociata* (1843), Solera fashioned stirring verses with political overtones. *Nabucco* took the Babylonian captivity of the Jews as its subject. Their yearning for freedom in choruses such as the famous "Va, pensiero" sounded a patriotic note to Italian audiences. *I lombardi*'s crusaders longing for their homeland in choruses such as "O Signore, dal tetto natio" struck a similar chord in Italy. Both operas became immediate hits. *Nabucco* alone enjoyed an unparalleled fifty-eight performances in its first two seasons at La Scala and soon drew international acclaim. Verdi followed these initial successes with a number of operas painted on vast canvases depicting political turmoil. Among them are *Ernani* (Venice, 1844), about a Spanish duke in conflict with the crown; *Giovanna d'Arco* (Milan, 1845), about the patriotic French saint; *Attila,* about resistance to invading Germanic tribes (Venice, 1846); *Macbeth,* about political unrest in Scotland (Florence, 1847); and *La battaglia di Legnano,* about the defeat of the Holy Roman Emperor by the Italians in the twelfth century (Rome, 1849).

In all, Verdi composed fourteen new operas in the decade between 1839 and 1849. Many of them were based on fashionable poets such as Schiller, Byron, and Shakespeare as adapted by the librettists Solera, Cammarano, and Francesco Maria Piave, Verdi's most frequent collaborator. These operas combine long-breathed melodic lines in the tradition of Bellini, rich and colorful orchestrations in the tradition of Donizetti, and vigorous accompaniments. They created what the contemporary critic Abramo Basevi called Verdi's "grandiose" style. The Rossinian conventions of the *introduzione,* three-part arias, four-part duets, and five-part finales persist in these operas, but Verdi exploits them with all the freedom and inventiveness developed to this time.

Maturity and "Second Period"

As Verdi's fame spread, the gravitational and financial attraction of Paris began to exert its influence. He traveled there in 1847 to supervise his revision of *I lombardi* as *Jérusalem* for performance at the Opéra. The composer also encountered a former acquaintance, the soprano Giuseppina Strepponi, who had sung in *Nabucco* at Milan. He lived with her from 1847 to 1849. Though he bought a home and land in Sant'Agata near Busseto during this period, he continued to spend a great deal of time between 1847 and 1857 in Paris, away from the gossip of Italian neighbors. He did not marry Strepponi until August of 1859.

At the same time his personal life took a turn for the better, Verdi also focused his operas on personal relationships between characters (rather than on grand political conflict), and he refined his style. These developments ushered in his "second period," beginning with *Luisa Miller* (after Schiller's *Kabale und Liebe;* Naples, 1849) and extending to *Rigoletto* (after Hugo's *Le roi s'amuse;* Venice, 1851), *Il trovatore* (after Gutiérrez's *El trovador;* Rome, 1853), and *La traviata* (after the younger Dumas's *La Dame aux camélias;* Venice, 1853, rev. 1854). The last three are Verdi's most popular and oft-performed operas, and in many ways they represent the final stage in the development of the Rossinian model.

La traviata (which might be translated "The Woman Who Strayed") provides an excellent example of Verdi's skill at midcentury. It utilizes "Rossinian" conventions to illuminate character so poignantly that it approaches a kind of psychological realism, and the subject matter itself has realistic aspects that we can understand today. The story came from a novel that the younger Dumas had based on his affair with the real-life Parisian figure of Alphonsine Duplessis. She was exquisitely beautiful and "kept" in luxury by various members of the high nobility until her death at the age of twenty-three from tuberculosis. In the plot as adapted by Piave, the female protagonist (Violetta Valéry) falls in love with a young man of modest means (Alfredo Germont). The boy's family disapproves, and his father (Giorgio Germont) persuades Violetta to leave Alfredo, gaining respect in the process for her nobility and self-sacrifice. She tries to return to her former life but pines so for the young man that her health collapses. As she lies dying, Alfredo returns with his remorseful father to be reconciled in her last moments.

The story presents multiple layers of realism. Lest we believe the situation of the dying courtesan overly dramatic, unmarried women had limited choices in nineteenth-century society, and "consumption" accounted for at least one quarter of all deaths in western Europe and the United States. Moreover, the "true facts" behind Dumas's fictional account were well known in Paris, where Verdi probably saw a play made from the novel in the company of Giuseppina Strepponi. This brought a personal note to the opera, for Verdi conducted an affair for over a decade with Strepponi, who had had two illegitimate children by previous lovers. When Verdi requested that the piece be produced in modern dress, he desired nothing more than explicit recognition of its current relevance (though his wishes were initially rejected in favor of a seventeenth-century setting).

A historical setting, however, could not prevent the mature Verdi and the talented Piave from achieving a very immediate musical and dramatic impact. After a delicate prelude that exposes the twin themes of "Love and Death" (one of the early titles for the opera), the collaborators launch into a classic *introduzione* (see Table 5.1). Compared with Rossini's for *The Barber of Seville*, however, (see Table 3.2), the "number" has become vastly more complicated and

TABLE 5.1   Schematic of the *Introduzione* for *La traviata*

SECTION	MATERIAL	KEY	DRAMATIC SITUATION
Chorus w/parlando soloists "Del invitato"	A	A	Introduction of main and supporting characters; sets scene.
Brindisi strophic aria "Libiamo"	B	B♭	Violetta toasts pleasure; Alfredo toasts love.
Duettino Waltz parlando lines over orchestral music, "Non gradireste"	C	E♭	Chorus departs; Violetta, Alfredo trade information.
Cantabile "Un dì felice"; Alfredo's reminiscence motive: "Di quell'amor"	D	B♭	Alfredo declares love; Violetta rejects him with laughing coloratura.
Waltz reprise parlando lines over orchestral music	C	E♭	Violetta allows Alfredo to pay call the next day.
Stretta choral parlando	A	A♭	Guests depart.

subtle. The solo characters now appear in the midst of an opening chorus in which the orchestra largely carries the texture while the singers declaim in rapid parlando texture. The encapsulated "aria" presents "realistic" music (that is, music the characters on stage actually hear): Alfredo and Violetta "sing" a drinking song called a Brindisi. The rest of the dramatic interaction unfolds in a duet, much of it over a waltz (also "realistic" music). When Alfredo and Violetta express their internal feelings, they adopt lyrical styles that display their different responses. Alfredo's elegant cantabile lines reveal his love in the haunting refrain "Di quell'amor" (Example 5.1), while Violetta's rapidly mocking coloratura declares that she has no love to offer. The waltz returns as background to their final arrangements, and then the guests' breathless departure at dawn mirrors their late arrival in repeated choral material. Bel canto and coloratura have been employed for characterization here, the music of the traditional choral opening and closing are finely attuned to the dramatic situation, and underlying orchestral music helps to weld the various situations into a continuous motion. Even the progressive sequence of keys propels the action: The prelude ending in E major serves as dominant to the beginning chorus in A major. It in turn serves as leading tone to B-flat major, which prepares E-flat major, dominant of A-flat major (the concluding key of Violetta's ensuing aria). Verdi creates an immensely complicated musico-dramatic structure in this

EXAMPLE 5.1   Beginning of Alfredo's plea from the *introduzione* of Verdi's *La traviata*, which will serve as a reminiscence motive

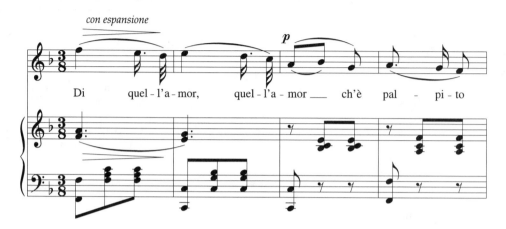

introduction by taking brilliant advantage of available vocal styles, orchestral accompaniment, and Rossinian conventions.

Violetta's three-part aria concludes the first act with another compositional tour de force. Piave employs the standard Rossinian outline (see Table 5.2) with great imagination. The strophic cantabile ("Ah, fors' è lui") finds Violetta musing on the possibility of true love, whereas in the *tempo di mezzo* ("Follie! Follie!") she rejects these idle thoughts to proclaim her independence and spirited pursuit of pleasure in a cabaletta. Verdi tracks the dramatic development assiduously. The cantabile begins with a melody in minor mode that gives way to

TABLE 5.2   Schematic for Violetta's Three-Part Aria from Verdi's *La traviata*, Act I

SECTION	*TEMPO*	*KEY*	*INCIPIT/CONTENT*
Cantabile	Andantino	f–F	"Ah, fors' è lui"; vs. 2: "A me, fanciulla" Violetta considers Alfredo's love.
Tempo di mezzo	Allegro	x	"Follie! Follie!"; Violetta rejects true love as folly.
Cabaletta	Allegro brilliante	A♭	"Sempre libera"; Violetta embraces the life of freedom and pleasure; AA′ form, interrupted by Alfredo's serenade, "Amor è palpito."
Coda			Violetta's coloratura and Alfredo's serenade in counterpoint.

a reminiscence of Alfredo's love motive (see Example 5.1) in the parallel major. The *tempo di mezzo* modulates to the relative major of a cabaletta featuring coloratura that has become the hallmark of Violetta's pursuit of pleasure. But here Alfredo's motive returns as a serenade of "realistic" music outside her window. She seeks to drown this out in the frenetic coloratura of her coda. The conflicting thoughts of soprano and tenor become a showcase for Verdi's counterpoint.

The four-part Rossinian duet between Violetta and Alfredo's father in the second act (see Table 5.3) offers another instance of Verdi's talent at characterization. The composer avoids the customary practice of having the singers borrow melodies from one another (compare Table 3.4). Germont's and Violetta's different positions and reactions result not only in different melodies but also in different keys and modes, as the schematic plainly shows. No diagram, however, can capture the depth of feeling invested in the various vocal lines. Germont's insinuations about Violetta's waning charms embody sinister persuasion (see Example 5.2), whereas the elegant lines setting her plea to have her sacrifice remembered at the beginning of the cantabile would melt a stone (see Example 5.3). Not until the cabaletta ("Morrò!"), when resolution has been reached, do Violetta and Germont actually hold phrases in common. Italian opera remains a singer's art for Verdi, in which melody and drama not only are brought into accord but also serve each other. Of course, the paired, repeated phrases and arched lines that promote even production throughout the singer's range persist. Verdi designed his roles for bel canto *and* acting, the reason the composer was at such pains to find the right singers for performances of his operas.

Outlining *La traviata*'s finales (for Acts II and III) would be pointless, because Verdi abandons the conventional five-part structure. Both unfold freely as a series of interactions between singers and the orchestra. Verdi and Piave,

TABLE 5.3   Schematic for Duet from Verdi's *La traviata,* Act II

SECTION	*KEY*	*CONTENT/INCIPIT*
I. Tempo di primo	A♭	Germont outlines family situation, "Pura siccome."
	c	Violetta replies she cannot bear to leave Alfredo, "Non sapete."
	f→A♭	Germont suggests that time will erode Alfredo's infatuation, begs Violetta to renounce him, "Un dì, quando."
II. Cantabile	E♭ (e♭)	Violetta accepts defeat, making Germont promise to remember her sacrifice, "Dite alla giovine."
III. Tempo di mezzo	x	Germont and Violetta agree that she will leave Alfredo, "Imponete."
IV. Cabaletta	g (B♭)	Violetta declares that she will die—Germont praises her noble sacrifice, "Morrò!"

EXAMPLE 5.2   Beginning of Germont's suggestion to Violetta that age will diminish Alfredo's love from duet in Act II of *La traviata*

however, adopt the conventional *device* of highlighting Alfredo and Violetta's fight at the end of the second act by placing it in the context of a festive gathering (a costume ball on a Spanish theme featuring gypsies and bullfighters). And the composer hits on a brilliant stroke for the conclusion of the opera by punctuating its vocal lines with a funeral-march accompaniment.

Throughout *La traviata* Verdi uses the orchestra to blend each declamatory "scene" (*scena* in Italian) into the lyrical sections. The instrumental writing also determines mood, and returning musical motives bind various parts of the opera together. This is equally true of the other operas in Verdi's second period, especially in *Rigoletto,* much of which unfolds in parlando style. Of course, accompanied recitative, reminiscence motives, and connection of outer and inner action were nothing new; all had developed in opera in the decades preceding Verdi. It was the composer's extraordinary ability to grasp the develop-

EXAMPLE 5.3   Beginning of cantabile from duet in Act II of *La traviata*

ments of previous Italian opera and use them with unprecedented inventiveness that made perennial favorites of his second-period operas.

The Third Period: Grand Opera and Its Influences

Once he had reached the pinnacle of success in Italian opera, Verdi turned his attention to French grand opera. Like Rossini and Meyerbeer before him, Verdi initially recast one of his Italian pieces for the Paris Opéra (*I lombardi* became *Jérusalem,* as mentioned earlier). Eventually he contracted to write an opera specifically for Paris, choosing Scribe to write the libretto. The result, *Les vêpres siciliennes* (Paris, 1855) was not particularly successful. *Simon Boccanegra* (Venice, 1857) captured some traits from grand opera, but without particular success. *Un ballo in maschera* (Rome, Teatro Apollo, 1857) was adapted from Auber's

Gustave III, and it treats the grand opera subject in an Italian way. *La forza del destino,* written for St. Petersburg (1862), has some features of grand opera. In 1864 the Académie des Beaux Arts elected Verdi to the chair vacated by Meyerbeer. Only then did Verdi celebrate an unqualified success at the Opéra with *Don Carlos* (libretto by Méry and Camille Du Locle; Paris, 1867). This lengthy work has stirring roles for a large cast, many beautiful solo passages, and also a first-rate scenic tableau in which heretics are burned at the stake. The story, modeled on Schiller's play of the same name, explores themes of individual liberty, political freedom, and ecclesiastical oppression, all issues of much concern to the composer.

In the 1860s Verdi's political ideals began to be realized. In the movement for the unification of Italy called "risorgimento," the composer had long served as both champion and symbol. His last name was taken as an acronym for "*Vittore Emanuele, Re D'Italia*" ("Victor Emmanuel, King of Italy"—the monarch Italians hoped would unite the country under secular rule). Cries of "Viva VERDI!" carried both cultural and political meanings. When Victor Emmanuel became King of Italy in 1861, Verdi ran for the newly formed Italian parliament. Unification was completed in 1871 when the French finally quit Rome and the papal lands were wrested from ecclesiastical control. In 1874 the composer was elected to an honorary position in the Italian senate, though he played no active role in deliberations.

During this period Verdi finally succeeded in combining elements of French grand opera and traditional Italian opera in a completely satisfying way. The result was *Aida* (1871), commissioned for the Cairo opera house in celebration of the new Suez Canal. Du Locle provided a prose libretto in French that Antonio Ghislanzoni rendered into Italian verse under Verdi's close supervision. The traditional forms of aria and duet, imaginatively construed, find a place here, as do scenic tableaux in the French tradition. The most famous of these is the triumphal scene, with its well-known march, its many extras, and its ballet. Verdi balanced vocal display, superb orchestration, and overwhelming spectacle so effectively in *Aida* that it has remained a favorite of audiences to this day.

Verdi's *Messa da Requiem* (1874) from this same period also proves a vocal and orchestral tour de force. The composer wrote the *Libera me* as part of a collaborative effort commemorating the death of Rossini in 1868. The death of the great Italian poet Alessandro Manzoni in 1873 prompted the composition of the remaining movements.

The German conductor and pianist Hans von Bülow characterized the Requiem contemptuously as Verdi's "most recent opera in church vestments," but that is precisely the work's strength. In the course of writing extended works for the stage, Verdi had mastered dramatic vocal line, effective choral disposition, brilliant orchestration, and command of overall structure. In combination with his early training in church counterpoint, the mixture proves extremely powerful. Nowhere is this so evident as in the *Libera me*. It begins with a soprano and choral recitative, followed by a brief lyrical section for soprano in the passage beginning "Tremens factus." The stormy *Dies irae* recalls its first appearance in the second movement, as does the contemplative passage for the words "Requiem aeternam" (see Example 5.4a). Verdi then summons all his powers for a reiteration of the passage *Libera me* ("Deliver me, O Lord, from eternal death on that tremendous day"), which ends with a choral fugue (see Example 5.4b). The final climax, beginning on the words "dum veneris judicare" ("and you shall come to judge the world by fire"), is as shattering as anything Berlioz accomplished in his Requiem. And the monotone chanting of the soprano as the last chords die away supplies theatrics of the best kind. Verdi's Requiem presents a worthy Italian successor to the tradition of the orchestral mass as exemplified in Beethoven's *Missa Solemnis* and Berlioz's *Grande messe des morts*.

The Fourth Period: The Experimentation of Old Age

Had Verdi composed nothing after *Aida* and the Requiem, he would still be remembered as the nineteenth century's greatest Italian composer. But like Beethoven, he could not set his creativity aside and simply retire. Verdi would have been comfortable: He had amassed a substantial fortune and become the equivalent of a country squire over the course of his career. He withdrew to his villa and farm at Sant'Agata from the time of the Requiem to 1879, but in that summer Giulio Ricordi (Verdi's publisher) suggested the possibility of a libretto from Shakespeare's *Othello*. It would be fashioned by Arrigo Boito, a critic and poet, and also composer of *Mefistofele* (Milan, 1868), an opera that enjoyed some success. Boito's skillful condensation of Shakespeare's play piqued Verdi's interest, but he first became accustomed to his new librettist by collaborating on a revision of *Simon Boccanegra,* performed at La Scala in 1881. He then turned his attention to a revision of *Don Carlos* in French with the original librettist, Du Locle. Shortened to four acts and brought closer to Schiller's play, it was translated into Italian and performed at La Scala in 1884.

Verdi did not finish *Otello* until 1885. Andrew Porter observes in his article for *The New Grove* that the opera has some standard features: "an *introduzione* in which the hero's entrance is framed between choruses, a *brindisi* [drinking song] . . . a duet finale to Act 2 (as in *Rigoletto*), a 4/4–12/8 ensemble finale to Act 3, a last-act *preghiera* [prayer-aria] for the heroine, a finale death scene for the hero." But beneath the "numbers" lie greater continuity, a delicate but constantly active orchestral texture, more declamatory vocal writing, and little of conventional bel canto style. The vocal line always predominates, often with many graceful melodies, but Verdi subordinates vocal effect to dramatic clarity and banishes coloratura altogether. We may be tempted to see the influence of Wagner in these features: Boito was a disciple, and Verdi acquainted himself

EXAMPLE 5.4A   Excerpt from last movement of Verdi's Requiem

with some of Wagner's writings and music in the 1870s. But *Otello* forms part of an Italian continuum. The outer action of *scene* blended increasingly into the inner action of arias and duets, and rapid alternation between declamatory and lyrical style became the norm in *introduzioni* and finales.

The final stage in these developments came in Verdi's last opera, *Falstaff* (Milan, 1893), with a libretto fashioned again by Boito after Shakespeare (*The Merry Wives of Windsor* and sections of *Henry IV*). The plot concerns the triumph of young love between Fenton and Nannetta over arranged marriage, and the confounding of Falstaff's philandering and conniving. In this work the orchestra becomes the witty chorus commenting on the rapid repartee between characters, carrying the action along on bubbling rhythms, and punctuating the dialogue. Rather than presenting a series of repeated motives à la Wagner, the orchestra creates coherence using ritornelli, ostinati, and repeated figures for segments that cannot be called "numbers." Most melodic reminiscences come in the vocal parts, and then usually in conjunction with repeated text (Fenton and Nannetta's "Bocca baciata," Quickly's "Reverenza," Falstaff's "Dalle due alle tre"). There is only one aria in set form, a "realistic" fairy song ("Sul fil d'un soffio"), presented as such by Nannetta in the third act.

EXAMPLE 5.4B   Excerpt of fugue from last movement of Verdi's Requiem, subject in tenor

Lacking the conventional aria, Verdi either has characters declaim monologues over orchestral passages or offers them sections of arioso with ritornelli. A prime example of the latter appears in Falstaff's self-congratulatory speech, "Va, vecchio John" (Act II, part 1; Example 5.5). An orchestral refrain frames the old knight's monologue and then makes a last appearance at the end of the scene. Ford's monologue in this same section is punctuated by a triplet figure very distantly related to "Dalle due alle tre." Although there seems to be no strict sequence of keys, various levels of interactions within scenes do generally assume the same key. Thus, the plotting of various characters in Act I, part 2, takes place mostly in E major, and Verdi reserves D-flat major for the lovers. The composer uses neither melodic repetition nor assigned key in a pedantic fashion, and this lends *Falstaff* its wonderful flexibility.

Verdi's lack of strict system and convention in *Falstaff*, however, does not preclude an occasional nod toward tradition. The rapid-fire ensemble sections often feature contrapuntal writing, a tradition in Italian comic opera. The finale

EXAMPLE 5.5   Excerpt from Falstaff's monologue in Act II, part 1, of Verdi's *Falstaff*

consists of a fugue such as one might find in a Rossini or even a Mozart ending. We can hear echoes of the fugal moral that sums up *Don Giovanni* in Falstaff's "Tutto nel mondo è burla" ("Everything in the world is a joke"; Example 5.6). *Falstaff* makes for a good-natured conclusion to Verdi's operatic career.

Verdi spent the years after *Falstaff* in philanthropy and musical experimentation. He concerned himself most with the establishment of the Casa di Riposo per Musicisti, a home for retired musicians that he built and endowed at his own expense. It houses aged Italian musicians to this day and affords them comfort in their declining years. Verdi published his last composition, a collection of *Four Sacred Pieces,* in 1898. He composed the "Ave Maria" (1889) on a puzzle scale that appeared in the *Gazzetta musicale.* Although Verdi wrote the piece for his amusement and did not think to have it performed, it does represent *fin de siècle* exploration of the furthest reaches of tonality. The remaining pieces for

EXAMPLE 5.6   Excerpt of concluding fugue from Verdi's *Falstaff,* subject in Fenton's part

chorus and orchestra also bear the imprint of late-nineteenth-century chromaticism, demonstrating Verdi's continued mental plasticity and artistic curiosity. The composer was so proud of the last piece in the collection, a "Te Deum," that he asked to have the score buried with him. His death from a stroke in January 1901 at the Grand Hotel in Milan, shortly after he had celebrated the holidays with Boito and Ricordi, was marked by mourning throughout Italy.

WAGNER

Background and "Romantic Operas"

Richard Wagner (1813–83), born in the same year as Verdi, holds an analogously central position in the history of German music and culture. Wagner, too, involved himself in political activity, though as a writer of cultural polemics rather than as a member of parliament. Unlike Verdi, Wagner explicitly styled himself as a visionary, and his originality and imagination cannot be denied. But these qualities should not blind us to the fact that he walked down an aesthetic path indicated by opera composers earlier in the nineteenth century, much as his great Italian contemporary did.

Wagner came from Saxony, the same region in Germany as Robert Schumann. His father, Friedrich Wagner, had risen to chief of police in Leipzig shortly before he died in November of 1813, just months after the birth of his youngest son. Less than a year later Friedrich's widow, Johanna, married Ludwig Geyer, an actor at the court theater in Dresden. She moved her whole family to the Saxon capital, and young Richard spent his childhood in its artistic circles. (Family acquaintances included Carl Maria von Weber, whom Wagner later credited with "arousing a passion for music in me.") Geyer died in 1821, but for a time his sister supported Johanna and her children. Richard received excellent schooling in Dresden, entering the Kreuzschule in 1822 for a literary education that included Latin and Greek.

When Johanna Wagner returned to Leipzig in 1828, Richard attended the Nicolaigymnasium, but he became so obsessed with theater and music that he neglected his studies there. During this time he wrote a student play entitled *Leubald*, which was much influenced by his reading of Shakespeare. Exposure to the rich concert life of Leipzig began to interest him in orchestral music, and he made a piano arrangement of Beethoven's Ninth Symphony, which he tried unsuccessfully to publish. He also took lessons in harmony from the director of the Euterpe Musical Society, Christian Gottlob Müller. These early activities bear a marked resemblance to those of Schumann, save for the fact that *he* aimed to become a piano virtuoso, whereas Wagner evinced no such solo talent.

In 1830 Wagner enrolled at the Leipzig university, and during his second term he encountered Christian Theodor Weinlig, cantor at the Thomaskirche. His lessons with Weinlig included counterpoint and general composition. Under his supervision the young composer wrote a Piano Sonata in B-flat, published by Breitkopf, and a Symphony in C, performed in Prague and Leipzig. In 1832 Wagner tried his hand at an opera libretto, *Die Hochzeit* (mostly lost). His practice of writing his own libretti persisted the rest of his life.

His studies complete in 1833, Wagner embarked on an apprenticeship in the musical theater. He began as a chorus master in Würzburg, a job his opera-singing brother Albert procured for him. He stayed for a year, helping to prepare productions by Cherubini, Weber, Beethoven, Auber, Rossini, Marschner, and Meyerbeer. He also wrote an opera there, *Die Feen,* with many similarities to Weber's *Oberon.* A music directorship of a traveling company followed in July of 1834, then an engagement at the Magdeburg theater lasting until 1836. During this period Wagner met his first wife, the singer Minna Planner; their marriage was stormy, with infidelity on her part and financial insecurity on his. He completed another opera, *Das Liebesverbot* (after Shakespeare's *Measure for Measure*), and he took up posts as music director successively in Königsberg (April 1837) and Riga (July 1837), departing suddenly in March 1839 just ahead of his creditors.

By a circuitous route that included Russia, East Prussia, and London, Wagner finally made his way in September 1839 to Paris, which he considered the center of operatic culture. In his work at various small German opera houses, he had come to admire the works of Spontini, Méhul, and Halévy, and he wrote letters to Meyerbeer and Scribe in advance of his arrival. But his hopes for a Paris production of his new grand opera, *Rienzi,* were bitterly disappointed. Instead he supported himself making arrangements of fashionable operas for piano and writing reviews for the *Gazette musicale.* Though a financial failure, Wagner's sojourn in Paris exposed him to a great deal of new music, including the novel orchestrations of Berlioz and the harmonic innovations of Liszt and Chopin. His stay in the French capital also introduced him to a great deal of progressive political thinking.

Wagner returned to Germany triumphantly in 1842, when the Dresden Opera agreed to perform *Rienzi.* Its overwhelming success led to the performance of a German romantic opera he had begun in Paris, *The Flying Dutchman* (1843). The two works induced the Dresden management to make Wagner conductor of the Royal Opera in February 1843. He had a controversial tenure there, celebrating success with some of his productions and championing the cause of German music. His next opera, *Tannhäuser* (1845), encountered opposition. Rejection of his 1848 proposal to reform the Saxon theater and the subsequent cancellation of the première of his next opera, *Lohengrin,* caused Wagner to lose faith in the government. He backed the revolutionaries in the Dresden uprising of May 1849 and fled to Switzerland with Liszt's help when the Saxon government issued a warrant for his arrest.

Wagner's earliest operas, *Die Feen* and *Das Liebesverbot,* are really student works, and *Rienzi* is a curiosity. *The Flying Dutchman,* on the other hand, forms a constant part of the modern repertory. It shows much of what Wagner had absorbed from the German, Italian, and French opera he conducted during his formative years, as well as hinting at the lines along which his future thoughts would run.

The plot of *Dutchman,* vaguely inspired by a Heine story and Wagner's voyage from Prussia to London, comes right out of German Romantic Idealism. A Dutch sea captain has sworn by the Devil that he will sail around the Cape of

Good Hope if it takes forever, and Satan holds him to the bargain. The captain and crew are doomed to cruise the seas throughout eternity. But there is an escape: The Dutchman may rest if he finds a woman so faithful that she will share his fate and die with him. During one of his periodic searches he encounters Daland, a Norwegian sea captain who has a "loyal" daughter, Senta. She has become obsessed with the legend of the Dutchman and with his portrait over her hearth. When he appears in the flesh, she falls immediately in love and casts herself into the sea with him, much to her father's and friends' horror. Satan's doom is lifted, the Dutchman's ship sinks beneath the waves, and its crew finds peace at last. The story explores the indistinct division between physical and spiritual reality that so intrigued German Idealists. It also sounds Wagner's favorite theme: redemption through love.

The opera represents a remarkable conglomeration of the various operatic traditions Wagner had encountered. The most prominent ingredient comes from the love of "characteristic" arias and choruses sung by common folk, elements Weber had borrowed earlier from opéra comique. Wagner composed his folklike sections for *Dutchman* first, among them Senta's reflexive ballad, which relates the plot of the opera (à la Rimbault's aria in Meyerbeer's *Robert le diable*—originally an opéra comique). The vocalizations at the beginning of Senta's piece, the heavy-footed accentuation of meter, the disjunct melody (just the opposite of bel canto in shape; see Example 5.7), and the strophic form all lend a folkish cast to the aria. The two sailors' choruses that begin the third act were also composed early, and the remaining folklike elements came next, including the "Helmsman's Song" in Act I and the "Spinning Chorus" at the beginning of Act II. Together these numbers give the opera its distinctive coloring and provide some of its most evocative moments.

Wagner used these "characteristic" sections of music as the starting point for the rest of *Dutchman,* though not in quite as consistent a fashion as he would later claim. Motives from the various folkish numbers, especially Senta's Ballad, return throughout the opera, and they are employed in a slightly more sophisticated and thoroughgoing manner than mere "reminiscences." A good instance appears in the accompanimental figuration for the opening of the Dutchman's first-act aria (see Example 5.8), which offers an ornamented variation of the vocalizations at the beginning of Senta's Ballad. Although there are other examples, long stretches of *Dutchman* feature no reminiscences at all. Motivic interconnection forms only one component of the opera's construction.

In much of *The Flying Dutchman* we can find traditional Italian formal conventions. The Dutchman's aria in the first act, for instance, presents a classic three-part cavatina (or entrance aria; see Table 5.4). Though Wagner includes the opening recitative as part of this number, regular meter actually commences with the "allegro molto agitato." We can hardly call it "cantabile," but then a slow beginning would be inappropriate to the dramatic situation. The "intermediate tempo" in parlando style reflects the Dutchman's bitterness and despair

EXAMPLE 5.7   Beginning of Senta's Ballad from Wagner's *Flying Dutchman*, Act II

at the prospect of salvation. Finally, a slow "cabaletta" (these also exist in Italian practice) states his conviction that he will not be released from his torment until the day of judgment. We can see Wagner thinking in the formal divisions he knew and admired from his extensive experience conducting Bellini and Donizetti.

The duet in the first act between the Dutchman and Daland also unfolds along the lines of an Italian structure. Seen as dramatic interactions, its stages include (1) initial exchange laying out the characters' positions, (2) internal reflection on the positions, (3) resolve on a course of action, and (4) reflection on the decision. The first and third sections generally involve dialogue in parlando style; the second and fourth tend to have longer verses and feature lyrical style. This is precisely what we find here (see Table 5.5). The "cantabile" nature

EXAMPLE 5.8   Beginning of Dutchman's aria in Act I of Wagner's *Flying Dutchman*

TABLE 5.4   Schematic for the Dutchman's Three-Part Aria from Wagner's *Flying Dutchman*, Act I

SECTION	TEMPO	KEY	INCIPIT/CONTENT
"Cantabile"	Allegro molto agitato	c	"Wie oft in Meeres"; Dutchman outlines his predicament.
Tempo di mezzo	Maestoso	x	"Dich frage ich"; Dutchman questions his fate and despairs of salvation ("Verb'ne Hoffnung!").
Cabaletta	Molto passionato	c	"Nur eine Hoffnung"; Dutchman awaits last judgment and release.

TABLE 5.5   Schematic for Duet from Wagner's *Flying Dutchman,* Act I

SECTION/TEMPO	KEY	INCIPIT/CONTENT
Tempo di primo/Moderato	g–G	Daland and Dutchman lay out their initial positions, the Dutchman his weariness ("Durch Sturm"), Daland his greed and the fact of his "faithful daughter" ("Wie wunderbar").
Cantabile/Allegro giusto	G	Daland and Dutchman reflect on situation to themselves internally ("Wie? Hört' ich recht"/"Ach! ohne Weib").
Tempo di mezzo/Animato	E♭–x	Daland and Dutchman hit on plan for Senta to wed Dutchman in dialogue.
Cabaletta/Allegro agitato	G	Dutchman and Daland celebrate decision, with a "faster tempo" beginning at "Gepriesen seid."

of the second section comes not in Daland's initial patter but in the Dutchman's long-breathed lines ("Ach! ohne Weib") in worthy bel canto style. A sprightly cabaletta at the end suits the happy resolution of both characters' concerns, beginning where Daland "praises" his good fortune at the chance meeting. Although outer and inner action merge smoothly into each other, they still fall into the old pattern of declamatory style for interaction and lyrical style for reflection. The Rossinian norms still hold.

Many parts of *Dutchman* reveal Wagner's thorough grounding in Italian style. The vocal writing generally falls in paired, repeated phrases primarily emphasizing the voice, with the orchestra as subordinated accompaniment. Cadenzas at the end of numbers such as Senta's ballad betray Italian operatic roots (though pervasive coloratura is lacking). And certain passages approach bel canto. Only the enriched harmonic language and heavier orchestration betray the Germanic tradition.

Wagner also inherited the Italian preoccupation with continuity. *Dutchman*'s "numbers" increasingly merge inner and outer action by prefacing arias, duets, and choruses with accompanied recitatives featuring elaborately worked orchestral interjections and short bits of arioso. Wagner takes this proclivity a step further by introducing a kind of hyperconnection. He leads the ends of arias and other numbers into the ensuing "scenes" by substituting deceptive for authentic cadences. (A classic example appears at the end of Senta's Ballad.) The composer also adds the option of linking one act to the next through continuous orchestral interludes.

From the preceding description, Wagner's *Flying Dutchman* would seem to be an uneven stylistic jumble, and it is precisely that. The intermixture of rich harmonic language, full orchestration, Italianate form, bel canto line, and folkloric number may strike us as naïve. But that is the opera's charm: It requires a certain wide-eyed credulity to enjoy a really good ghost story.

The two remaining "Romantic operas" from Wagner's Dresden period, *Tannhäuser* and *Lohengrin,* progressively achieved more stylistic consistency than *Dutchman* and continued even further down the path of continuity between numbers. Wagner combined two unrelated tales for *Tannhäuser,* a story in *Des Knaben Wunderhorn* of a turn away from earthly pleasure to pious religiosity (parodied by Heine) and a medieval saga of a singing contest (reported in E. T. A. Hoffmann's *Die Serapionsbrüder*). The composer never quite found *Tannhäuser's* final form, though the Paris version may be the most compelling of its four incarnations (Dresden 1845 and 1847; Paris, 1861; Munich, 1867). *Lohengrin* combines ancient myths in which bewitched human beings are trapped in the forms of swans with medieval Christian myths about knights of the Holy Grail. Both works feature numbers (including some fine arias and scenic tableaux) and both are transitional between the transparent synthesis of *Dutchman* and Wagner's mature style.

The Creation of the "Music Drama"

The failed 1848 revolution in Germany and Wagner's dealings with the Saxon government disillusioned the composer in a number of ways. They caused him to lose faith in the Enlightenment tenets of German "liberalism,"* which included presumptions of fundamental rationality, individuality, and the rule of law. It also prompted him to rethink the organization of the musical theater and the nature of opera, particularly German opera.

Wagner was unable to bring his new ideas to fruition in Dresden, since he fled to Switzerland in May of 1849. He landed in Zurich, and he settled there after trying his luck unsuccessfully in Paris for the first half of 1850. His proposal for a new kind of opera came in a series of tracts that had distinct political overtones, the most important being *The Artwork of the Future* (1849) and *Opera and Drama* (1851; rev. 1868). He gave his dramaturgical and political ideas a concrete form in a libretto titled "Siegfrieds Tod," which eventually grew into four parts. The extended cycle became *Der Ring des Nibelungen* (1852), for which Wagner began composing music in 1853. He would not complete it until 1874, though he finished work on the first two installments, *Das Rheingold* and *Die Walküre,* by 1856 and began the third, *Siegfried,* in 1857. At that point Wagner abandoned the *Ring* for *Tristan und Isolde,* inspired by his affair with the wife of a family friend. He finished it in 1859, but not before his own wife discovered the illicit relationship. They separated in 1858, and Wagner moved to Venice, then to Paris in 1860.

---

*Not to be confused with American "liberalism" in the latter half of the twentieth century, which Europeans would call "social progressivism."

Wagner's third Paris sojourn was as disappointing artistically as the first two. He succeeded in having *Tannhäuser* performed there in 1861 after revising it for French tastes, but it flopped. He used his diplomatic contacts in Paris, however, to win a partial amnesty in German and Austrian lands. From 1861 to 1864 he lived variously in Venice, Karlsruhe, Vienna, and Stuttgart, always moving just ahead of his creditors. In 1862 he wrote a libretto for *Die Meistersinger von Nürnberg,* and he started work on its music.

In 1864 Wagner finally enlisted a patron equal to his extravagant theatrical vision in the person of the newly crowned, teenage King Ludwig II of Bavaria. Ludwig settled Wagner's many debts, paid him a generous stipend, and offered him a contract to finish the *Ring.* Wagner moved briefly to Munich, and shortly thereafter began another infamous affair, this time with Cosima von Bülow, wife of a famous conductor and daughter of Franz Liszt. She eventually bore the composer three children, the first in 1865 while Bülow was rehearsing the premiere of *Tristan und Isolde.* The affair and Wagner's general excess caused such an uproar at court that Wagner was forced to leave Munich, and he settled again in Switzerland near Lucerne. He remained there until 1872, marrying Cosima after her divorce in 1870. Meanwhile, Ludwig continued his interest in Wagner from afar, and his Royal Opera presented first performances of *Meistersinger* (1868), *Rheingold* (1869), and *Walküre* (1870).

Wagner's concept of these "music dramas" stemmed from what he saw as the defects of earlier nineteenth-century opera, especially Italian and French opera. He outlined these in a series of rambling historical tracts (mainly the lengthy *Opera and Drama*), from which some fairly clear overall principles emerge despite the logical inconsistencies in the composer's writing. Wagner thought that nineteenth-century opera ignored drama in favor of what he called "absolute" musical considerations and empty scenic display. "Absolute" vocal melody à la Rossini fed the demand for beautiful production and singers' virtuosity. It demanded repeated, symmetrical phrases, gradual rise and fall of the line, and elaborate ornamentation, whether this suited the dramatic import of the text or not. According to Wagner, absolute vocal writing made a recital of what was supposed to be theatrical entertainment, and it did not take advantage of the expanded modern orchestra. By the same token, "absolute" instrumental music fell into the regular harmonic and metrical patterns of dance music, which ran at cross-purposes with dramatic inflection. In French opera, the demand for scenic spectacle overrode the needs of the dramatic situation, leading to grandiose "effects without causes."

To remedy these various failings, Wagner insisted that the dramatic conception or "poetic intent" of an opera should govern all other elements of musical theater. This meant:

1. A work would not divide into discrete "numbers," as if it were a concert featuring self-contained musical pieces.

2. A libretto would avoid poetry with regular meter, regular syllable count, and end rhyme conditioned by musical periodicity. Instead, alliteration between words on each line of poetry (called *Stabreim*) would provide coherence by means of repeated consonants.

3. Vocal lines would avoid virtuosic display, bel canto, and regular, repeated phrases in favor of declamatory melody inflected by the moment-to-moment import of the text. Because the text could describe the physical world, it appealed to the intellect, and it logically articulated the outer action.

4. The orchestral accompaniment would play an active role in the drama. It, too, would avoid periodic phrasing during vocal passages, instead providing harmonies modulating to fit the meaning of the text. The orchestra would also have its own melody composed of motivic presentiments (*Ahnungen*) and recollections (*Erinnerungen*)—later designated "leitmotifs" by the musicologist Wilhelm August Ambros. Music could not describe, but it could intimate feeling, and so it would carry the inner action and create mood.

5. The poet-composer would focus on dramatic interactions between characters rather than scenes inserted merely to produce spectacle.

Partly to fulfill this last condition, and partly for nationalistic reasons, Wagner decided that the proper subject matter of opera should be ancient myths that had originated in folkloric German religious practice. He borrowed this idea from the Greek theater of antiquity, which he much admired. (The German philosopher Friedrich Nietzsche later amplified this theory in *The Birth of Tragedy from the Spirit of Music*.) By tapping folkloric religion, Wagner hoped to bring the intuitive and irrational back into balance with the intellectual and rational elements of drama.

Wagner was not entirely revolutionary in his goals. We have seen earlier that Italian opera from Rossini on concerned itself with increased continuity. Rossinian introductions and finales combined outer and inner action, and gave a more prominent role to the orchestra. Italian *scene* articulated text with greater attention to dramatic inflection, and multisectional arias and duets lent a sense of dramatic motion to set pieces. Wagner simply took these trends several steps further. It was their combination with the German symphonic tradition and the expanded orchestra of Berlioz and Meyerbeer that created Wagner's unique style.

Wagner's concept of "music drama" took its first concrete shape in *Der Ring des Nibelungen*. The composer pieced the plot together by combining old German and Norse myths with a medieval saga of family feud and heroic deed. The first two music dramas introduce the contest between Wotan, king of the gods, and Alberich, the Nibelung ruler of the subterranean world, for ultimate power invested in a magic ring fashioned by Alberich (thus the title *The Nibelung's Ring*). The last two music dramas record the history of the continuing tribulations of Wotan's grandson, Siegfried, on account of the ring.

Wagner organized his music dramas by scene, and a good example of how he adapted earlier operatic structure appears at the beginning of Act II in *Die*

Walküre. The scene divides into two major dramatic interactions. The first consists of a brief dialogue between Wotan and his Valkyrie daughter, Brünnhilde, who is instructed to defend his son, Siegmund, in a coming battle. This first interaction ends with music in the key of B minor, a presentiment of the famous "Ride of the Valkyries" that opens the third act. The second interaction in the scene unfolds as a duet between Wotan and Fricka, his wife. She reproaches her husband for protecting his illegitimate son, and he relents, promising to withdraw his aid. Based on a coherent scheme of related keys, the duet betrays the vestiges of traditional four-part structure (see Table 5.6). With the exception of a brief interjection by Brünnhilde, the whole unit transpires in C minor-major and the relative E-flat major-minor, with an excursion to A-flat minor (subdominant to E-flat or submediant to C minor, spelled enharmonically as G-sharp).* Wagner has retained the conventional stages of the argument: (1) initial statement of characters' positions, (2) internal reflection on positions, (3) decision about a course of action, (4) reflection on the outcome (see the duet from *Dutchman,* Table 5.5). He also retains the melodic practice in the voice parts of casting reflective moments in lyrical style, whereas interchanges in dialogue

TABLE 5.6   Schematic for Duet from Wagner's *Walküre,* Act II, scene 1

SECTION	*KEY*	*CONTENT/INCIPIT*
I. Initial confrontation	c→E♭	Fricka reproaches Wotan for siding with Siegmund against Hunding, whose wife Siegmund has stolen ("Wo in Bergen"). Wotan defends himself on the grounds that Siegmund loves Hunding's wife ("Was so schlimmes").
II. Internal reflection	E♭→a♭(=g♯)	Fricka laments her husband's mistreatment and condoning of infidelity ("So ist es aus"); includes long cantabile ("O was klag ich").
III. Resolution	C–c	After more objections ("Nichts lerntest du"), Wotan withdraws his protection from Siegmund and forbids Brünnhilde's intercession (ends with brief interlude in Valkyrie key of B minor).
IV. Reflection on resolution	E♭	Fricka celebrates victory in arioso ("Deiner ew'gen Gattin").

---

*Making sense of key in Wagner involves accepting the equivalence of parallel major and minor mode, as well as enharmonic equivalence. Cadences are frequently deceptive.

feature parlando style. He punctuates the interchanges with orchestral interjections, just as previous composers had done.

The unique feature of Wagner's writing lies in his way of employing orchestral interjections, which introduce and develop leitmotifs (literally: "connecting motives"). In the duet between Wotan and Fricka, the most prominent leitmotifs include those associated with Siegmund's magic sword (Example 5.9*a*), Wotan's various treaties and oaths (5.9*b*), and his misfortunes (5.9*c*). "Associate with" is the key phrase here, for leitmotifs *do not denote any one object or event*. A motif alludes to *all* the events or objects affiliated with it, past, present, or future. When the orchestra plays a motif,* the effect is subliminal. Leitmotifs create a symphonic texture that lends coherence to the music drama, whether we recognize their significance consciously or not. In fact, because the leitmotifs change and develop over the course of a music drama, we *cannot* make all the connections as we listen.

Wagner's use of *Stabreim* works in a similar interconnective fashion. Repeated sounds within one line of poetry bind the various words and thoughts. A good example from Act II, scene 1, of *Walküre* comes in Fricka's outraged exclamation at the end of section 2:

So *f*ühr es denn aus,	Then *f*inish it up,
*f*ülle das Mass:	*F*ill the measure *f*ull:
die Be*t*rogene laß auch zer*t*reten!	Let the be*t*rayed be *t*rampled too!

EXAMPLE 5.9   Leitmotifs in Wagner's *Walküre* associated with (*a*) sword, (*b*) rules and treaties, (*c*) Wotan's frustration

---

*In moments of intense emotion or deep significance singers intone leitmotifs as well.

The English version, if shouted vehemently, will give the effect of connecting the words "finish," "fill," and "full" or "betrayed" and "trampled" by means of alliteration. The absence of regular syllable count and meter discourages the paired, even phrases that Wagner regarded as damaging to dramatic inflection. The composer borrowed the idea of *Stabreim* from German medieval verse, and it lends an old-fashioned poetic sound to his libretto. Together with the rich, punctuated orchestral texture, *Stabreim* provides the unique sonic quality of the *Ring*.

Eventually Wagner would use his new symphonic technique to structure scenes in novel ways. Scene 4 from Act II of *Walküre* presents a good example of how the composer could organize a duet by developing a leitmotif in response to the dramatic action. In this scene Brünnhilde announces to Siegmund that he will die because Wotan has withdrawn his protection. When she offers him the chance to join Wotan in Valhalla, Siegmund declines for the love of Sieglinde, the woman with whom he has run away. Brünnhilde is so moved by his passion that she decides to protect Siegmund herself.

Robert Bailey demonstrates that Wagner began his work for this scene with the musical idea we hear first in the brass (see Example 5.10a). Wagner used this idea to generate the longer leitmotif in Example 5.10b that forms the basis for section 1 of the duet (see Table 5.7). As the argument between Brünnhilde and Siegmund grows more heated, the composer halves the note values of the leitmotif for section 2, and halves them yet again for section 3, effectively doubling the tempo twice. The scheme of keys provides coherence by circling around F-sharp minor-major (sometimes spelled as G-flat major), the mediant A-sharp minor (B-flat minor), and the relative major of A. The increasing tempo of the developing leitmotif reflects the growing tension of the conflict brilliantly, and it reminds us of Beethoven's use of motivic repetition to control the perception of musical time. Wagner applied the lessons he had learned so well from the revered master's symphonic procedures. In this scene the orchestra truly becomes an equal player.

EXAMPLE 5.10A Head motive that prefaces Brünnhilde's announcement of Siegmund's death in Wagner's *Walküre,* Act II, scene 4

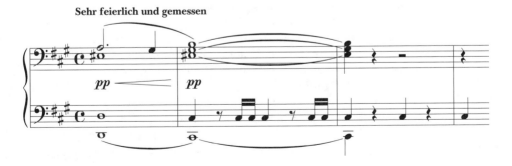

EXAMPLE 5.10B   Leitmotif underlying Wagner's *Walküre,* Act II, scene 4, with embedded head motive in mm. 2–3, 3–4

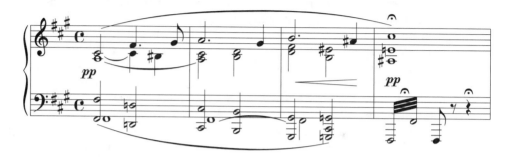

TABLE 5.7   Schematic for Act II, scene 4, from Wagner's *Walküre*

DRAMATIC ACTION	KEY	INCIPIT/LEITMOTIF SPEED
I. Brünnhilde appears to Siegmund, announces death, that he is chosen for Valhalla.	f♯→F♯ (G♭)	"Siegmund! Sieh auf mich"/ full note values
Siegmund questions her and declines to go if Sieglinde stays behind.	f♯→F♯ (G♭) A→f♯	"Der dir nun folgt"/full values "So grüße mir Walhall"/full values
Brünnhilde informs him he will die because his sword will fail.	f♯→a♯ (b♭)	"Du sahst der Walküre"/full values
Interlude: Siegmund addresses sleeping Sieglinde.	a♯ (b♭)	"Weh! Weh!" (motif from Act I)
II. Siegmund vows to kill Sieglinde and himself if he must leave her.	f♯→C	"So jung und schön"/leitmotif in diminution (C for "sword" motif)
III. Brünnhilde relents, promising to protect Siegmund in the battle.	f♯→A	"Halt ein! Wälsung!"/leitmotif in double diminution

Combined with *Stabreim* and the many diminished chords used to avoid full cadences, the technique yields a distinctive musical landscape.

Wagner went on to expand the range of this distinctive sound in his remaining operas from this period, including *Tristan* and *Meistersinger. Tristan* in particular explores the further reaches of chromatic harmony in response to its subject matter. The composer fashioned a language of harmonic deception for a tale of marital infidelity. But these techniques have a precedent in his earlier practice: He simply elevates his penchant for deceptive cadences to a harmonic principle in *Tristan* (see Example 5.11). *Meistersinger* presents a complementary opposite and Wagner's only mature comedy. Its harmonic vocabulary is largely diatonic, and its text features end-rhymed (though metrically irregular) verse in

EXAMPLE 5.11   Beginning of Wagner's prelude for *Tristan und Isolde*

response to its subject matter. A historical music drama about a guild of song writers from the sixteenth century required apposite poetry. Both *Tristan* and *Meistersinger* follow the composer's dictum that the dramatic conception must govern text and music.

Tristan and *Meistersinger*, together with the first half of the *Ring*, also reveal a darker side to Wagner's art, for he invests them with a radical philosophy. In each of these music dramas friction arises from the conflict between law or societal convention and irrational will or passion. In *Walküre*, Wotan looks benignly on incest (Siegmund and Sieglinde are twins) and adultery, all in the name of love. Wotan's frustration derives from his inability to transcend law (of which he is the guardian). *Tristan* also glorifies adultery in the name of love, and *Meistersinger* advocates art unfettered by rules. Moreover, in each music drama a naturally gifted and heroic individual leads the way in overthrowing conventional morality and law.

Wagner meant his message politically as well as philosophically, a fact his admirers understood only too well. They later fashioned a politics of emotion in defiance of traditional "liberalism." Coupled with the ideal of communality based on intense nationalism in Wagner's music dramas and writings, this approach spawned a proto-national socialism. The composer bears a strong, if indirect responsibility for Nazi philosophy, and Hitler's official adoption of Wagner's music represents a good deal more than mere coincidence.

Even *Meistersinger*, a comedy that seems to overflow with charitable tolerance and wise moderation, has an unsavory element. Wagner intended the figure of Beckmesser, the town clerk, as a caricature of Eduard Hanslick, an antagonistic critic. What is more, Hanslick was Jewish. Wagner had published an article in the *Neue Zeitschrift* some years earlier decrying "Jewishness in Music." This symbolism was understood quite clearly when *Meistersinger* annually formed the artistic centerpiece of the Nazis' party congress in Nuremberg, the place where they promulgated their anti-Semitic edicts. The music dramas of Wagner's middle period are exceptionally powerful works of art, full of brilliant creativity, imagination, and exceptional technique. But we must approach their message critically.

Last Years: Bayreuth and the "Unified Work of Art"

One of the factors that had discouraged Wagner from completing the *Ring* was the lack of an opera house that could do justice to his vision of a "unified work of art" (*Gesamtkunstwerk*). He had formulated the concept in *The Artwork of the Future* (1849), and it entailed the combination of all the arts (poetry, music, dance, painting, and architecture) in the united service of a dramatic ideal. Even the performance space became part of the concept. For a time Wagner hoped that Ludwig II would build a theater in Munich devoted solely to the realization of "total works of art." But these plans dissolved in 1868, and the composer became convinced that he would need to make a completely fresh start.

Wagner chose Bayreuth as the logical site for the creation of his new theater, partly because of its political symbolism. It lay halfway between Berlin and Munich, capitals of the two large German states that the composer hoped to see united. Though Bayreuth already had an opera house, he deemed it inadequate and decided to build a completely new facility. An executive committee was formed in February 1872, and Wagner arrived in April to supervise financing, planning, construction, and staffing of a "festival theater" (*Festspielhaus*).

The architecture of the theater reflected its creator's aesthetic and social philosophies. The auditorium as outlined in "Bayreuth (das Bühnenfestspielhaus)" would have no boxes. The seats would slope upward gradually like those of a Greek amphitheater, though without making a complete semicircle (see Figure 5.1). Wagner's technical reason for this arrangement concerned lines of sight: "We were governed entirely by the laws of perspective, which could lengthen as the rows of seats ascended, but which always required a head-on orientation to the stage." Preservation of sight lines also motivated the decision to cover a deeply sunken pit, thus hiding the "technical apparatus" of the orchestra and also creating a " 'mystical foreground' of supernaturally resounding music" between the audience and the stage. Wagner meant all these architectural choices to increase the sense of communion among the spectators at his music dramas.

The construction of the new theater and plans for the festival gave Wagner much to do. He had completed the third act of *Siegfried* and all of *Götterdämmerung*, the last two installments of the *Ring*, just before reaching Bayreuth. Now the printed scores and orchestral parts had to be prepared. The composer toured as a conductor to raise money for the new theater, auditioned singers, engaged technicians, and also oversaw the building of a new villa for his family. King Ludwig eventually came through with a loan to complete construction of the theater, and rehearsals began for the *Ring* in August 1875.

The premiere of the complete *Ring* took place in August 1876, with Ludwig and Wilhelm I of Prussia in attendance. It had taken twenty-eight years from the time of the first sketch to the first complete performance. Given the extended period of composition and the interruption between the two halves, the *Ring* exhibits a remarkable consistency. It earned Wagner fame but not fortune: His festival showed a large deficit in its first seasons. For a time Wagner contemplated moving to the United States, but the Bavarian treasury came to the rescue once again in early 1878.

Wagner's last undertakings included a final music drama and the founding of an artistic journal. He had begun the prose sketch for *Parsifal* in 1857 but did not complete the libretto until 1877 and the music until December 1881. In his last years he also began to publish *Bayreuther Blätter* to disseminate his more radical ideas. He had reached the height of his compositional power and

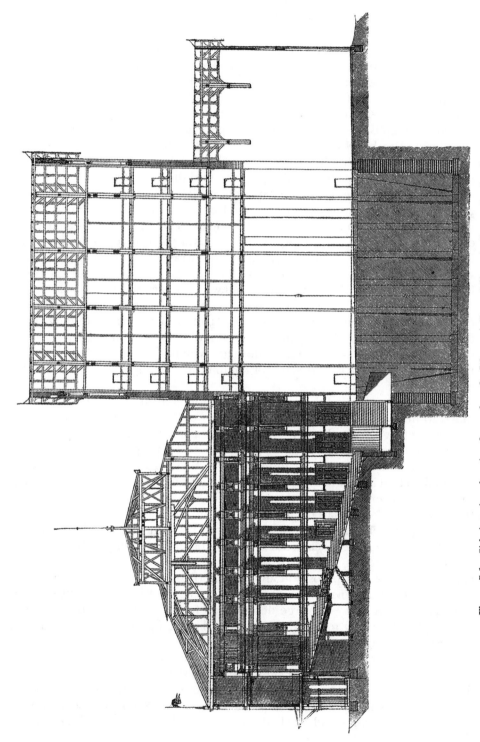

Figure 5.1 Side interior elevation from plans for Wagner's Festspielhaus in Bayreuth, showing upward sloping rows of amphitheater seats, extremely deep orchestra pit, and extensive stage. Music Library, University of North Carolina at Chapel Hill.

philosophical influence in these two projects. *Parsifal* strikes Wagner's admirers as his most sublime music drama, whereas to others it appears to be a murky exposition of pseudomedieval religiosity. In any event, its music is beautiful. In the summer of 1882 *Parsifal* received sixteen performances, after which Wagner left Bayreuth to winter in Venice. But his health deteriorated, and he died there of a heart attack in February 1883.

Wagner has had more influence on subsequent generations than any other nineteenth-century composer. His collected writings span sixteen volumes (excluding letters), and the literature about him is extensive. The darker side of his political legacy has received mention earlier, and it should not be underestimated. But Wagner's positive contribution to the dramatic arts is just as substantial, especially his notion of a "unified work of art." Of course, we can discern its influence easily in operas by Debussy and Puccini, and even in American musical comedies. But if we abstract the principles of Wagner's music dramas (text declaimed with appropriate dramatic emphasis in conjunction with orchestral support creating mood and supplying coherence), then it has an undeniable connection to modern film. Though we may smile at this thought, the cinema presents us with "unified works of art" that create compelling dramatic illusions. In film the techniques of architecture, painting, lighting, special effects, acting, the hidden orchestra playing leitmotifs all conspire in a way that we could not imagine without Wagner's extraordinary vision. The popular nature of these *Gesamtkunstwerke* would have gratified him immensely.

FRENCH OPERA AFTER MIDCENTURY

French opera from the second half of the nineteenth century has not fared as well in the modern repertory as its Italian and German counterparts. It seems odd that the thriving operatic institutions of Paris, so attractive to Verdi and Wagner, did not produce a French composer of equal stature. The Opéra continued to flourish with lavish support by the government. The rival Théâtre-Lyrique, a company begun in 1851, offered a substantial repertory for two decades, and the Opéra-Comique continued to present an extensive roster of premieres. In addition, Jacques Offenbach's Bouffes-Parisiens played many satirical operettas that toured internationally with great success. Yet from this teaming milieu, only a handful of notable works by native composers remain in the repertory, and only one of these, *Carmen,* holds a consistent place.

The relatively scant representation of French works from the vast output of the later nineteenth century may result from the uncertain terrain of genre. The tradition of grand opera no longer stimulated the imagination of French composers as it once did. When we think of works by a composer such as Jules Massenet (1842–1912), we do not immediately summon up *Le cid* (Opéra, 1885), but *Werther* (drame lyrique; Vienna, 1892) or even *Thaïs* (comédie lyrique; Opéra,

1894). The cutting edge of style shifted to mixed genres such as the "opéra romanesque," the "opéra-feerique" (fairy-tale opera), or the ever present opéra comique. All these forms embraced more intimate themes in preference to vast, politically charged canvases. This change in taste may have responded to the passing of France's last monarchy in 1871 and the final triumph of middle-class government. In any event, immediate, personal subject matter certainly accounts for the continued interest today in pieces such as Gounod's *Faust* and Bizet's *Carmen*.

Faust

More than any other work of the century, Charles Gounod's *Faust* liberated French opera from the expectations and conventions of grand opera. Gounod (1818–93) came from an artistic family. His father had won a Second Prix de Rome in painting, and his mother, a pianist, gave her son his first lessons. Charles received a classical education at the Lycée St. Louis and private lessons in music from Anton Reicha before entering the Conservatoire in 1836. The young Gounod showed extraordinary promise, following in his father's foot-steps with a Second Prix de Rome in 1837 and a Grand Prix de Rome in 1839. During his Roman sojourn he came to admire the sixteenth-century polyphony of the Sistine Chapel Choir, and he also made the acquaintance of Fanny Mendelssohn Hensel, sister of the great composer. She reinforced Gounod's proclivity for "classical music" by introducing him to Bach, Beethoven, and the works of her brother. After Gounod left Rome in 1842, he traveled to Vienna, then to Berlin for a visit with the Hensels. He also took time to stop in Leipzig to hear the Gewandhaus Orchestra. For a time Gounod thought of entering the priesthood, and he assumed a post as organist of the Missions Etrangères. During this period he wrote sacred music, including a number of masses.

Eventually Gounod gave up thoughts of becoming a cleric and decided to try his hand at opera, the most prestigious French genre. The famous soprano Pauline Viardot encouraged him in his first try, *Sapho* (Opéra, 1851), which failed in spite of critical praise. A grand opera, *La nonne sanglante* (Opéra, 1854), met a similar fate. For a time the composer had to support himself by directing a large male choral society. Finally in 1858 he turned to the Théâtre-Lyrique, a company with a much more flexible charter than the Opéra. During the ensuing decade, Gounod wrote five successful operas for the Lyrique, of which *Faust* received the most acclaim in France and abroad. In the nineteenth century the work held a primary place in the roster of many companies. The Metropolitan Opera chose *Faust* to open its new house in 1883, and the work appeared so often during its first years that it became known jokingly as the "Faustspielhaus."

Faust takes its story indirectly from Goethe's play as adapted by Michel Carré in his *Faust et Marguerite*. Carré focused only on the first part of Goethe's masterpiece, and then mostly on the affair between Faust and Gretchen (Marguerite in the French version). In the libretto by Jules Barbier, the elderly Faust, desiring the return of his lost youth, summons the demon Mephistopheles. He makes a bargain for Faust's soul in return for youthfulness, and then leads him on a series of revels. In the course of one of these, Mephistopheles introduces the now handsome young man to the beautiful and innocent Marguerite, who is seduced. She eventually bears Faust a child, kills it, and is sentenced to die. But in her last moments Faust returns to declare his love, and this combined with her prayers for forgiveness redeems her, to Mephistopheles' consternation.

Designated an "opéra dialogué" at its inception, *Faust* originally included spoken text between the numbers, but it was not exactly an opéra comique. Its intermixture of genre with supernatural and sacred subject matter gave Gounod wide stylistic latitude, and he drew on his love of antique polyphony as well as on operatic tradition to fashion a synthesis. In *Faust* we find the coloristic choruses and strophic songs of an opéra comique as well as elements of grand opera and formal counterpoint.

A good example of this intermixture comes in the beginning of Act III, set in Marguerite's garden. We find her singing a famous ballad from Goethe's *Faust*, "The King of Thule." Gounod goes out of his way to make this strophic aria sound modal, beginning its first phrase with A Dorian (similar to natural minor, but with the sixth degree raised; see Example 5.12). Marguerite interrupts the tale constantly with her dreams of Faust, and the remainder of the song changes mode several times, falling mostly in harmonic minor. The effect is cleverly old-fashioned and helps create the Gothic atmosphere of the opera. Gounod follows the ballad with a more "operatic" aria, the "Jewel Song," reflecting Marguerite's delight in a precious casket of gems Faust has given her. This number draws on coloratura (see Example 5.13), and juxtaposed with "The King of Thule," it displays her peculiarly naïve susceptibility to Mephistopheles' scheming. The duet between Faust and Marguerite at the end of this act unfolds in a "high" operatic style, though in only three parts: a tempo di primo ("Laisse-moi"), a cantabile ("O nuit d'amour), and an ending ("Ah! partez!") that combines a tempo di mezzo and a cabaletta. If the number never generates quite the drama of an Italian duet, it adds to the intriguing mixture of styles, nonetheless.

Gounod's experience with choral writing forms another ingredient in *Faust*'s stylistic synthesis. There are coloristic numbers à la opéra comique, such as the famed "Soldiers' Chorus" from Act IV, scene 3 (Example 5.14), and contrapuntal numbers, such as the even more famous waltz chorus at the end of Act II. The underlying style of this waltz might be characterized as "popular." Both these selections are chestnuts of the operatic repertory, reflecting their composer's flair for engaging tunes.

EXAMPLE 5.12   Beginning of Marguerite's ballad "The King of Thule" from Act III of Gounod's *Faust*

The last ingredient in *Faust* comes from its supernatural themes, both demonic and angelic. Mephistopheles has two appropriately diabolical arias, both strophic: a "Song of the Gold Calf" in Act I and a suggestive serenade beneath Marguerite's window in Act IV, scene 5. There is a witches' Sabbath in Act V, with music that might have come out of the German tradition. And finally Gounod adds a rather saccharine sacred style for Marguerite's scene in church and for the angelic chorus that announces her redemption at the end. This last component in the rich stylistic array of *Faust* probably accounts for its progressive disappearance from the stage in the second half of the twentieth century. The style seems a bit maudlin to modern listeners.

Whatever its later reception, however, nineteenth-century audiences devoured *Faust*. It became so popular in France that Gounod rewrote it for the Opéra by adding recitatives and also a ballet. (Mephistopheles tempts Faust

EXAMPLE 5.13   Beginning of Marguerite's "Jewel Song" from Act III of Gounod's *Faust*

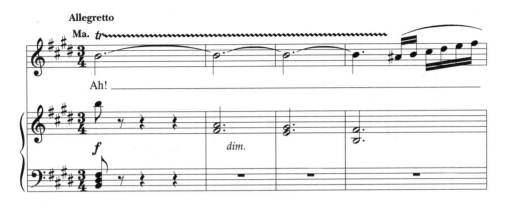

with beauties of the past in Act V, scene 1.) In this guise the piece set a new fashion and freed later French composers from grand opera's requirement for political themes and overwhelming spectacle. Without Gounod's stylistic intermixture as a model, Bizet's *Carmen* would be unthinkable.

Carmen

Georges Bizet (1838–75) came from an artistic family, with musicians on both sides. His father taught singing in Paris, and his mother was an accomplished pianist. His parents determined early that Georges should follow in the family business, and they entered him in the Conservatoire early, when he was just ten years old. Among his other studies, he took counterpoint with Pierre Zimmerman, whose ill health often forced him to rely on his son-in-law, Charles

EXAMPLE 5.14   Beginning of "Soldiers' Chorus" from Act IV of Gounod's *Faust*

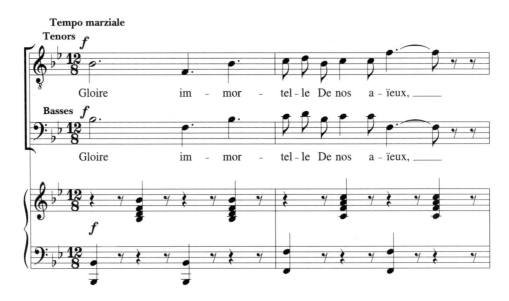

Gounod. Gounod liked his young pupil and engaged him to make arrangements of numbers from his operas. Throughout his life Bizet admired Gounod as an artist and absorbed much of his style at first hand.

As his studies at the Conservatoire progressed, Bizet evinced talent both as a performer and as a composer. He won first prizes in the competitions for piano in 1852 and for organ and fugue in 1855. He also studied composition with the opera composer Halévy, whose daughter he later married. Like Gounod, Bizet took a Second Prix de Rome in 1856 before winning first prize in 1857, just before his nineteenth birthday. He spent three idyllic years in Italy, enjoying the warm climate and becoming acquainted with Ernest Guiraud, a fellow prizewinner who would later play a role in the history of *Carmen.*

Given his promising start and his abundant talent, we might expect Bizet to have been a great success upon his return to Paris in 1860. But his career fared poorly. First his mother died in 1861, and then he declined to teach at the Conservatoire or to tour as a concert pianist. (Liszt considered him among the best players in Europe.) In 1863 he tried his hand at *The Pearl Fishers,* an opera premièred by the Théâtre-Lyrique in September to an indifferent public reception. The piece had some beautiful moments, however, and a series of aborted operas commissioned by the Lyrique followed. In 1867 Bizet completed *The Lovely Maid of Perth,* and though it received good critical notices, it, too, failed with the public. The repeated lack of success threw the composer into despair, and for a time he contemplated moving to America. He persevered nonetheless, and in the summer of 1871 he turned his attention to the Opéra-Comique.

Though his first attempt at opéra comique, *Djamileh*, failed completely in 1872, the composer finally celebrated an unqualified success with some incidental music for a revived play at the Vaudeville, *L'arlésienne* (*The Lady of Arle;* 1872). In its arrangement for concert performance this music created a sensation and displayed Bizet's talent for painting colorful, folkloric portraits by adapting traditional tunes. Following this triumph, the composer began work on *Carmen*. Completion was interrupted by a lost grand opera entitled *Don Rodrigue* (never performed) and a highly successful oratorio, *Patrie*.

In October 1874 *Carmen* finally went into rehearsal at the Opéra-Comique. Trouble with the censors over the "racy" material, with the nervous directors, and with the chorus ensued, and the piece did not appear in its first performance until March 1875. The middle-class public at the Comique and the conservative press expressed shock. In the meantime, Bizet became quite ill with a throat abscess, and he died of a heart attack in June 1875, believing that *Carmen* too was a failure. But a production with recitatives by Guiraud mounted at the Vienna Court Opera in October 1875 made a sensational hit. Brahms attended over twenty performances, and composers as diverse as Tchaikovsky and Debussy were transfixed by the piece. It has remained a mainstay of the repertory ever since.

Carmen offers one of the first examples of "realistic" opera—that is, opera focused on the life of the working classes in their personal interactions and struggle for survival. Based on a popular novella by Prosper Merimée, the story concerns a Gypsy woman (Carmen) working in a Seville cigarette factory who seduces an army corporal (Don José). She persuades him to forget his fiancée (Micaëla), then to release her from the stockade against orders, and finally to desert the army and join her band of smugglers. When he has finally ruined his reputation completely, she jilts him for a matador (Escamillo). Don José stalks her and finally stabs her to death when she refuses to return to him. Even though the librettists, Henri Meilhac and Ludovic Halévy (Bizet's uncle) toned down the original story, many considered the subject matter too seamy to be staged at all, let alone presented at the family-oriented Comique. But the "realistic" setting pitted José's middle-class values against Carmen's love of freedom, and this conflict ultimately proved both alluring and sympathetic.

Bizet's genius in composing the music for the opera lay in harnessing the synthesis of folkloric and elevated styles developed in Gounod's *Faust* to portray the conflicting values of Carmen and José. Carmen represents the exotic (what some modern-day critics translate as "the Other"). Bizet attaches a distinctive style to her first memorable appearance in Act I. Her cavatina consists of a strophic song about love, in which she tells the onlookers (including Don José) that love knows no law, knows no rationale, and is changeable and free. To capture the folkloric and Spanish aspects of Carmen, Bizet casts the song in the rhythms of a tango-like dance from Havana or a "Habanera" ("Havanaise"), with a melody from Sebastián Iradier's collection of songs, *Fleurs d'Espagne* (Paris, 1864). The descending melodic line is chromatic, emphasizing Carmen's exotic nature (see Example 5.15), and the accompaniment is staccato, underlining her directness. The shift from minor to major mode in each verse of the song reflects her message about the mutability of affection. In each subsequent solo number for Carmen (the Seguidilla in Act I, the Gypsy Song that opens Act II), Bizet features a staccato (or pizzicato) accompaniment, dance rhythms, chromaticism in the melody, and strophic form. Carmen's consistency of style mirrors her candor. She embodies unyielding, elemental attraction.

In contrast to Carmen's exotic, Gypsy style, Bizet uses more conventional "operatic" writing to characterize Don José's attachment to middle-class propriety. We first hear him extensively in a duet with his fiancée, Micaëla, in Act I ("Parle-moi de ma mère"). The number falls roughly in the three-part form seen earlier in the duet between Faust and Marguerite, and it owes a heavy debt

EXAMPLE 5.15   Beginning of "Habanera" from Act I of Bizet's *Carmen*

to Gounod's lyrical style. Especially in the last section when José and Micaëla sing in counterpoint, the lines take on a legato quality with gradual rise and fall that could only be called cantabile. Another example of this style comes in José's "Flower Song" (Act II), where he declares his undying love for Carmen. The legato syncopation in the string accompaniment supports a smooth and gracious line for the tenor (see Example 5.16). As for José's recent promise to marry Micaëla, this inconsistency is mirrored in occasional changes in José's style. Could the sighing lover be the same devil-may-care soldier of the marching song, "Dragon d'Alcala"?

The fundamental differences between Carmen's and Don José's personalities and musical styles charge their moments together. In their second-act duet ("Je vais danser") Carmen begins her invitation to pleasure with her usual dance

EXAMPLE 5.16   Excerpt from José's "Flower Song" in Act II of Bizet's *Carmen*

style, while we hear José pleading for Carmen's understanding of duty (he must return to barracks, not dishonor his uniform) in almost bel canto tones. Carmen answers in matter-of-fact declamations, accompanied by pizzicato strings. She will have none of middle-class mores. Her style is consistent, her honesty complete, and it follows her into the final chorus of the act ("Suis-nous à travers"). When she proclaims her love of liberty above all, we believe her because Bizet has portrayed her so consistently.

Other components from the tradition of opéra comique contribute to the eclectic mixture Bizet inherited from Gounod. The large number of choruses, for instance, adds the voice of the common people. The soldiers' ensemble and the choir of street urchins at the beginning of Act I, the choral scene surrounding Escamillo's "Toreador Song," and the chorus of smugglers in Act III, scene 1, all lend *Carmen* folkloric and realistic color. And a reminiscence motive, sometimes called the "Fate motive," recurs at various critical junctures. (The orchestra plays it prominently just before the curtain rises on Act I.)

Bizet shows his consummate mastery of the various traditions available to him in the second scene of Act III. We have already learned the outcome of Carmen and José's entanglement in the previous scene: "Death, first for me, then for him," she sings ominously in the famous card trio ("Mêlons, coupons"). The festivities outside the bullfighting arena come straight out of the grand-opera tradition of scenic tableau. But the pomp is far from the "effect without cause" Wagner derided. Instead, it prepares us for a contest of wills, not the one inside between matador and bull, but the one outside. As Carmen and José battle to prevail, the exclamations of the crowd watching the bullfight inside become a chilling backdrop to their struggle. Bizet then uses vocal style—Carmen's short, direct utterances as opposed to José's bel canto pleading—to maintain the character of the players.

The question that has intrigued commentators in the many years since the first performance of *Carmen* concerns who is victim. Modern feminist commentary tends to portray Carmen as the object of stereotypical male aggression. Strong-willed women threaten male dominance, and so they must die. Although there is a grain of truth to this view, we can also see *Carmen* as a clash between competing internal instincts in all human beings, the amorous and possessive on the one hand at odds with the libertarian on the other. In the end, we admire Carmen for her honesty, courage, and self-control. José becomes the victim not so much of Carmen as of passions he is too weak to restrain. Nietzsche would write of the last scene in *Carmen*:

> I know no case where the tragic joke that constitutes the essence of love is expressed so strictly, translated with equal terror into a formula, as in Don José's last cry, which concludes the work:
>
> > *"I'm the one that killed her,*
> > *Ah Carmen! My darling Carmen!"*
>
> Such a conception of love (the only one worthy of a philosopher) is rare: it elevates the work of art above thousands of others.

Bizet's use of style—the exotic and coloristic against the familiar operatic—places the dilemma of love in deep relief. He succeeded in convincing listeners such as Nietzsche that "number operas" presented a worthy alternative to Wagnerian music drama. Indeed, Nietsche's praise of *Carmen* comes in the context of a diatribe against his former mentor, entitled *The Case of Wagner*. History has proved Nietzsche mostly wrong: Wagnerian music drama prevailed in the twentieth century. But *Carmen* has much to commend it, especially in its opéra comique version rather than in the one with inferior recitatives fashioned by Guiraud after Bizet's untimely death. *Carmen*'s triumph derives not from its structure but from its combination of realistic subject matter with eclectic style. Bizet's ability to characterize a fundamental dilemma of the human condition by using music lends his masterpiece universal appeal.

FURTHER READING

Giuseppe Verdi

The standard account of Verdi's operas (and, incidentally, his life) remains Julian Budden's three-volume *Operas of Verdi* (I, New York and London, 1973; II, London, 1978; III, New York and London, 1981). Andrew Porter's article for *The New Grove Masters of Italian Opera* (New York, 1983) is also worth reading.

Richard Wagner

Ernest Newman has provided the most complete (though not the most critical) biography in *The Life of Richard Wagner* (New York, 1933–46), but this should probably be supplemented by Curt von Westernhagen's newer and more accurate *Wagner: A Biography* (Cambridge and New York, 1978). Carl Dahlhaus's take on Wagner's aesthetics remains the best, *Richard Wagner's Music Dramas* (Cambridge and New York, 1979). Robert Bailey summarizes form and compositional process for Wagner's *Ring* succinctly in "The Structure of the *Ring* and Its Evolution," *19th Century Music* I (1977), 48–61. For the political implications of Wagner's activity, see William McGrath's *Dionysian Art and Populist Politics in Austria* (New Haven and London, 1974).

Charles Gounod

Steven Huebner provides the best summary of Gounod's works for the musical theater in *The Operas of Charles Gounod* (New York and Oxford, 1990).

Georges Bizet

Winton Dean's biography still has great merit, *Bizet,* 3rd ed. (London, 1975). For more recent criticism of *Carmen,* Susan McClary entertains an interesting feminist reading in *Georges Bizet's* Carmen (Cambridge, 1992).

CHAPTER *6*

The Life of the Concert Hall after Midcentury

A survey of the newspapers and musical journals from almost any major European city beginning in the 1870s would reveal an increasingly familiar concert life. Indeed, by the 1890s almost all the institutions we currently take for granted had been established. The major orchestral societies, such as the Berlin Philharmonic, the Vienna Philharmonic, and the Amsterdam Concertgebouw, took their final shape during the second half of the nineteenth century. Chamber music moved decisively into smaller recital halls that offered subscription series to the general public. Songs entered the domain of professional singers, who offered whole evenings devoted to nothing but Lieder in public recital.

The Germans had already traveled quite a long way down the road of the public concert, though they did not establish *Liederabende* or regular chamber-music subscriptions firmly until the 1860s and 1870s. Even performances limited solely to orchestral literature played by ensembles of professional musicians developed surprisingly late in many large German cities. Once regularized, however, these kinds of subscription series called forth the talents of composers who would write mostly for the concert hall, as Brahms, Bruckner, and the youthful Strauss did. The German example induced France to follow suit as a matter of national pride. Composers such as Franck, Saint-Saëns, and Fauré devoted far more energy to this venue than previous generations had done, and they generated an extensive literature. In many ways, the history of music in the last part of the nineteenth century becomes increasingly an account of the concert hall.

THE GERMAN CONTENTION

"The undersigned have long followed with regret the activities of a party whose organ is Brendel's *Neue Zeitschrift für Musik*," Johannes Brahms, Joseph Joachim, and a group of like-minded friends declared in an 1860 *Manifesto*. They went on to condemn the "New German School" as "contrary to the fundamental essence of music." Wagner's polemics, amplified by his admirers, had finally divided the advocates of German music into openly warring factions.

The dispute came to embrace many facets of music and aesthetics, including the growing dichotomy between "absolute" and "programmatic" music, between "historicism" and "modernism," between "Apollonian" and "Dionysian" art. It extended to (or perhaps resulted from) political and cultural differences between conservatives and radicals. Unfortunately, none of these simple binary oppositions accurately characterize the shifting currents of the period, which often seem puzzling to us. Both sides claimed artistic descent from Beethoven, they shared harmonic vocabulary and musical techniques, and both responded to the gradual drift away from the old Romantic Idealism toward the new "scientific" positivism.

No one document casts the inclination toward positivism in such bold relief as Eduard Hanslick's *On the Beautiful in Music: An Essay on the Revision of the Aesthetics of Composition* (*Vom Musikalisch-Schönen: Ein Beitrag zur Revision der Ästhetik in der Tonkunst*, Leipzig, 1854). Hanslick, originally trained in Prague as a lawyer, served much of his life in Vienna as music critic for *Die neue freie Presse,* and he later became the first professor of music history at the University of Vienna. He was a staunch ally of Brahms, the butt of Wagner's Beckmesser caricature in *Die Meistersinger,* and leader of the movement that advocated "musical autonomy" or "art for art's sake."

The concept of "musical autonomy" increasingly moved aesthetics away from the old Romantic precepts of Neo-Platonism. "A complete musical idea brought to realization," Hanslick wrote in his treatise, "is intrinsically beautiful, is an end in itself, and is not the means for representing emotions or thoughts" (III, ¶5). And just to make himself perfectly clear he added, "Sonically animated forms are the sole and exclusive content and subject of music" (III, ¶6). Through successive editions of his widely disseminated treatise, Hanslick systematically purged *any* hint of external association as aesthetically appropriate. He even excluded the Romantic notion that music might be imbued with "spirit" or might communicate "ideas." Positivism required that the nonrepresentational art of music not pretend to more than aestheticians could logically demonstrate. The beauty of music lay, then, in the very fact that it *was* abstract and autonomous. Because the intellectual fascination of abstractly patterned sound became the only point of music, rules of correct voice-leading, proper chord progression, and clear form—all gauged by traditional practice—were paramount to Hanslick, Brahms, and their fellow travelers.

Disciples of the New German school rejected musical autonomy as narrow, overly intellectualized academicism. They scoffed at rules upheld for their own sake and derided what they saw as a slavish adherence to outmoded rigor. Ironically, however, positivism also gripped the New German school, prompting composers to more exact correspondence between programmatic cause and musical effect. And even the followers of Wagner and Liszt could not ignore the implications of music history as a new academic discipline, if for no other reason than the fact that "music of the future" required the concept of the "past" to define it. These central currents of the age may explain why we can find common threads running through the music of Brahms, Bruckner, and Strauss, despite the polemics that surrounded them.

Brahms and Neoclassicism

Johannes Brahms (1833–97) inherited leadership of the "Leipzig school" in the second half of the nineteenth century, though he never resided permanently in that city. Born in the hanseatic port of Hamburg, Brahms came from a musical family. His father played double bass in the city orchestra, and he selected a well-known piano teacher, Otto Cossel, for his son's first lessons at the age of seven. Cossel soon recommended that Johannes study composition and piano with Eduard Marxsen. Though Brahms would later claim he "learned absolutely nothing" from Marxsen, the virtuoso must have provided good training at the keyboard at least. Brahms developed into a talented pianist with formidable technique, and he played a mixed repertory of Bach, Beethoven, and some of the Parisian virtuosi such as Thalberg and Herz. He also arranged music for the popular concerts at the Alster Pavilion, where his father played.

In 1850 a Hungarian refugee violinist, Eduard Reményi, persuaded Brahms to accompany him on a European tour that took the seventeen-year-old pianist to Hanover, Göttingen, and Weimar, where he met Liszt. It was his encounter with the Schumanns in October 1853, however, that proved decisive. Robert immediately designated Brahms "a genius" in his household accounts, and he immediately announced this fact to the musical world in an article for the *Neue Zeitschrift*. Brahms was impressed by Robert and smitten by Clara. He rushed to her aid in the throes of a youthful crush when her husband was stricken in 1854. It remains a matter of conjecture whether their relationship had more than platonic aspects, but there can be no doubt that Clara held artistic sway over her young admirer. They remained lifelong friends and confidants.

Prompted by the Schumanns' interest in music history, Brahms began a concerted study of old theory treatises in 1854. He concerned himself especially with figured bass (which runs like a thread through many of his surviving sketches), voice-leading, and counterpoint. And he took entirely to heart the precept Schumann had learned from Thibaut that modern composition should be built on the foundation of earlier classics. These included works by Beethoven, Bach, and Mozart; sixteenth- and seventeenth-century sacred music; and traditional folk music.

Brahms's output during his early years reflects his intense involvement with his German artistic heritage. His first publications came understandably in the realm of piano, not a series of brilliant variations on well-known operas of the day à la Herz or Thalberg via Marxsen, but weighty sonatas (opp. 1–2, 5) in the tradition of Beethoven and Schubert. True, there was a set of *Variations on a Theme by R. Schumann* (op. 9; 1854), but it was hardly light fare. Even more indicative were the *Variations and Fugue on a Theme by Handel* (op. 24; 1861), which followed more along the lines of Beethoven's *Diabelli Variations.* When Brahms did turn his attention to the Parisian piano tradition, he chose *Ballades* (op. 10; 1856). These were explicitly "songs without words" inspired by Herder's translations of Scottish ballads to the point of reproducing the meter of the poetry. If Schumann believed Chopin's weighty essays in the genre to be inspired by poetic ballads, Brahms took the notion quite literally.

During his first decade of composing Brahms also contributed a series of richly textured chamber works for piano and strings (the trio, op. 8; two piano quartets, opp. 25–26; and a stunning piano quintet, op. 34), as well as two ravishing string sextets (opp. 18 and 36). All this chamber music written between the ages of twenty and thirty-one includes intricate and ingenious motivic working à la Beethoven, a good deal of finely crafted counterpoint, and an elaborate, precisely regulated harmonic palette. Brahms often based his large-scale tonal architecture on Schubert, as Schumann had done.

A good example of these musical qualities appears in the first movement of the Sextet in B-flat major, op. 18 (composed 1858–60, published 1862). Its main theme begins richly with two celli in counterpoint, accompanied by a single viola (Example 6.1). The phrase structure of the melody in the first cello combines a three-measure cell with a two-measure fragment, and then proceeds to further fragmentation and recombination of various melodic bits. Meanwhile, the second cello offers phrases of different, overlapping lengths. In one sense this is an irregular Beethovenian "Satz" (2 + 2 and fragmented continuation). But it also has the hallmarks of an almost Baroque "spinning out" that Schoenberg later called "continually developing variations" ("immer entwickelte Variationen"). Many of Brahms's themes combine these qualities of spunout melody and contrapuntally shifting accent.

Opus 18's first movement delineates form by means of clear, largely diatonic cadences and presents us with an almost textbook scheme (see Table 6.1). The main theme consists of a "small binary" form extending to Schubert's "heavenly lengths." The approach to the dominant key-area through a mediant also reminds us of Schubert. But where Schubert would integrate this tonal

EXAMPLE 6.1   Beginning of main theme from Brahms, Sextet, op. 18, mvt. I

digression unambiguously into the second theme (see, for instance, Table 2.4), Brahms places it ambiguously at the end of the transition (not really part of the "cantabile" melody that follows). The scoring for six instruments in three matched pairs allows for an unusual amount of cleverly disguised counterpoint. (Stretto, not fragmentation, becomes Brahms's favorite device for dissolving model-sequence progressions.) And when we return to the original key by means of an augmented sixth chord, its flatted third degree (B–double flat spelled as A) moves so subtly up to B-flat that the chromatic motion is almost imperceptible. Brahms kept form and harmony under strict control at all times.

One of the most remarkable facets of Brahms's output from his first decade moved beyond the traditional to the neoclassical in a group of pieces that referred explicitly in form, style, or both to historical antecedents. During stints from 1857 to 1860 in Detmold as a court musician, the composer wrote two serenades for orchestra (opp. 11 and 16) modeled on Mozart's serenades,

TABLE 6.1   Schematic for Brahms, op. 18, mvt. I

SECTION	SUBSECTION	KEY	MEASURES
Exposition			
	Mth	B♭:I	1–43
	trans.	I→iii	43–84
	Sth	V	85–106
	Closing	V	107–136
Development			
	Bridge	X	137–140
	Core		
	Model 1		141–152
	sequence		153–164
	extension (3 × 2)		165–170
	stretto		170–172
	Model 2		173–176
	sequence (extended)		177–181
	varied sequence		182–186
	dissolution		187–191
	Model 3		192–199
	sequence		200–207
	stretto fragmentation		208–213
	Retransition (via G♭⁺6/V)		214–233
Recapitulation			
	Mth (shortened)	I	234–269
	trans.	I→vi	269–309
	Sth	I	310–332
	Closing	I	333–362
Coda		I	363–398

even to the inclusion of archaic minuets. With choirs in Detmold and Hamburg in mind, he wrote a series of motets (opp. 29 and 37) as well as a host of other choral pieces (opp. 12, 27, and 30) based variously on Bach's motets or on seventeenth-century German choral music. Brahms also turned his attention to what Thibaut called "classical" folk melodies by arranging a large number of traditional tunes for voice and piano (*14 Folksongs for Children* and *28 German Folksongs,* both 1858). There was even a series of unpublished gigues, sarabandes, and gavottes for piano, as well as several fugues and chorale preludes for organ.

This early neoclassicism culminated in a crowning masterpiece, *A German Requiem* (op. 45), begun in 1857 and finished in 1868. In choosing his title Brahms certainly had in mind the first part of Schütz's *Concert . . . in Form einer teutschen Missa* from the *Musikalische Exequien,* not so much its style as the tradition of North German Protestantism and use of biblical texts in the vernacular. The direct frame of musical reference came from Handel's *Messiah*, a fact particularly evident in the sixth movement of the *German Requiem*. As in *Messiah*, Brahms selected excerpts from scripture to provide the words. After a brief invocation from Hebrews 13:14, Brahms moves to the famous passage from 1 Corinthians 15:51, "Behold, I tell you a mystery." The association with Handel's setting of this same text for solo baritone in recitative becomes all the stronger for Brahms's assigning it to the same solo voice with a similar melodic approach. Though Brahms gives much of the remaining text to the choir, the allusion to Handel is unmistakable. It continues at the end of the movement, a fugal setting of Revelation 4:11 ("Herr, du bist würdig zu nehmen Preis und Ehre und Kraft") that recalls Handel's final chorus in *Messiah* ("Blessing and honor, glory and power be unto him that sitteth upon the throne," Revelation 5:12), even to the homophonic exclamations that punctuate both fugues at intervals. Lest anyone in the audience at the Bremen premiere (1868) of *A German Requiem* miss the frame of reference, the program included "I know that my redeemer liveth," "Behold the Lamb of God," and the "Hallelujah" chorus from *Messiah*.

Brahms's early devotion to the study of music history and to compositional neoclassicism persisted all his life. He had personal acquaintance with many prominent music historians of his day and served on the advisory boards of *Denkmäler Deutscher Tonkunst* and *Denkmäler der Tonkunst in Österreich*. He also edited two volumes of the complete Handel edition for Chrysander as well as pieces by Schubert and Schumann, and he collected autographs of Haydn's, Mozart's, and Schumann's works. Brahms composed two more sets of historically modeled choral motets (opp. 74, 110). He structured the chaconne that concludes his Fourth Symphony after Bach's finale to the unaccompanied Violin Partita, BWV 1004. And he ended his career by publishing a set of *Eleven Chorale Preludes* for organ (op. 122; 1896) modeled on Bach's *Orgelbüchlein*.

Brahms's involvement with music history did not render his activity remarkable in itself: Wagner chose historic or archaic subjects for most of his operas. But Brahms's *scholarly* pursuit of this discipline, one of the new humanistic "sciences," possessed all the hallmarks of that rational positivism that formed one component of nineteenth-century European "liberalism."* Brahms conducted a systematic study of old music to provide concrete models for his own, whereas Wagner employed historical material as a means of creating atmosphere. Wagner regarded all this as an academic charade:

> I am acquainted with famous composers whom one can meet disguised at concert masquerades, today in the costume of a street musician [a dig at Brahms's folk-song

---

*Nineteenth-century European liberalism should not be confused with twentieth-century American liberalism, which more resembles social democracy. In Europe "liberalism" generally connotes rationalism, free agency for the individual, rule of law, and laissez-faire economics. Wagner advocated a socialism with nationalistic roots.

settings] . . . , tomorrow in the Hallelujah-wig of Handel, another time as a Jewish czardas player [a slur on Brahms's *Hungarian Dances* and his association with Reményi], and then again as an ostensibly genuine symphonist in a number Ten [a slap at Brahms's First Symphony hailed by critics as "Beethoven's Tenth"].

To Brahms the systematic exploration of these various styles and techniques constituted rational and orderly progress.

Brahms's move to Vienna in 1863, just as the city embarked on an eclectically historical urban renewal, seems altogether fitting. Having torn down its encircling medieval fortifications, Vienna filled the void with the famous Ringstraße decorated with historically styled buildings. The professional middle classes, empowered in the new constitutional government, appropriated the symbolism of the past to establish their legitimacy in the present. For instance, in adopting late German gothic style for the Rathaus (see Figure 6.1), the city fathers invoked the authority of the free medieval German commune. The Greek temple that inspired the Parliament building took its cue from Athenian

Figure 6.1   The gothic-style Viennese Rathaus, constructed as part of the Ring development, 1872–83. Courtesy Austrian National Tourist Office; photo: Markowitsch.

Figure 6.2   The classically styled Austrian Parliament Building, constructed as part of the Ring development, 1874–83. Courtesy PhotoDisc, Inc.; photo: Neil Beer.

democracy, going so far as to place a statue of Pallas Athena herself in front of the edifice (see Figure 6.2). The adoption of these and other historical styles for the many public and private buildings around the new boulevard also symbolized pride in art history as an orderly system of knowledge proper to the middle-class intelligensia.

Brahms came to Vienna initially to accept a post as conductor of a choral society populated by this same professional middle class. The Singakademie specialized in the performance of early music by such composers as Bach, Handel, Schütz, Isaac, Hassler, Eccard, and Gabrieli. Brahms would later go on to do a brief stint as music director of the Musikverein, performing branch of the Gesell-schaft der Musikfreunde. In this role he conducted oratorios by Handel, passions and cantatas by Bach, and pieces by Palestrina and Lassus. Given this learned repertory, it comes as no surprise that Brahms numbered many members of the professional middle classes among his friends—for example, the great Austrian surgeon Theodor Billroth and lawyer-cum-musicologist Eduard Hanslick.

After the success of *A German Requiem* in 1868 Brahms could afford to live on the income from his compositions, and he performed mostly as a guest pianist and conductor. (His brief tenure with the Musikverein in the early 1870s was a matter of prestige rather than economic necessity.) Increasing financial security gave the composer confidence to publish in the more ambitious genres of the string quartet and symphony. He completed his First Symphony, op. 68, in 1877 at the relatively advanced age of forty-four. Its progression from the C minor first movement to its C major finale in conjunction with the last-movement theme's resemblance (see Example 6.2) to the chorale in Beethoven's Ninth led to the famous "Beethoven's Tenth" label. Three more symphonies appeared between 1878 and 1886 (opp. 73, 90, and 98), as well as the Second Piano Concerto (in four-movement symphonic format), the *Academic Festival Overture*, the *Tragic Overture*, and the *Variations on a Theme by Haydn*. Through these weighty additions to the orchestral repertory Brahms became known as "first among contemporary masters of serious music," as the citation for an honorary doctorate from Breslau University put it.

Aspects of his earnest approach to the orchestral literature surface in all Brahms's symphonies, from the imposing First in C minor and the Second (op. 73) in a pastoral D major to the somber Fourth (op. 98) in E minor. But the most tightly constructed and revealing of Brahms's symphonies may be the intriguing Third (op. 90; 1884). Just a glance at the first few measures (Example 6.3) discloses Brahms's layered combination of modal harmonic ambiguity, contrapuntal intricacy, and "continually developing variation." Though the

EXAMPLE 6.2 Beginning of main theme from Brahms, First Symphony, mvt. IV

EXAMPLE 6.3   Opening of Brahms, Third Symphony

composer proclaims F major boldly in the opening sonority, we immediately find the flute, oboe, and horn tracing an F minor chord melodically in their first three measures. This modal borrowing in turn deflects harmonic progress briefly to A minor and D-flat major chords in measures 4–5. And as we puzzle over this modal ambiguity, the motto (F–A♭–F) works its way contrapuntally through the contrabassoon, bass trombone, and contrabass, while its inversion (minus the intervening C) animates the descending melody in the first and second violins. The continual variation of this motive in one form or another occupies much of the main theme.

The layers of musical interplay reach even deeper in the Third Symphony. The melody and the rhythmic hemiola in measures 3–4 of the violins invoke various passages from the first movement of Robert Schumann's Third Symphony, as Robert Bailey points out. And if that were not enough, F–A–F had significance for Brahms as his personal motto, *"Frei aber froh"* ("single but happy")— a retort to Joachim's gloomier *"Frei aber einsam"* ("single but lonely"). This completes the circle of associative reminiscence, for Brahms, Schumann, and Albert Dietrich had planned a collaborative F.A.E. violin sonata in 1853 to honor Joachim. These interleaved features of intellectual play led Brahms's critics to characterize his writing as too intricate and cerebral for symphonic composition. He had applied an intimate, chamber-music aesthetic and style, they claimed, to works meant for a broader public stage.

The formal outline of the Third Symphony's first movement, however, shows that Brahms could invest his symphonic writing with an accessible clarity of design *and* musical intricacy (see Table 6.2). If one just listens without consulting the score, the various sections of the sonata form introduce themselves easily enough. The composer cues them in classic fashion by means of texture, rhythm, and melodic structure, and the compact size of the movement makes it easy to follow. But a look at the notes reveals that Brahms carried the implications of Schubertian and Schumannian tonal logic one step further (see Tables 1.4 and 3.1). The secondary theme *and* closing of the exposition now fall in the mediant (in the submediant for the recapitulation), with the mechanism of major-minor intermixture plainly evident. The composer delays return to the major tonic at the end of the movement until the coda. Only a master composer could indulge these tonal excursions without ruffling the feathers of his audience. The cadences are so clear, the movement from key to key so subtle, that the remarkable combination of flat and sharp keys goes almost unremarked.

The remaining movements unfold in classic form, the second in a ternary pattern with a series of "developing variations" in its *A* theme, the third as a gracious waltz in minor mode instead of a scherzo. The intriguing sonata-rondo finale follows Schumann's dictum of "recalling what the previous [movements] contained" by quoting from the *B* section of the second movement and also by fading away quietly in its coda to strains of the main theme from the first movement. This last gesture serves as fitting homage to Schumann, whose own Third

TABLE 6.2 Schematic for Brahms, Third Symphony, mvt. I

SECTION	SUBSECTION	KEY	MEASURES
Exposition			
	Mth	F:I (i)	1–14
	trans. 1	I→III	15–35
	Sth	III	36–48
	trans. 2	III→iii	49–60
	Closing	iii	61–70
Development			
	Bridge	X	71–76
	Core	X	
	Model 1		77–82
	varied repeat		83–89
	Model 2		90–91
	sequence		92–93
	fragmentation		94–97
	dissolution		98–100
	Model 3		101–104
	sequence		105–108
	dissolution		109–111
	Retransition	♭VII-♭v-⁺6/F	112–119
Recapitulation			
	Mth	I	120–135
	trans. 1	I→VI	136–148
	Sth	VI→I	149–157
	trans. 2	I→vi	158–169
	Closing	vi	170–180
Coda		vi→I	181–224

Symphony Brahms cites and who would have approved of the ingenious musical craftsmanship woven into every measure of op. 90.

If the Third Symphony took its cue from Schubert and Schumann, Brahms leaped back a generation to Beethoven and even further to Giovanni Battista Viotti (1755–1824) in the first movement of his Violin Concerto, op. 77 (1879). The second-generation Romantics had dispensed with the initial orchestral "ritornello" in their concerti, favoring a three-part sonata form instead. Although listeners may have followed this regularized approach more easily (it resembles the structure of an overture or the first movement of a symphony), it did not afford the soloist as much time to prepare as did the older "double exposition." The Mendelssohn Violin Concerto, for instance, puts the soloist on the spot after only two measures of orchestral vamp before he introduces the main theme. This abruptness may explain why Brahms, collaborating with the violin virtuoso Joseph Joachim, returned to the older practice of having the orchestra introduce a good deal of the thematic material before the soloist enters (see Table 6.3).

Mozart could have found his way through this scheme with ease, up to and including the cadenza indicated only by a chord with a fermata over it. Though most violinists today choose the cadenza written by Joachim, they are free to improvise at will, a latitude many nineteenth-century composers did not allow performers. Only Brahms's unusual harmonic shifts (occasioned in part by his constant modal ambiguity) would strike a late-eighteenth-century composer as odd. The rest of the concerto, with its slow movement derived from the main theme of the first and its concluding gypsy rondo, follows the traditional scheme.

Brahms's concentration on intricate traditional craftsmanship in instrumental music seems to have excluded opera, but he did not avoid solo vocal music altogether. There was still the realm of the Lied, and here the composer gained a preeminent place. The roots of his style lay appropriately in the *Volkslied,* and it seems altogether fitting that Brahms considered "Vergebliches Ständchen" ("Useless Serenade," op. 84, no. 4; 1882) his favorite. He wrote Hanslick, "For this one song I would give all the others." The composer took the text from Andreas Kretschmar and Anton von Zuccalmaglio's *German Folksongs with their Original Tunes* (Berlin, 1838–40), believing it an authentic product of oral tradition (though von Zuccalmaglio had actually written it as a paraphrase of a Rhenish folksong).

"Vergebliches Ständchen"

Er:	**He:**
Guten Abend, mein Schatz,	Good evening, my treasure,
Guten Abend, mein Kind!	Good evening, my child!
Ich komm' aus Lieb' zu dir,	I come out of love for you,
Ach, mach mir auf die Tür,	Ah, open the door for me,
Mach mir auf die Tür!	Open the door for me!
Sie:	**She:**
Mein' Tür ist verschlossen,	My door is locked,
ich laß dich nicht ein;	I'll not let you in;
Mutter, die rät mir klug,	Mother warned wisely,
Wärst du herein mit Fug,	If I let you in willingly,
Wär's mit mir vorbei!	All would be over for me!
Er:	**He:**
So kalt ist die Nacht,	So cold is the night,
So eisig der Wind,	So icy the wind,
Daß mir das Herz erfriert,	That my heart will freeze,
Mein' Lieb' erlöschen wird,	My love will be extinguished;
Öffne mir, mein Kind!	Open up for me, my child!

TABLE 6.3   Schematic for op. 77, mvt. I

SECTION	SUBSECTION	KEY-AREA	MEASURE
Exposition I (orchestra)			
	Mth (ritornello)	D:I–i–I	1–40
	trans. 1 & 2	I→i	41–77
	Closing	i	78–89
Bridge (violin entrance)			
		i–I	90–135
Exposition II (violin & orchestra)			
	Mth	I→v/V	136–175
	trans. 1	v/V→V	176–205
	Sth	V	206–235
	trans. 2	V→v	236–245
	Closing	v	246–271
Development			
	Core	X	
	Model 1 (ritornello gesture)		272–279
	sequence		280–287
	Model 2		288–295
	repetition & sequence		296–303
	Model 3		304–319
	repetition & sequence		320–331
	fughetta		332–348
	Model 4		349–350
	sequence		351–352
	sequence		353–354
	sequence		355–356
	sequence		357–358
	sequence		359–360
	Retransition	dom. pedal	361–380
Recapitulation			
	Mth	I	381–416
	trans. 1		393–444
	Sth	III→I	445–474
	trans. 2	i	475–488
	Closing	i	489–512
Coda			
	Mth (ritorn.)	♭VI→I	513–524
	Cadenza	X	525–526
	Mth (ritorn.)	I	527–571

Sie:	**She:**
Löschet dein' Lieb',	If your love is extinguished,
Laß sie löschen nur!	Then let it go out!
Löschet sie immerzu,	Let it go out forever,
Geh' heim zur Bett, zur Ruh',	Go home to bed, to sleep,
Gute Nacht, mein Knab'!	Goodnight, my boy!

The dialogue in the text places it roughly in the genre of the romance or the ballad, but Brahms's setting is hardly dramatic. Rather, he superimposes the irregular scansion of von Zuccalmaglio's poetry on a more foursquare German *Ländler,* as Walter Dürr points out. Through successive verses the composer then varies this folk dance, ornamenting it slightly for the second verse, presenting a minor variation for the third verse, ending with a more chromatic variation. At regular intervals the piano alone drives the melodic and hypermetric structure forward, providing a scaffolding for the irregular verse. This deceptively simple folk song carries the tradition of the "polyrhythmic Lied" to a new level in which the instrumental part no longer accompanies, but the other way around. The poetry is a pretext for a folkish set of instrumental theme and variations. Nor is "Vergebliches Ständchen" an exception among Brahms's songs: Many wrap folk or folklike conceits in an elaborate pianistic style.

In his later years Brahms carried his proclivity for superimposing instrumental style on Lieder even further in the more declamatory and elevated *Four Serious Songs,* op. 121 (1896). For their lyrics the *Serious Songs* use four biblical passages that impose absolutely no requirements for musical periodicity to match poetic regularity. The third song of the set, with its text from Ecclesiasticus 41:1–2, is particularly instructive.

Four Serious Songs, no. 3

O Tod, o Tod, wie bitter bist du!	Oh death, oh death, how bitter art thou!
Wenn an dich gedenket ein Mensch,	When a man contemplates you,
Der gute Tage und genug hat,	Who has a good life and enough,
Und ohne Sorge lebet;	And lives without care;
Und dem es wohl geht in allen Dingen,	And who fares well in all things,
Und noch wohl essen mag!	And who still eats well!
O Tod, o Tod, wie wohl tust du dem Dürftigen,	Oh death, oh death, how good thou art to the needy one,
Der ja schwach und alt ist,	Who is weak and old,
Der in allen Sorgen steckt,	Who is lost in care,
Und nichts Bessers zu hoffen, noch zu erwarten hat;	And has nothing better to hope for, nor to expect;
O Tod, o Tod, wie wohl tust du!	Oh death, oh death, how good thou art!

EXAMPLE 6.4A   Beginning of Brahms, "O Tod," from the *Four Serious Songs*

Schoenberg, among others, noted the distinct similarity between the opening of this song (Example 6.4a) and that of the main theme from the first movement of the composer's Fourth Symphony. Both spin out descending thirds in continually developing patterns that include various kinds of inversion. In "O Tod" Brahms uses the complementary inversion of the ascending sixth to emphasize the reversal of sentiment for "oh, death, how good thou art" (Example 6.4b) in conjunction with major mode. The similarity to the first movement of the Fourth Symphony emphasizes the instrumental nature of this melody: Brahms no longer distinguishes between instruments and voices, employing the same developing variations for both. As the composer pursues motivic development in "O Tod," its phrase structure becomes increasingly irregular and its harmonic language more abstruse. The opening progression i–VI–iv–II (V/V) around a circle of thirds gives the singer something to ponder

EXAMPLE 6.4B   Second section of Brahms, "O Tod," in major mode

when it causes a melodic leap upward of an augmented octave from C-natural to C-sharp in measure 2 and then to the seventh of this secondary dominant in measure 3. Deceptive resolution of the F-sharp secondary dominant to the mediant (falling back to the tonic) provides another surprise.

Schoenberg saw Brahms's combination of developing melodic variations, irregular phrase lengths, and harmonic deception as the hallmarks of a "progressive." The composer's propensity for avoiding exact repetition of musical units required more advanced concentration, Schoenberg reasoned, and led to the "modern" practices of twelve-tone composition. Whether we adopt Schoenberg's teleological view of music history or not, we can see that Brahms grew increasingly daring toward the end of his life. If he began as a young fuddy-duddy, he ended as an old turk.

Brahms's progressive traits at the end of his career manifest themselves particularly in his late works for piano. Whereas Schumann wrote experimental piano miniatures at the beginning of his career, Brahms saved his for the end. Opuses 116 through 119 comprise sets of intermezzi, capriccios, and assorted other shorter pieces, all of them composed in 1892.

The most extreme example of the composer's late style comes in his Intermezzo, op. 119, no. 1, in B minor. Again we find the motif of descending thirds (see Example 6.5a), here in perpetually extending series. Just as Brahms seems to present the tonic in the first measure, it slips away under the dint of continuing arpeggios to form a subdominant seventh chord. Where the composer should offer clear cadences, as in the motion from the last beat of measure 4 to the first beat of measure 5, he avoids producing the tonic root (B), offering a deceptive cadence instead. The *B* section of the piece (mm. 17–42) does fall securely in D major, but this reverses its traditionally developmental function in ternary form. The two outer sections should offer tonal stability, with the tonal instability of the middle section standing in contrast. Even at the end of the

EXAMPLE 6.5A Beginning of Brahms, Intermezzo, op. 119, no. 1

EXAMPLE 6.5B End of Brahms, Intermezzo, op. 119, no. 1

piece, where Brahms finally settles on an unambiguous B minor chord, the result is somehow unsatisfying because he reaches the tonic by arpeggiating downward, G-E-C♯-A♯-F♯-D-B (see Example 6.5b). This is technically a thirteenth chord on B, but Brahms treats the upper four notes as a doubly diminished seventh chord that contracts inwardly to a B minor triad in the right hand. The effect is cryptic and unsatisfying to the ear, however we might rationalize it.

The metric insubstantiality and the tonal ambiguity of this intermezzo resemble more the music of a composer such as Debussy, save for one signal difference. Where Debussy (even Schumann, for that matter) would have attached a programmatic title to help explain the tonal ambiguity (or at least account for it to the amateur listener and player), Brahms offers no such comfort. For a less positivistic composer op. 119, no. 1, would suggest elusive "Raindrops in Springtime," for others ephemeral "Autumn Leaves," but for Brahms it is simply "Adagio." An exercise in tonal and rhythmic ambiguity in its positivistic sense constitutes just that and nothing more. A piano miniature is not a "means for representing thoughts or feelings" outside the musical idea itself.

By the end of his life Brahms had become the grand old man of German absolute music, awarded "Pour le Mérité" of the Order of Peace by Kaiser Wilhelm and created Commander of the Order of Leopold by Emperor Franz Joseph. Slowly but surely his compositional activity waned after 1890, and he systematically destroyed all his abandoned or incomplete works and sketches. In the spring of 1896 Clara Schumann died; Brahms followed less than a year later, in April 1897. He bequeathed a legacy of piety toward music history, rigorous compositional technique, and also intellectual curiosity to his successors, Schoenberg and Webern among them. In many ways they perpetuated Brahms's highly erudite and abstractly technical approach to music, but not always with his gift for leavening even the most severe piece with a measure of sentiment.

Bruckner and Monumentality

In the annals of Viennese criticism the Wagnerian challenge to Brahms came in the form of Anton Bruckner (1824–96). Though Bruckner did admire Wagner immensely, his output was conditioned just as much as Brahms's by Viennese conservatism. Bruckner ventured little further than Brahms outside the realms of "absolute music," and he, too, bowed to the weighty history of sacred music and the traditions of Viennese instrumental music. Bruckner was also well versed in counterpoint, and he taught this subject in his later years along with harmony and orchestration at the Vienna Conservatory. However much partisan detractors (Hanslick among them) pitted him against Brahms, Bruckner shared more with his ostensible rival than his contemporaries admitted.

Just as Brahms's music reflected his North German heritage, so Bruckner's found its roots in his Austrian Roman Catholicism (a parochial difference that provided ammunition for his supporters). Bruckner was born into a musical family in a small village outside Linz, Austria. His father served as a church organist and schoolteacher, and his mother sang in the church chorus. Anton received his first lessons from his father, learning both organ and violin. After his father died in 1837, Bruckner's mother arranged for her son to become a chorister at the monastery of St. Florian (also in the vicinity of Linz), where he continued study of organ and violin.

Like Schubert, Bruckner decided after his voice broke to become a schoolteacher. Several minor posts from the age of seventeen and more study of organ and composition eventually led to a position at St. Florian. He taught school there, took composition lessons in nearby Enns, attended organ recitals in Linz, and gradually assumed the duties of organist at the monastery. Eventually he tried his hand at some large-scale masses for soloists, chorus, orchestra, and organ, which led to the suggestion that he study harmony and counterpoint through a correspondence course with Simon Sechter at the Vienna Conservatory.

In 1855, at the same time he began his study of more advanced composition, Bruckner won a post as organist at the Linz cathedral, where he spent the next thirteen years. He became a preeminent performer, adept also in theory, harmony, counterpoint, and composition. In 1861, at the age of thirty-seven, he applied for a diploma certifying his abilities from the Vienna Conservatory, and he won the special praise of the examiners for his improvisation on a fugue subject. In 1862 he completed his musical education by studying orchestration with Otto Kitzler, a cellist and assistant conductor at the Linz Municipal Theater. During this time Buckner also attended a performance of *Tannhäuser,* and he was so impressed that he journeyed to Munich for the premiere of *Tristan und Isolde,* making Wagner's acquaintance in the process. The two men got along famously (largely because Bruckner idolized Wagner), and the older composer inspired his new friend to renewed vigor in composition, especially of masses and symphonies.

Bruckner's masses and symphonies brought him again to the attention of Johann Herbeck (conductor at the Gesellschaft der Musikfreunde in Vienna and also one of his examiners at the conservatory). Herbeck eventually sponsored Bruckner for a professorship at the conservatory, and helped him secure a position as organist at the imperial chapel as well as a government stipend for composing. In 1868, at the age of forty-four, the self-effacing, provincial musician moved to Vienna, where his music gained acceptance very slowly in the face of concerted opposition from Hanslick. He triumphed eventually, however, receiving the Order of Franz Joseph in 1886 and an honorary doctorate from the University of Vienna in 1891. He died at the height of his fame in 1896 while composing the finale of his Ninth Symphony.

A good sample of the influence exerted on Bruckner by his long tenure as an organist in Roman Catholic churches appears in a motet such as "Os justi," written in 1879 for the Feast of St. Augustine.

"Os justi"
Gradual for the Common of Doctors
(Psalm 37:31–32)

Os justi meditabitur sapientiam,	The righteous man contemplates wisdom,
et lingua ejus loquetur judicium.	and his tongue speaks justice.
Lex Dei ejus in corde ipsius:	The law of God is in his heart,
et non supplantabuntur gressus ejus.	and his steps do not slip.
Alleluia.	Alleluia.

One of the peculiar features of this piece is its key signature of no flats or sharps, which places it in a Lydian mode to which Bruckner adheres strictly. He bolsters this antique "church mode" with textures that reflect a late-nineteenth-century understanding of Renaissance sacred music. The *a cappella* motet opens homophonically but soon introduces a long imitative passage for the text "et lingua ejus loquetur judicium" (see Example 6.6). Bruckner returns to homophonic texture for the remainder of the gradual, ending with a section of chantlike monophony for the "Alleluia."

The concluding homage to plainchant reminds us how deeply nineteenth-century musicians became involved in the history of sacred style. Just as the rediscovery of Bach's choral music moved Brahms to historically modeled motets, so the renewed interest in Palestrina and the tradition of Roman Catholic chant prompted Bruckner's emulation. Various "Cecilian Societies" in the German-speaking parts of Europe fostered the *a cappella* performance of chant beginning in the eighteenth century, and the movement gained momentum in the nineteenth. France also saw new research into medieval plainchant, with study revolving especially around the monastery of Solesmes. Scholars there published facsimiles of old chant manuscripts and undertook the revision of Roman Catholic chant to reflect what they believed were the earliest musical practices. Positivistic historicism marked these efforts just as much as it did the Bach revival. We can hear the effects in some of Bruckner's motets (even though contemporaries found his approximation of early church style questionable).

Bruckner's symphonies in their turn also hearken to a tradition, combining elements of the Beethovenian and Schubertian heritage of Viennese composers. A good example appears in the first movement of Bruckner's Fourth Symphony (written 1874; revised 1878–80; see Table 6.4). The composer begins

EXAMPLE 6.6   Fugato from Bruckner's motet "Os justi" (1879)

TABLE 6.4   Schematic for the *Romantic* Symphony, mvt. I (1878 version)

SECTION	SUBSECTION	KEY-AREA	MEASURE
Exposition			
	Main theme	E♭: I	1–50
	transition	I→V/V	51–74
	Secondary theme	♭VII→♭III→	75–118
		♭VII→V/V	
	Closing	V	119–192
Development		X	
	Bridge		193–216
	Core		
	Model I		217–228
	sequence (partial)		229–236
	fragmentation (2 × 2)		237–240
	dissolution		241–252
	Model II		253–256
	sequence		257–260
	fragmentation (7 × 2)		261–273
	dissolution		274–278
	Model III		279–282
	sequence		283–286
	dissolution		287–288
	Model IV		289–292
	sequence		293–296
	Model V		297–304
	sequence		305–312
	sequence		313–320
	frag. & diss.		321–333
	Retransition		334–364
Recapitulation			
	Main theme	I	365–412
	transition	I→x→I	413–436
	Secondary theme	♯V→VII→	437–484
		V/V→V	
	Closing (abridged)	I	485–500
Coda		x→I	501–573

his exposition in a manner highly reminiscent of the opening of Beethoven's Ninth; the *pianissimo* string tremolo and the descending fifth bespeak this allusion (see Example 6.7). But unlike Beethoven, Bruckner does not build his melody from motivic fragments. Instead, he repeats phrases in sequence à la Wagner, often presenting them antiphonally between various instrumental voices or

EXAMPLE 6.7   Opening of Bruckner, Fourth Symphony, 1878 version

choirs. Bruckner's construction of massive climaxes from repeated patterns recalls Schubert, as does the contrasting secondary theme that explores both subtonic and mediant key-areas. Like Brahms, Bruckner prepares these distant keys by means of shifts between parallel major and minor modes. But he is much more willing to modulate abruptly or by means of direct chromatic scale in the Wagnerian manner.

The remaining movements of the symphony include a haunting march ("Andante") in C minor that takes its motivic cue from the main theme of the first movement. The composer casts the Andante as a series of loose variations, and it offers much interesting counterpoint. The third movement presents a spirited scherzo in B-flat major that opens in classic fashion with "hunting" motives (for horns) related to the main theme of the first movement. Here Bruckner displays his mastery of brass used in chorus. He tends to deal with instruments in groups as if they represented stops on an organ (though he refrained from adopting Wagner's expanded ensemble). The trio to this movement offers a gracious Austrian *Ländler* by way of contrast, both in orchestration (for strings and woodwinds) and in tempo. The sonata-form finale does not sustain the obvious thematic bonds that link the other three movements, and it seems less inspired. Bruckner ran the risk of empty bombast in his massed orchestrations, especially when his melodic material was less compelling.

Bruckner mentions a program in his correspondence about the Fourth Symphony, something unique to this work among his symphonic output. The references consist of vague generalities setting various scenes. At one point he says of the first movement, "Medieval city—morning mists—knights ride out of the gate—forest shadows surround them—twittering of birds," corresponding, respectively, to the main theme (morning), transition (knights), secondary theme (birds), and so forth. The composer later gives a different frame of reference for the first movement in which brass instruments herald the New Year from the towers of the parish church in Linz. Bruckner designated the second movement a "serenade . . . in which an enamored country lad visits his beloved but does not gain entry" (thus the cantabile theme). The "hunting" scherzo speaks for itself, and Bruckner denied any concrete associations with the last movement. Aside from the easily discerned topoi—"hunting" motives, cantabile secondary themes, and the like—the programmatic cues take us little further than much of Brahms's "absolute music." The music creates mood, but specific programs seem to have played no important or pervasive role in Bruckner's approach to composition.

Bruckner did not have Brahms's range or his intellectual proclivities. He wrote no memorable concerti, his Lieder and string quartets go largely unperformed, and his symphonies hardly form a mainstay of the orchestral repertory. But his unique way of treating instruments contributed something novel to the Viennese musical scene. And his tendency to contrast and overlap shifting masses of sound would influence one of his famous admirers, Gustav Mahler. Without Bruckner's use of antiphonal choirs of instruments and his occasional Austrian folkishness as precedent, Mahler's symphonic counterpoint and folk-like nationalism would be almost unthinkable.

Strauss and *Jugendstil*

It remained for the generation of composers after Brahms and Bruckner to seize the legacy of the "New German School" and capture the positivism of the age in the service of program music. Richard Strauss's consummate technical artistry draws out the implications of Wagnerian musical language in the service of *Jugendstil,* the German avant-garde at the turn of the century.

Strauss (1864–1949) had a distinguished musical pedigree. His father, Franz Joseph, occupied a position as principal horn in Munich court orchestra. In this capacity he played at the first performances of Wagner's *Tristan, Meistersinger, Rheingold, Walküre,* and *Parsifal,* and he was considered a virtuoso by no less than the conductor Hans von Bülow. Franz heartily disliked the "Music of the Future" and even held Brahms in suspicion. When Richard evinced talent on the piano, Franz had him study Haydn, Mozart, Beethoven, Mendelssohn, and Schumann, beginning at age three with the harpist of the Munich court orchestra. Strauss's mother came from a well-to-do family with a large brewery, and her young son had a solid, upper-middle-class academic education at the Ludwigsgymnasium and later at the University of Munich.

Although Strauss did not become a virtuoso (he was an able pianist and violinist), he quickly excelled at composition. He studied counterpoint, harmony, and instrumentation with Friedrich Wilhelm Meyer (one of Hermann Levi's assistants), and he composed regularly from the age of six. By the age of sixteen he had written a String Quartet, a Symphony in D minor, and a Piano Sonata in B minor, among other pieces, all of which received public performances in Munich to much acclaim. Soon his works made their way to Dresden, Berlin, and Meiningen, where Bülow had trained one the finest orchestras in Europe. Bülow commissioned a piece from Strauss for his ensemble (it turned out to be a Suite in B-flat) and invited the nineteen-year-old composer to conduct its first performance in 1884.

This initial pass at conducting led to a career: Bülow engaged Strauss the following year as an assistant. And when the older conductor departed shortly afterward, the young Strauss was left in charge of the orchestra. A series of assistant conducting posts followed, at Munich in 1886 and at Weimar in 1889. By 1894 his reputation had risen to such an extent that Munich asked him back as Kapellmeister, and he began conducting in Bayreuth with the approval of an admiring Cosima Wagner. Strauss also undertook a series of international guest engagements, in Holland, Spain, France, and England. By 1896 Berlin summoned him to the post of chief conductor of its Royal Opera, and he also took charge of the Berlin Philharmonic. In this role he championed the works of modern composers, including his friend Gustav Mahler, Reger, Elgar, and Sibelius.

Strauss often made guest appearances to conduct his own works, which were primarily instrumental until the end of the century. (His opera from this period, *Guntram,* never enjoyed success.) At first he adopted the style of Brahms, something highly evident in works such as the *Burlesque* for piano and orchestra. Much of the older composer's approach to the texture of piano and to intense motivic work appears in this piece, as it does in most of Strauss's early symphonies, serenades, and other conventional works. An early apprenticeship in the traditional, academic style marks the careers of many *Jugendstil* artists. But beginning with *Aus Italien* and *Macbeth* (both originating in 1886), Strauss took a decidedly Lisztian turn under the influence of Alexander Ritter, a violinist in the Meiningen orchestra and a nephew-in-law of Wagner. These first examples of program music follow transparent precedents, *Harold in Italy* for *Aus Italien* and the concert overture for *Macbeth*.

With *Don Juan* (1889), however, Strauss began calling his titled compositions "tone poems" (*Tondichtungen*), and he entered a realm much more responsive to the external demands of program. It seems at first glance as if *Don Juan* will also fall into the formal patterns of the concert overture. It begins with what appears to be the exposition of a sonata form (see Table 6.5), but long stretches of tonal stability where the development ought to be, combined with the entrance of two very distinctive new themes, render continued analysis along conventional lines untenable. The third episode, which looks at first to be a "recapitulation," actually acts more as a development of previous ideas. Various attempts to fit the structure into rondo form prove equally unsatisfying.

Strauss provides a succinct guide to the structure of his tone poem at the beginning of his score, however, in the form of three episodes from Lenau's poem "Don Juan." The first excerpt characterizes the great lover himself at the height of his passion: "I would traverse the magic circle, immeasurably wide, of multifariously charming, beautiful femininity in a storm of pleasure...." Strauss's second excerpt portrays Don Juan moving from conquest to conquest, always in search of the novel (thus the two new themes in this section, interwoven with the motives of Don Juan's nature from the first section). The third segment of Strauss's program finds the lover viewing his life in retrospect: "A beautiful storm drove me but has subsided...." After poignant remembrances of his former powers, his ardor dies away ("the fuel is consumed, and the hearth grows cold and dark"), an event mirrored by Strauss's denouement. The composer has moved away from absolute musical form, letting the external inspiration guide him more literally in his choice of musical events.

TABLE 6.5   Schematic for *Don Juan,* op. 20 (1889)

SECTION	*SUBSECTION*	*KEY-AREA*	*MEASURE*
Episode I			
	"Main theme"	E: I	1–39
	transition	I→V	40–89
	"Second theme"	V	90–148
	"Closing"	i	149–168
Episode II			
	Dev. of Mth	I→iii	169–196
	Tranquil theme	III	197–312
	Noble theme	III	313–350
	dev. of themes	x	351–423
	"retransition"	V pedal	424–473
Episode III			
	Var. on Mth	I	474–509
	Noble theme	I	510–555
	Var. on Mth	♭II→I	556–585
	Denouement	I	586–606

Strauss also adopts a more daring sonority and musical vocabulary in *Don Juan* than in his previous works. His orchestra expands on its Wagnerian predecessor, with extra flutes, English horn, harp, and an enlarged percussion section quite foreign to either Brahms or Bruckner. Moreover, Strauss deploys the instruments in wider ranges, opening up the texture and avoiding the middle-range density of the Viennese school. Though Strauss's cadences remain squarely tonal and relatively clear, he seems much more willing to indulge chromatic color for its own sake. He is particularly fond of introducing harmonies that act as chromatic upper or lower neighbors to the prevailing key. This habit expands to temporary digressions in key, like the brief one to F major in the third episode of the piece (see Table 6.5). Strauss had mastered the Brahmsian lessons of motivic development and counterpoint completely. But Strauss's melodies stress cantilena (see Example 6.8), and his counterpoint avoids Brahms's convoluted motivic density in favor of imitation based on long-breathed phrases. This style of writing would serve Strauss well in his later operas.

Strauss went on to consolidate his positivistic approach to the tone poem with *Death and Transfiguration* (1889), *Till Eulenspiegel's Merry Pranks* (1895), *Thus Spake Zarathustra* (after Nietzsche's treatise; 1896), *Don Quixote* (after Cervantes' novel; 1897), and *A Hero's Life* (1898). Each of these adopts a free, episodic structure based on its program (just as his failed opera, *Guntram,* takes a rather literal approach to the relationship between leitmotif and drama).

The closest correspondence between program and instrumental music comes in *Don Quixote,* which unfolds as a set of "Fantastic Variations on a Theme of Knightly Character," op. 35. It was a brilliant stroke on Strauss's part to cast episodes in Cervantes' story as a set of variations involving the "knight of the sorrowful countenance," represented by a solo cello, and his faithful servant, Sancho Panza, given voice by a solo viola. Each of the prime characters (Don Quixote, Sancho Panza, and Dulcinea) receives his or her distinctive melody,

EXAMPLE 6.8 Violin melody at beginning of "Main theme" from Strauss, *Don Juan* (1889)

the Don's being the most pervasive (see Example 6.9). And the colorful scenes provide Strauss with a pretext for employing all manner of strange scales, harmonies, and instruments, as we can see in a brief inventory:

> *Introduction:* Strauss presents us with Don Quixote; he dreams of all the chivalric tales he has read and of an ideal maiden, whom he names Dulcinea (roughly translated, "the sweet one"). But he lets his imagination carry him away. Chaotic fragments of fantasies about battles, magicians, and quests begin to boil in his brain, until he becomes unhinged and decides to set out into the world in the self-proclaimed role of a knight errant.
>
> *Theme:* "The knight of the sorrowful countenance" appears as a solo cello in minor mode. He is joined by a hapless and sometimes disrespectful squire, Sancho Panza, whose bumbling theme often appears in the bass clarinet, the tenor tuba, and later the viola.
>
> *Variation 1:* The Don happens on a group of windmills, which he imagines to be evil giants. The theme of his motivating ideal, Dulcinea, also appears in the violins. The stroke of the timpani records his fall as one of the windmill vanes strikes down his lance.
>
> *Variation 2:* Don Quixote mistakes an approaching cloud of dust for the sign of an approaching army, but discordant bleating in the muted brass reveals nothing more than sheep. The Don kills several of them before enraged shepherds stone him. Sancho Panza is left to pick up the fallen hero.
>
> *Variation 3:* Sancho (represented by the viola) tries to talk his master back into his senses, but the Don is too filled with thoughts of Dulcinea and glory. The two argue back and forth. The deluded knight waxes eloquent on chivalry, ending with a magnificent statement of his imaginary beloved's beauty and virtue in the violins.
>
> *Variation 4:* The knight encounters a religious procession represented by muted trumpets playing a chantlike melody. Don Quixote imagines they are Muslim infidels, and charges them, only to be struck down by one of the pilgrims, who continue on their way. Panza must revive the crumpled knight again.
>
> *Variation 5:* Don Quixote spends a restless evening thinking of Dulcinea, whose theme finally appears explicitly in his thoughts, surrounded by an ecstasy of harp glissandos.

EXAMPLE 6.9   Don Quixote's theme from Strauss, *Don Quixote* (1897)

Variation 6: When the knight and his squire reach El Toboso, the town in which Dulcinea supposedly lives, Sancho Panza tries to pass off a common peasant as the woman of his master's dreams. A dancelike variation of her theme in alternating meters appears in gypsy style in the oboes, accompanied by tambourine.

Variation 7: Duped by a huckster, Don Quixote and Sancho sit blindfolded astride a "magic" wooden horse, which supposedly can fly through the air. In fact, giant bellows give the impression of a gale rushing past, represented in the orchestra by chromatic scales in the woodwinds, parallel chordal motion in the brass, and a wind machine in the percussion section.

Variation 8: In a fable borrowed from the Percival Legend, the Don stumbles upon a small wooden boat, which he takes to be an enchanted barge. In fact, the dinghy takes him downstream to a gristmill, where his boat plunges over the millrace. The millers rescue him and Sancho from drowning. The Don give thanks in a prayerful woodwind passage closing the variation.

Variation 9: The knight and his squire next meet a caravan on the road, consisting of a noblewoman's coach accompanied by two monks. Don Quixote convinces himself that the monks (their chanting can be heard in the bassoons) are really sorcerers abducting a princess. As he charges the group, they flee.

Variation 10: Hoping to end Don Quixote's mad exploits, a fellow townsman from La Mancha, Samson Carrasco, pretends to be "The Knight of the White Moon" (his theme appears in triplet figures for the winds). He challenges the Don to a joust, defeats him, and demands that The Knight of the Sorrowful Countenance return home. Crushed by his defeat, accompanied by the sorrowing Sancho (whose theme is interwoven here), the Don rides back to La Mancha, where he briefly imagines taking up the rural life again to the tune of a shepherd's piping.

Variation 11: Overcome by grief at abandoning his quest, the Don dies of a broken heart. But as he expires, we are reminded by a major-mode version of his theme of the inner nobility of all those deluded individuals who entertain magnificent, if unrealistic dreams.

In his pursuit of more direct correspondence with the program of *Don Quixote,* Strauss produces ever more dissonant and less clearly tonal music, though the basic tonal background remains. The programmatic references also elicit a sonic tour de force. Strauss brings instrumental music as close to positivistic realism as it legitimately dares without descending to mere cartooning. At the same time, he provides a truly novel alternative to the severity of "absolute music."

Strauss's songs can take a similarly "illustrative" approach to the setting of poetry. A particularly striking example appears in "Ruhe, meine Seele!" op. 27, no. 1 (1894), which he presented to his wife, the soprano Pauline de Ahna, on their wedding day.

"Ruhe, meine Seele!"

Nicht ein Lüftchen regt sich leise,	Not a breeze stirs softly,
Sanft entschlummert ruht der Hain;	Gently slumbering, the glade rests;
Durch der Blätter dunkle Hülle	Through the leaves' dark covering
Stiehlt sich lichter Sonnenschein.	Steals the bright sunshine.

Ruhe, ruhe, meine Seele,	Rest, rest, my soul,
Deine Stürme gingen wild,	Your storms ran wildly,
Hast getobt und has gezittert,	You have raged and trembled,
Wie die Brandung, wenn sie schwillt!	Like the surf when it swells!
Diese Zeiten sind gewaltig,	These times are momentous,
Bringen Herz und Hirn in Not,	Bringing trouble to heart and mind,
Ruhe, ruhe, meine Seele,	Rest, rest, my soul,
Und vergiß, was dich bedroht!	And forget what threatens you!

On one level of meaning, Strauss reacts to the idea of "rest" by setting Karl Henckell's verse as metrically inactive recitative. We gain almost no sense of poetic scansion or meter from the declamatory, narrowly inflected vocal melody or from the block chords that dominate the piano accompaniment from beginning to end (see Example 6.10). Predictably, however, at the end of the second

EXAMPLE 6.10   Opening of Strauss, "Ruhe, meine Seele!" (1894)

stanza Strauss adds scalar flourishes between chords to depict the "surf" that carries into "momentous" times. He also allows the dynamic level to "swell" for these lines to *forte,* before returning to the predominantly soft last couplet. Finally, the underlying harmonic motion works on a different semantic level, enchaining a series of seventh chords. These move first toward an uneasy cadence on a B major dominant seventh at the end of the first stanza, then on a B-flat minor-major seventh at the end of the second stanza. Only in the postlude does the accompaniment "forget that which threatens it" and come to "rest" on the C major tonic implied by the key signature. It would be wrong to leave the impression that all Strauss songs adopt this literal approach; some present fairly straightforward strophic settings of text. But Strauss was willing to take a much more representational view of music's role than either Brahms or Bruckner, bringing Wagner's operatic aesthetics into the concert hall.

THE *ARS GALLICA* REPLIES

As the "German propaganda machine" (Virgil Thomson's term) for music cranked into high gear during the nineteenth century, the importance of French art after the generation of Berlioz, Liszt, and Chopin began to wane. Opera, which had always stood at the center of Parisian musical prestige, continued unabated. But the works of Meyerbeer held less sway on the stage, and we tend to remember Verdi's works for the Opéra better than those of Jules Massenet (to take just one instance). German music increasingly dominated concert life, especially the works of Haydn, Mozart, Beethoven, Mendelssohn, and the "progressive" Schumann. "A French composer who was daring enough to venture into the terrain of instrumental music," Camille Saint-Saëns wrote retrospectively in 1885, "had no other means of having his work performed than to give a concert himself and invite his friends and critics. As for the general public, it was hopeless even to think about them. The name of a living French composer had only to appear on a poster to frighten everybody away."

After the defeat of Napoleon III at Sedan in 1870 and its blow to national pride, French composers sought a way to reassert their native art in the concert hall. To that end, a group of composers including César Franck, Camille Saint-Saëns, and Gabriel Fauré founded the Société Nationale de Musique (its motto: "Ars gallica"—"French Art") in early 1871 with the express purpose of presenting the chamber and orchestral music of French composers to Parisian musicians and audiences. The Société bore some relationship to the London Philharmonic Society or the Viennese Gesellschaft der Musikfreunde, both established at the beginning of the century.

For all their nationalistic fervor, French composers for the concert hall after midcentury owed much of their inspiration to German composers, but rather than siding with one or the other of the two opposing German camps, the French borrowed from both. For that reason, individual composers melded features of the Weimar-Bayreuth and the Leipzig-Vienna "schools."

A good example of this mixed influence appears in the person of César Franck (1822–90). Franck, like so many musicians prominent in France, was actually born in Liège (part of present-day Belgium), the son of a German mother and an ethnically German father. But César studied at the French-influenced Liège Conservatory, and his family moved to Paris during their son's adolescence. This brought entry to the Conservatoire and the support of Reicha, Meyerbeer, Liszt, Halévy, Chopin, Thomas, and Auber, among others. The young Franck had thought to become a piano virtuoso, but his gift for counterpoint also led in the direction of composition. He took Conservatoire prizes in both piano and counterpoint during his student days, but eventually composing proved his strongest suit.

Franck's early compositions included a group of celebrated Piano Trios, op. 1; the oratorio *Ruth;* the symphonic poem *Ce qu'on entend sur la montagne;* and an unfinished opera, *Le valet de ferme.* None of these proved sufficiently viable to pay the rent, and the young composer finally took a job as a church organist. In this capacity he became an "artistic representative" for the famous builder of nineteenth-century French organs, Cavaillé-Coll, and he secured a position at the newly built church of Sainte Clothilde. Franck also taught organ to a number of prominent students, including Henri Duparc and Vincent d'Indy, and he would eventually succeed to the post of organ professor at the Conservatoire. His manual technique grew to be legendary, as did his improvisations, which formed the basis for a substantial body of organ works. His position as the first secretary of the Société Nationale de Musique furthered his career as a composer for the concert hall. (He would never compose a truly successful opera.)

Franck's works for the concert hall included a series of virtuosic pieces for piano solo, chamber music, and a goodly number of pieces for piano and orchestra, the *Variations symphoniques* (1885) being the most frequently performed today. His six symphonic poems appear relatively little on programs, though orchestras sometimes perform and record *Les Eolides* (1876) and *Psyché* (1888). The one piece still solidly ensconced in the repertory is his D minor Symphony (1888), first performed at the Concerts du Conservatoire in 1889. It demonstrates the peculiar synthesis of German influences on French concert-hall repertory in several ways.

In its thematic relationships, Franck's Symphony in D Minor takes its cue from the composer's mentor, Franz Liszt. Many of the melodies in the three-movement piece proceed from one another by a process of thematic transformation (see Examples 6.11a–6.11d). And, in fact, the introductory theme to the first movement bears more than a passing resemblance to the beginning of Liszt's *Les préludes* (see Example 4.13a). Franck's harmonic language and penchant for chromaticism reflect not only his acquaintance with Liszt but also his admiration for Wagner, whose Prelude to *Tristan* he first encountered in 1874.

EXAMPLE 6.11A   Opening from Franck, Symphony in D Minor, mvt. I

EXAMPLE 6.11B   Second theme from Franck, Symphony in D Minor, mvt. I

EXAMPLE 6.11C   Theme from Franck, Symphony in D Minor, mvt. II

EXAMPLE 6.11D   Opening theme from Franck, Symphony in D Minor, mvt. III

In the structure of his D minor Symphony Franck takes his cue more from Schumann. For instance, the material of the "slow introduction" to the first movement merges into the main theme as in Schumann's First, Second, and Fourth Symphonies, and the last movement quotes episodes from the first two like the finale to Schumann's Second. The form of the first movement follows a pattern similar to that for the first movement of Schumann's Third Symphony, in which the main theme repeats strophically (instead of a repeat for the whole exposition; compare Table 6.6 with Table 4.1). The haunting slow movement, with its English horn solo accompanied by harp and pizzicato strings, may be the most famous of the three. The finale concludes triumphantly in major mode, following a plot traced by every symphonic composer since Beethoven. Franck's orchestration, save for the harp, expands little on the conservative orchestra employed by Brahms. This symphony without program offers a French reading of the "absolute" tradition. Franck's music has fallen somewhat out of favor today, perhaps because it combines Wagnerian chromaticism with a regular phrase structure that can seem mechanically overwrought. But the D minor Symphony displays sturdy craftsmanship, like the rest of Franck's music, and it offers some glorious moments well worth hearing.

Camille Saint-Saëns (1835–1921), Franck's most famous musical co-conspirator in the Société Nationale, followed the pattern of child prodigy and keyboard virtuoso. He grew up in Paris, raised by his mother and a great-aunt who taught him piano at the very young age of two and one half (the boy's father died just after he was born). Charles-Camille (for that was the boy's full name) played his first recital in the Salle Pleyel at age ten, with a program featuring Beethoven and Mozart. He entered the Conservatoire at age thirteen, taking piano, organ, and later composition with none other than Halévy. His virtuosity both at the keyboard and with the pen earned him the admiration of Rossini, Gounod, Liszt, and Berlioz, who once commented wryly that "Saint-Saëns knows everything but lacks inexperience."

During his lifetime Saint-Saëns excelled immediately at almost everything to which he put his hand. His piano concerti, tone poems, symphonies, songs, and chamber music all triumphed. He also had success (unlike Franck) in the genres of opéra comique, grand opera, and the more modern *drame lyrique.* During the last part of the century he held the widest reputation of any French composer, and he enjoyed honors comparable to Brahms's, such as honorary doctorates from Cambridge and Oxford. Saint-Saëns championed the "moderns" of his youth: Schumann, Wagner, and Liszt (who became a staunch supporter), and he even brought the music of Musorgsky's *Boris Godunov* to Paris, though he had doubts about its soundness. His catholicity of taste and extensive involvement in the French musical scene made him instrumental in founding the Société Nationale du Musique.

Saint-Saëns's contemporary fame has not translated into an extensive role in the modern repertory, perhaps because his extraordinary compositional virtuosity

TABLE 6.6   Schematic for Franck's Symphony in D Minor, mvt. I (1888)

SECTION	SUBSECTION	KEY-AREA	MEASURE
Exposition			
	Mth	D:i→iii	1–48
	Mth	iii→III	49–98
	trans.	x	99–128
	Sth	III	129–174
Development		x	
	Bridge		175–198
	Core		
	model 1		199–205
	sequence		206–212
	model 2		213–216
	sequence		217–220
	dissolution		221–226
	model 3		227–230
	sequence		231–234
	fragmentation 2×2		235–238
	dissolution		239–244
	model 4		245–254
	sequence		255–266
	model 5		267–272
	sequence		273–278
	dissolution 3×2		279–284
	model 6		285–288
	sequence		289–292
	model 7		293–296
	extension		297–300
	sequence		301–304
	model 8		305–308
	sequence		309–312
	sequence		313–316
	dissolution		317–322
	Retransition	V pedal	323–330
Recapitulation			
	Mth	i→ii→I	331–388
	trans.	x	389–418
	Sth	I	419–464
Coda		I→i	465–521

can appear facile at times. His opera *Samson et Dalila* (first performed in Weimar, 1877) still holds the stage, his piano concerti receive some performances, and his *Danse macabre,* a tone poem for violin and orchestra, surfaces occasionally. But we generally hear only the tip of his large output.

One of Saint-Saëns's more frequently performed pieces, the Third Symphony, op. 78 (1886), offers us a glimpse of his style and the influences on it. The composer wrote the piece on commission from the London Philharmonic Society, and that may account for its rather grand instrumentation, which includes a variety of percussion, piano, and a very prominently featured organ. At first glance the *Organ* Symphony's two movements might appear rather novel. But the two movements each subdivide into two major sections, yielding the conventional four (see Table 6.7).

All the sections of the symphony share the same melodic material. The theme for the Adagio results from transforming the secondary theme of the preceding Allegro. The opening of the scherzo varies a countertheme from the recapitulation of the Allegro (m. 236) and later quotes the first movement's main theme directly, as does the ensuing trio. The finale reworks the main theme from the first movement in a series of variations much freer than a diagram can suggest. The model for this almost continuous series of movements seems to have been the "symphonic fantasy" found in Schumann's D minor Symphony. Influence from the Leipzig school also appears in the almost Mendelssohnian regularity of Saint-Saëns's phrase structure. And although the sequence of keys in the *Organ* Symphony reveals an expanded chromatic palette, it is hardly as sinuous as that in Franck's D minor Symphony. Saint-Saëns shares with his compatriot, however, an organist's love of counterpoint, of which both composers were past masters.

The theme of an organist's craft also runs through the career of Saint-Saëns's pupil Gabriel Fauré (1845–1924), yet another cofounder of the Société Nationale de Musique. Fauré's family came from the minor aristocracy and resided in the provinces. His father took a post as a school administrator (director of the Ecole Normale at Montgauzy), and his young son spent many hours playing the harmonium in the school chapel. Gabriel's father decided to enroll him at age nine in the newly established Ecole de Musique Classique et Religieuse in Paris to prepare him for a career as a church musician. The young Fauré spent eleven years there studying organ with Clément Loret, counterpoint with Joseph Wackenthaler, and piano and composition with Saint-Saëns after the death in 1861 of the Ecole's founder, Louis Niedermeyer. Through Saint-Saëns, Fauré became acquainted with the works of Schumann, Liszt, and Wagner, as well as gaining an important contact with the musical scene in Paris.

After graduating from the Ecole de Musique, Fauré pursued a career as an organist and choirmaster, first in Rennes, then in Clignancourt near Paris, in Paris at St. Sulpice, and finally at the Madeleine during Saint-Saëns's absences. In 1896 Gabriel became chief organist at the Madeleine and succeeded

TABLE 6.7   Schematic for Saint-Saëns's Third Symphony (1886)

MOVEMENT	*SECTION*	*SUBSECTION*	*KEY*	*MEASURE*
I.				
	Sonata-allegro			
		Intro.	c	1–11
		Mth	c	12–83
		trans.	c→D♭	84–101
		Sth	D♭	102–131
		Closing (Sth)	F	132–158
		Dev.	x	159–232
		Mth.	c	233–275
		trans.	c→F	276–300
		Sth	F→D♭	301–349
	Adagio (theme and double var.)			
		Theme	D♭	350–402
		var. 1	D♭	403–423
		var. 2 (Mth)	d♭	424–438
		var. 3	D♭	439–477
II.				
	Scherzo			
		scherzo	c	1–70
		trio	C→A♭→G	71–206
		scherzo	c	207–276
		trio (bridge)	A♭→G	277–375
	Finale (variation on Mth)			
		Intro.	C	376–383
		Theme (Mth)	C	384–391
		var. 1	C	392–399
		var. 2 (fugue)	C	400–428
		interlude	G	429–461
		var. 3 (fugue)	g	462–503
		var. 4	x	504–546
		interlude	E→C	547–579
		var. 3 (fugue)	c	580–609
		var. 5	c	610–630
		Coda	G→C	631–671

Massenet as professor of composition at the Conservatoire. Fauré would number Ravel, Enescu, and Nadia Boulanger among his composition students. He eventually became director of the Conservatoire and something of a celebrity, awarded the Grand Croix of the Légion d'honneur in 1920 and lionized by the younger generation of French composers.

As the admiration of younger composers might indicate, Fauré was a transitional figure between the generation of Franck and Saint-Saëns and later French modernists. We can think of him as an "Art nouveau" composer. Although generally using conventional tonal language in his music, he began to test its boundaries by using it in untraditional ways. A good example appears in his Requiem, op. 48, composed in stages between 1888 and 1893, and reorchestrated in 1900. It began life as a liturgical piece for its composer's use at the Madeleine, but finally assumed the shape of a concert-hall work for full orchestra and chorus, premiered at the Trocadéro Palace during the Parisian World Exhibition.

One remarkable departure from the earlier tradition of setting the requiem mass as a multimovement composition for chorus and orchestra lies in Fauré's decision to omit the *Dies irae*. Where this vision of the last judgment had formed a dramatic chapter in Berlioz's and Verdi's requiems (a version of which even Brahms indulged in his *German Requiem*), Fauré had little time for the sequence's theatrical effects. Instead, he confines himself to the responsory *Libera me* and adds the gentle *In Paradisum*, both from the burial service. The French *Art nouveau* in music sought a graceful, almost distant and ethereal surface, rather than the grandiose display of German *Jugendstil*. To avoid theatrical bombast even further, Fauré limits himself to just two soloists for his Requiem, soprano and baritone. His full orchestration omits percussion, save timpani, and restricts the employment of brass. By these means the composer achieves an overall effect at once solemn and delicate.

Fauré's harmonic palette in the Requiem reinforces the delicacy of his orchestration. Though he uses mostly functional harmonies, the composer feels free to dispense with them at will, and he often repeats alternations between two chords so frequently that we lose a sense of progression altogether. A good example appears in the opening of the *In Paradisum* (Example 6.12), where the tonic chord (D-F♯-A) alternates with a supertonic seventh chord over a pedal A-natural. The repeated B-natural acts as appoggiatura in the tonic, as the fifth of the supertonic, but lends a note of gentle ambiguity. Could the first chord possibly be a submediant seventh progressing to the supertonic? Even were we to hear the B as a chord tone, probably not; it would be more like a sixth added to a major tonic. The ostinato of the repeated bass notes and alternating harmony suspends a sense of tonal motion, just the ethereal effect Fauré sought in treating the eternity of paradise. His relatively late appointment to teach composition at the Conservatoire (at the age of fifty) resulted directly from this kind of tonal "radicalism." It lies far from the hyperchromaticism of the German school, however, presenting instead an empirically conditioned, local suspension of diatonic harmonic progression.

Fauré's refined ability to set text by means of delicate tonal indirection made him a superb composer of songs, often called *mélodies* on programs of the Société Nationale. One of his best settings comes in response to Paul Verlaine's "Clair de lune," op. 46, no. 2 (1887).

EXAMPLE 6.12 *In Paradisum* from Fauré, Requiem (1888)

"Clair de lune"

Votre âme est un paysage choisi	Your soul is a chosen landscape
Que vont charmants masques et bergamasques,	Where charming maskers and mummers stroll,
Jouant du luth et dansant et quasi	Playing the lute and dancing,
Tristes sous leurs déguisement fantasques.	Almost sad beneath their fantastic disguises.
Tout en chantant sur le mode mineur,	While singing in a minor mode
L'amour vainqueur et la vie opportune,	Of triumphant love and the easy life,
Ils n'ont pas l'air de croire à leur bonheur,	They seem not to believe in their happiness,
Et leur chanson se mêle au clair de lune,	And their song mingles with the moonlight,
Au calme clair de lune triste et beau,	With the tranquil moonlight, sad and lovely,
Qui fait rêver les oiseaux dans les arbres,	That makes the birds dream in the trees,
Et sangloter d'extase les jets d'eau,	And the fountains sob with ecstasy,
Les grand jets d'eau sveltes parmi les marbres.	The tall, slender fountains amid the marble statues.

Fauré adds the subtitle "menuet" to this song, and the piano accompaniment does indeed provide the generally four-square phrases of the triple-meter, minor-mode dance alluded to in the poem. Fauré creates the equal here of the German polyrhythmic Lied. For when the voice enters, its line shares little with the melody of the dance, generally moving in longer note values and sometimes presenting irregular phrases that contradict the phrases of the minuet. The use of the minuet has a neoclassical air about it and recalls in its technique (though not in mood) Brahms's superimposition of a folk text on a *Ländler* in "Verge-bliches Ständchen" (discussed earlier).

Fauré's frequent use of the lowered seventh degree in the natural minor scale lends an antique modal flavor to "Clair de lune." But his most elegant harmonic effect occurs when he separates the last four lines of Verlaine's text by a modulation to the relative major (see Example 6.13). The composer chooses not to arrive immediately on the major tonic, but begins with the subdominant (a G-flat triad in the key of D-flat). He then vacillates between the subdominant and the dominant seventh (built on A-flat). For the last line of text, Fauré dwells on the secondary dominant, but instead of moving through the dominant, proceeds directly to a two-note sonority (D-flat/F). This dyad serves ambiguously as a pivot back to the minor home key of B-flat (by simple addition of the minor root). Delay of gratification, release of tension, and the bittersweet collapse back into minor mode all relate directly to Verlaine's sexual symbolism concerning "the tall slender fountains amid the marble statues." But in the course of pursuing harmonic congruence to the meaning of the poetry, the composer almost succeeds in detaching the chords from their function. The key word here is "almost," for *Art nouveau* composers such as Fauré indicated the direction in which modernism lay without themselves crossing over into the promised land.

EXAMPLE 6.13   Excerpt from "Clair de lune" (1887) by Fauré

Whether Fauré actually arrived in the new country of modernism, however, he devoted much energy to the genres of the concert hall that previous generations of his countrymen (aside from Berlioz) had heeded so little. Fauré had no lasting success at the opera, but his extensive output of songs, suites (usually from incidental music), piano miniatures, and chamber music left an enduring legacy for Claude Debussy, Maurice Ravel, and Les Six. They, too, invested a good deal of time in pieces for the concert hall, where they carried on much of their avant-garde experimentation.

FURTHER READING

Johannes Brahms

The magisterial four-volume biography by Max Kalbeck has never appeared in translation, and it contains many anomalies and mistakes at any rate. The best recent treatment in English comes from Michael Musgrave, *The Music of Brahms* (Oxford and New York, 1994), which might be supplemented by various issues of *Brahms Studies.*

Anton Bruckner

Bruckner remains terra incognita in English, but Stephen Johnson's brief *Bruckner Remembered* (London, 1998) makes a start.

Richard Strauss

Strauss has received a good deal of attention of late. Bryan Gilliam's *The Life of Richard Strauss* (Cambridge, 1999) offers a solid, if abbreviated primer against which to set Matthew Boyden's *Richard Strauss* (Boston, 1999) and Tim Ashley's *Richard Strauss* (London, 1999). Norman Del Mar's *Richard Strauss: A Critical Commentary on His Life and Works* (London, 1962–69) presents a three-volume magisterial biography in the older vein.

César Franck

Laurence Davies has contributed the fairly reasonable *César Franck and His Circle* (Boston, 1970), which might well be supplemented with Vincent d'Indy's treasurable old *César Franck* in a translation by the indefatigable Rosa Newmarch (repr. New York, 1965).

Camille Saint-Saëns

How could Saint-Saëns have garnered two lengthy biographies recently—Brian Rees's *Camille Saint-Saëns: A Life* (London, 1999) and Stephen Studd's *Saint-Saëns: A Critical Biography* (London and Madison, NJ, 1999)? Saint-Saëns's *Musical Memories* (*Ecole buissonnière*) in an ancient translation by Edwin File Rich (London, 1919) also makes for interesting reading.

Gabriel Fauré

For the elusive and beloved Fauré we have Jean-Michel Nectoux's compendious *Gabriel Fauré: A Musical Life* in a translation by Roger Nichols (Cambridge, 1991).

CHAPTER 7

The Diversity
of Nationalism

The term "nationalism" brings with it many shades of meaning for the history of music. In some ways it summons notions of the artistically patriotic or political, and in this sense it would include music by Beethoven, Schubert, Berlioz, Liszt, Chopin, Schumann, Wagner, Verdi, Brahms, and almost any other nineteenth-century composer we can name. In another sense the term often involves overtones of the exotic, or what some scholars of culture now call "the Other"—that is to say, music from cultures other than the traditionally dominant regions of European music making—Germany, Italy, and France. The word "exotic" also connotes "the strikingly, excitingly, or mysteriously different or unusual." Composers often use highly distinctive, or "characteristic," local color in this latter sense to create various shades of musical nationalism.

Some people will see the category of musical nationalism as a catchall designed for the sake of convenience, but this view has its pragmatic appeal. The term will serve here as a pretext to view some later nineteenth-century composers in Russia, Scandinavia, the Hapsburg Empire, England, and the United States who wanted to assert their patriotism or to cultivate local musical color. Even then we must understand that composers framed almost all their "exotic" music in the European mainstream.

The several connotations of "nationalism" suggest that the term had no single aesthetic tenet. Diversitarian and particularist threads held over from

Romanticism sometimes motivated nationalistic art. But it does not simply represent a mere extension or some special subgenre of Romanticism. The desire for realism and naturalism provided just as strong an impetus as the penchant for the fantastic. We must examine each case, then, for the multiplicity of aesthetic and political impulses that moved a composer to assert nationalism in a particular work.

RUSSIA

In the spring of 1867 Mily Balakirev led a concert for an international meeting of Slavonic ethnographers that included pieces by Glinka, Dargomïzhsky, Rimsky-Korsakov, A. F. Lvov, and Balakirev himself, among other composers. Vladimir Stasov, an indefatigable polemicist for Russian music, concluded his review of the festivities by hailing the abilities of the "mighty little group" (*moguchaya kuchka*) of native composers displayed in the evening's entertainment. By this time art music had been cultivated in Russia for just a little over a century, and during the eighteenth century much of it had been imported from western Europe. Stasov felt that the ascendancy of native composers writing identifiably Russian art music was at hand, and he hoped the delegates to the ethnographic conference would carry home with them the memory of his countrymen's "poetry, feeling, talent, and skill."

The group of composers listed by Stasov by no means reflected a tightly knit society. Three of them came from an earlier generation: Alexey Lvov (1798–1870), Mikhail Glinka (1804–57), and Alexander Dargomïzhsky (1813–69). Together they had helped found a school of Russian national art music based on Western examples but also incorporating folk song. In the West we hear their compositions relatively seldom in concert. (The lack of familiarity with Glinka's *Life for the Tsar* counts as our loss.) Instead, we tend to focus our listening more on the contributions of the younger generation, represented in the 1867 concert by Nicolay Rimsky-Korsakov and the composer-conductor Balakirev (1837–1910).

Balakirev had gathered a number of disciples and friends around him, including not only Rimsky-Korsakov but also Modest Musorgsky, Alexander Borodin (1833–87), César Cui (1835–1918), and even, for a brief period, the young Pyotr Il'yich Tchaikovsky. The group attracted by Balakirev represented a kind of loosely associated Russian *Davidsbund,* which various composers entered and left fluidly. Western writers would later equate the mighty *kuchka* with a core of just five artists: Balakirev, Cui, Borodin, Musorgsky, and Rimsky-Korsakov. But that definition is probably too narrow, given what Stasov originally had in mind.

Russian composers of the nineteenth century tested the whole range afforded them by classical music, from the highly westernized to the more strongly localized. Most pieces reflect a variety of influences, with affinities to western European models joined by more or less exotic elements. Among the composers who play the largest role in our current performing repertory are Musorgsky, Rimsky-Korsakov, and Tchaikovsky. They will serve here as worthy representatives of the "Russian School" in the second half of the nineteenth century.

Musorgsky

Modest Musorgsky (1839–81) came from a well-to-do landowning family living in the Pskov district of north central Russia. He could trace his lineage back to medieval princes, and though his family had lost their noble title, his paternal grandfather served as an officer in the tsar's bodyguard. The young Modest's musical education began on the family estate of Karevo, where his mother taught him piano. He became adept in short order, good enough to play a Field concerto in his parents' salon at age nine. He continued studying with Anton Herke, a pupil of Henselt, at age ten. After a solid general education with a tutor and later in a preparatory school, he entered the elite Cadet School of the Guards in 1852 to follow in his grandfather's footsteps. Though he dabbled in composition throughout this period and even tried his hand at an opera, he had little formal instruction in harmony or counterpoint and remained essentially a talented dilettante pianist.

After graduating and receiving a commission in the elite Preobrazhenksy Regiment, Modest met another officer and dilettante musician, César Cui, and through him made the acquaintance of Mily Balakirev in 1857. Musorgksy persuaded Balakirev to give him lessons in musical form based on study of Beethoven's symphonies in four-hand arrangements and also on pieces by Schubert, Schumann, Glinka, and others. In the summer of 1858 Modest decided to resign his military commission in order to pursue composing, and he continued his studies with Balakirev.

Musorgsky would have been free to pursue his career as a gentleman composer had the emancipation of the serfs in 1861 not demolished his fortune. His family lost their estates at Karevo, and Modest took a series of jobs in the civil service that barely kept body and soul together. He shared rooms at various points with Rimsky-Korsakov and other bachelor friends, sometimes living off the largesse of his siblings or middle-class patrons. But he never established a stable social life, and there is some speculation that homosexual crushes on his straight male friends left him frustrated and bitter when they eventually married.

During all his tribulations Musorgsky managed to compose. He focused most of his energy on songs and opera, trying his hand at a treatment of *Salammbô* (based on a play by Flaubert; 1863–66) and *The Marriage* (a setting of Gogol's prose comedy; 1868), the latter under the influence of Dargomïzhsky's naturalism in *The Stone Guest.* Not until he hit on the idea of a libretto based on Pushkin's *Boris Godunov* in late 1868, however, did Musorgsky find a subject that inspired his best efforts. Condensing scenes in Pushkin's play to create his own libretto, the composer finished his vocal score for the first version of *Boris* in July 1869 and the orchestrated full score at the end of December. But the opera committee of the Maryinsky Theater rejected the work in February 1871, and then rejected a revision completed in mid-1872. Only the publication of a piano score in early 1874 and a benefit performance of the opera shortly afterward prompted the inclusion of *Boris* in the repertory. In 1873 Musorgsky began composing a new opera, *Khovanshchina,* left incomplete at his death, and in 1874 yet another opera, *Sorochintsy Fair* (based on a Gogol short story), also unfinished. In the meantime he wrote a number of songs, including two notable cycles, *The Nursery* (1870) and *Songs and Dances of Death* (1875–77). The latter was set to poetry by Count Arseniy Golenischev-Kutuzov, with whom the composer shared living quarters for two years. Also during this period the composer wrote his set of piano miniatures, *Pictures at an Exhibition* (1874), in memory of the painter Victor Hartmann. Increased drinking after the marriage of Golenischev-Kutuzov in 1875 rendered Musorgsky's composing more sporadic, and he died of alcoholism in 1881.

Musorgsky's masterpiece, *Boris Godunov,* illustrates the intermixture of nationalist and Western elements that came to influence the Russian music of this period. Musorgsky drew his initial inspiration from Pushkin's historical drama (1825) on the Russian "Time of Troubles" at the end of the sixteenth and beginning of the seventeenth centuries. During this period of dynastic struggle the Godunov family briefly came to power before succumbing to peasant and aristocratic unrest that eventually brought the Romanov dynasty to the throne. Musorgsky distilled Pushkin's twenty-odd scenes initially into seven. These focus not so much on a single plotline as on the progressive psychological instability of Boris, whom Pushkin portrayed as having come to the throne by murdering the Tsarevich Dmitri (the last legitimate heir of Ivan the Terrible). Musorgsky intersperses pictures of Godunov's steadily decaying mental state with scenes of growing political disorder that reflect (or are reflected by) the tsar's derangement. Plagued by remorse, challenged by an impostor pretending to be the assassinated Dmitri, and beset by insurrection among his courtiers, Boris dies of an almost Dostoyevskian guilt. *Crime and Punishment* as well as Musorgsky's opera were very much products of the Russian 1860s, when literature exploring the mind's inner workings enjoyed a tremendous vogue.

In his first version of *Boris* (1869) Musorgsky attempted an *opéra dialogué* that converted Pushkin's verse into prose set naturally, with a minimum of lyrical intrusions in a declamatory vocal line (even for the chorus). When the Maryinsky theater committee rejected this version on the grounds that it contained no female lead, Musorgsky rethought the whole opera. He not only added an act showing the false Dmitri with Marina Mniszech in a Polish plot to take over Russia, but also added more folk music, more lyrical writing, and a concluding scenic tableau set in the Kromy Forest. The piece came to resemble something very like a French grand opera in theme and shape (personal tragedy amid political turmoil in five acts, the first of which appears as a "prologue"). *Boris* in its second version combines some *kuchkist* naturalism with the influence of Western operas such as Meyerbeer's *Les Huguenots* and Verdi's *La forza del destino* or *Don Carlos*. There are even a number of reminiscence motives after the practice of several composers, Glinka, Berlioz, and Wagner among them.

The most famous part of the opera, the Coronation Scene (Prologue, scene 2), will give some idea of the interwoven elements that produced *Boris*. The first ingredient results from Musorgsky's empirical approach to harmony, which greets us at the scene's opening. Here two major-minor seventh chords with roots a tritone apart (A-flat and D) alternate to mimic the tolling of large bells, while ostinati from the notes of these same chords imitate the ringing of smaller bells (see Example 7.1). This sonic realism suspended harmonic function, suggesting to later composers the use of chords for their intrinsic sonority rather than as part of a prescribed hierarchy. Musorgsky drew the pitches in this passage, moreover, from an octatonic scale that partitions the octave into eight tones by regularly alternating whole and half steps (in this case C D E♭ *F* G♭ A♭ A *B*).* Finally, the alternating tritone becomes a reminiscence motive, recalled later in Act II, when Godunov reports seeing visions of the slain Dmitri. In this way the composer links the tsar's illicit accession to power with the murder of his predecessor's heir. Throughout *Boris* Musorgsky avails himself freely of a variety of scales and harmonizations, intermixing them according to the dramatic needs of the moment in ways that encouraged other composers to expand their vocabulary beyond the limitations of common-practice tonality.

The second salient element of the Coronation Scene appears in its chorus taken from the traditional Russian folk song "Slava!"

**Excerpt of the Opening Chorus from the
Coronation Scene in Musorgsky's *Boris Godunov***

Ush kak na nyebye solntsu krasnomu, slava, slava!	Like the bright sun in the sky, Glory, Glory!
Ush i slava na Rusi tsaryu Borisu! Slava!	Is the glory of Russia's Tsar Boris! Glory!

This song, Richard Taruskin explains, originated in yuletide as an accompaniment to fortune-telling for the coming year (thus the refrain "Glory!" or "Glorious!"). It made its way into the earliest collection of Russian folk songs assembled by Nikolay Alexandrovich Lvov and Johann Gottfried Pratsch (1790).

---

*The italicized pitches from the collection do not appear in this passage.

EXAMPLE 7.1   Excerpt from beginning of the Coronation Scene in Musorgsky's *Boris Godunov*

Beethoven took "Slava!" from this collection for use in the *Razumovsky* quartet, op. 59, no. 2. And other composers in the early nineteenth century incorporated the song in their operas, notably for extolling the nobility. In this sense, it comments ironically in *Boris* as a hymn (see Example 7.2) praising a man who has usurped the throne by violent means. Musorgsky plays with the tune and develops it beyond its simple boundaries, feeling free to adapt folk material to suit his artistic ends. In fact, Musorgsky created much of the folkish-sounding material in *Boris* from partial or whole cloth. Authentic tunes appear rarely, though the composer included several in the Kromy Forest scene at the end of

EXAMPLE 7.2   Beginning of folk song "Slava!" from the Coronation Scene in Musorgsky's
Boris Godunov

his 1872 revision. Whether authentic or manufactured, however, folk or folklike material served the ends of musical nationalism.

The third element of the Coronation Scene lending *Boris Godunov* its distinctive flavor is the tsar's monologue at the heart of the tableau.

**Boris's Monologue from the
Coronation Scene in Musorgsky's *Boris Godunov***

Skorbit dusha!	My heart is heavy!
Kakoy-to strakh nevolni	Strange, dark forebodings
zloveshchim pryedchuvstviyem	and evil presentiments
skoval mnye syerdtse.	oppress my spirit.
O, pravyednik, o, moy otyets erzshavni!	Oh, Merciful One, oh, my Almighty Father!
Vozri s nyebyes na slyozi gryeshnikh slug	Look down from heaven on the tears of Thy sinful servant,
i nisposhli ti mne svyashchennoye vlast blagoslovyenye.	and send down Thy blessing upon my reign.
Da budu blag i pravyedyem kak ti,	May I be just and merciful as Thou,
da v slavye pravlyu moy narod.	and in glory rule over my people.
Tyepyer poklonimsya pochiyushchim vlastitelyam Rusi.	Now let us go kneel before the tombs of Russia's former rulers.
A tam szivat narod na pir,	Then the people are summoned to a feast,
vsyekh, ot boyar do nishchyevo slyeptsa,	all, from the nobles to the blind beggars,
vsyem volni vokhod,	all are invited,
vsye gosti dorogiye.	all as honored guests.

The passage begins naturalistically with declamation, moves in its second section ("Oh, Merciful One . . .") to something slightly more lyrical, and then to full-blown arioso in its third section ("Now let us go . . ."). Naturalistic setting of speech carries with it nationalist overtones: Musorgsky meant to capture the peculiar accents and rhythms of Russian prose, stylized for dramatic presentation, to be sure. Act I, scene 1, between the monks Pimen and Grigory, falls mostly in this naturalistic style, which has its own distinctive aesthetic attractions. With its many consonants, Russian would seem to make a poor singing language, but quite the opposite is true: Its inflections form a rich and beautiful sonic pattern.

The arioso that marks much of Boris's part often places musical values on a par with speech accent, and these passages are shot through with reminiscence motives, either in the orchestra or in the voice line itself. Before Boris begins singing his monologue in the Coronation Scene, we hear a single melodic line, played first by woodwinds, associated with Boris's fear and "dark forebodings." It returns to preface these same sentiments, to take just one example, for Boris's monologue in Act II, where the guilty tsar confesses his fears to his son.

Some scholars have designated *Boris Godunov* a realistic opera, but it lies far from the aesthetic that presents the life of working-class folk or peasants. Musorgsky gives us grand opera in the tradition of Verdi's *Don Carlos*, in which history consists of the deeds of great rulers. We can only lament the lack of a faithful performing edition. More recent "original" versions unfortunately conflate the 1869 score with the 1872 revision. The Rimsky-Korsakov version, which displayed *Boris* to the West for almost sixty years from its publication in 1908, comes closest to the 1872 version but reorchestrates extensively, reworks voice-leadings, extends the material of the Coronation Scene, and reverses the order of the two scenes in Act IV. Rimsky had a certain feeling for the music of his erstwhile roommate, and his version has much to be said for it. But *Boris* should also be available in its original 1872 form, which speaks most clearly of its composer's musical nationalism.

A similar fate has befallen Musorgsky's other well-known piece, *Pictures at an Exhibition,* which modern audiences know best in Ravel's orchestration based on Rimsky-Korsakov's edition. As admirable as this version may be, it disguises something of the tradition in which *Pictures* falls, that is, the genre of the virtuosic piano miniature. The influence of Schumann and even more of Liszt makes itself felt in these short, interconnected pieces that commemorate the "characteristic" art of Victor Hartmann. The composer had met Hartmann first in 1870, and the architect became an admirer and confidant. When Hartmann died suddenly in 1873, Musorgsky grieved deeply, and an exhibition of his drawings in February 1874 prompted the composition of this musical tombeau. Hartmann believed that Russian architecture should draw its inspiration from folk designs, though he was far from a "realist." In fact, Musorgsky seized on some of his more fantastic drawings for *Pictures,* including a clock in the shape of Baba Yaga's hut and a city gate for Kiev in the form of a Russian war helmet.

"Characteristic" patterns mark Musorgsky's music from the very opening of the piece, which begins with a "Promenade" featuring alternating metrical groupings of five and six beats together with a pentatonic melody (Example 7.3). The five-beat meter invokes the pentasyllabic verse of Russian wedding songs, which were regarded by some nineteenth-century Russian ethnographers as "the most ancient and most indigenous of all folk poetic genres" (Taruskin observes). Other writers notice the similarities of the melody in the "Promenade" to "Slava," seen earlier in the Coronation Scene of *Boris Godunov.* Russian folk song does not generally feature pentatonic scales, but then, Musorgsky aimed to create the perception of local color, and for this he often used emblems of what *sounded* folklike to more cultivated listeners. In fact, no writer has found authentic folk material in *Pictures,* for all its highly original and distinctive writing.

EXAMPLE 7.3   Opening of "Promenade" from Musorgsky's *Pictures at an Exhibition*

Allegro giusto, nel modo russico, senza allegrezza, ma poco sostenuto

Some of the other "characteristic" emblems in *Pictures at an Exhibition* include the use of drones ("Il vecchio castello"), ostinati ("Bydlo"), irregular harmonic progressions, shifting modes, and suggestions of heterophonic texture (in which no one part in a harmonized setting carries *the* principal melody). The "Promenade" exhibits some features of changing mode and heterophony, as do certain passages in "Catacombae." The chorale-like passage in "The Knight's Gate" (changed in some editions to "The Great Gate") means to invoke Russian sacred music in its irregular phrasing and block chordal texture, though this reflects the practice of hymnody sanctioned in the nineteenth century by the Imperial Chapel, not the practice of ancient Orthodox chant.

Above all, *Pictures* is marked by a pragmatic empiricism that permitted Musorgsky to use any necessary means in evoking the image at hand. The composer employs no invariable tonal system, or scale, or mode, but selects whatever pitches summon association. Some of these sounds may indulge imitation (the rumbling of the oxcart in "Bydlo"); some indulge suggestion (the frenetic melody of "The Ballet of the Unhatched Chicks"), and some association (the augmented seconds in " 'Samuel Goldenberg' and 'Schmuÿle' "); others rely on simple assertion (the abrupt leaps that serve to astonish at the beginning of "The Hut on Hen's Legs"). Musorgsky could not have proceeded in this way had he received a standard conservatory training. And thus the importance of his connection to the *kuchkist* circle that cultivated an identity apart from the mainstream of western European art. His influence on later composers was immense, even on an American such as Aaron Copland expounding on the roots of *Our New Music* (1968):

> Modest Musorgsky, creator of *Boris* and the most important member of the Russian Five, is the archetype of the pioneer in music. Living in an atmosphere saturated with Italian and German music, he nevertheless was able to extricate himself from the conventions and prejudices of the time.

Rimsky-Korsakov

If Copland gives the remaining members of Balakirev's circle less credit than Musorgsky as "pioneers," we should remember that without the good offices of Nicolay Rimsky-Korsakov (1844–1908), his former roommate's music would have taken much longer to gain public notice. But Rimsky was more than a mere musical executor; he was an accomplished composer and teacher in his own right. He came from a family distinguished in the civil and military service. His father was a provincial governor, and his much older brother became director of the College of Naval Cadets in St. Petersburg just a few months before Nicolay Andreyevich enrolled at age twelve. He had taken piano lessons from the age of six, and these continued while he studied to become a naval officer. While in the Russian capital, he availed himself of its concert life, attending both opera and orchestra performances. In 1861 he met Balakirev, Cui, and Musorgsky, and the older men encouraged his bent toward composition. Though he wished to leave the navy for a career in music, Rimsky served on a sailing vessel as a midshipman for over two years before returning in 1865 to St. Petersburg. There Balakirev took him in hand, developing the young naval officer's talent for orchestration and conducting his works in concerts at the Free School of Music.

   Toward the end of the 1860s Rimsky-Korsakov turned his attention increasingly to music and was deeply impressed by Berlioz's 1868 concert in St. Petersburg (with the *Symphonie fantastique* and *Harold in Italy* on the program). The young naval officer began an ambitious number of works, including a programmatic symphony on oriental themes and an opera, *The Maid of Pskov*. In 1869 Balakirev entrusted him with completing the orchestration of Dargomïzhsky's *The Stone Guest,* and for a brief period in 1871–72 Rimsky shared quarters with Musorgsky while the latter was revising *Boris Godunov.*

   The fateful turning point for Rimsky-Korsakov came in June 1871, when the director of the St. Petersburg Conservatory appointed him a professor of composition and orchestration. He undertook autodidactic study of harmony from Tchaikovsky's textbook and counterpoint from texts by Cherubini and Bellermann. In 1873 he resigned his naval commission, only to assume a civil post as Inspector of Naval Bands. Gradually he became an entrenched academic, composing in the more traditional genres, including the string quartet and the symphony. After the death of Musorgsky in 1881, Rimsky-Korsakov busied himself with preparing his friend's manuscripts for publication. If he concerned himself in the 1880s mostly with the composition of instrumental music, he ended his career with a series of operas, among them *Mlada* (1891), *The Tsar's Bride* (1899), *The Tale of Tsar Saltan* (1901), and *The Golden Cockerel* (1908). He also exerted significant influence as a teacher, numbering Stravinsky and Prokofiev among his pupils.

Although Rimsky-Korsakov must count among the major composers of Russian opera, the West knows him better in the concert hall from works such as *The Russian Easter Overture* and *Scheherazade*. This latter work is particularly emblematic of Russian "orientalism," which became almost synonymous with Russian exoticism through the offices of Sergey Diaghilev. He presented a choreographed version of *Scheherazade* as part of the 1910 Ballets Russes season in Paris, and it has enjoyed currency in orchestral repertory ever since.

Significantly, Rimsky-Korsakov was moved to compose *Scheherazade* while orchestrating another piece of Russian orientalism:

> In the middle of the winter [1888], engrossed as I was in my work on *Prince Igor* [by Borodin], I conceived the idea of writing an orchestral composition on the subject of certain episodes from *Scheherazada*. . . . I had in view the creation of an orchestral suite in four movements, closely knit by the community of its themes and motives, yet presenting, as it were, a kaleidoscope of fairy-tale images and designs of Oriental character. . . .

In its structure *Scheherazade* has much in common with Berlioz's programmatic symphony-cum-concerto, *Harold in Italy*, which had made such a large impression on the young Rimsky-Korsakov. Although technically a four-movement symphony, *Scheherazade* features an obbligato violin solo representing the voice of the title character. The composer explicitly associates the opening unison phrase with Sultan Shakhriar, the "stern spouse" to whom Scheherazade tells her stories every night to delay her execution. The four movements, then, represent four of her "tales," bearing the titles "The Sea and Sinbad's Ship," "The Story of the Kalender Prince," "The Young Prince and the Young Princess," and "The Festival in Baghdad." But as in the case of program music in this vein, the piece has an "absolute" side as well, according to Rimsky:

> Originally, I had even intended to label Movement I of *Scheherazada* Prelude; II, Ballade; III, Adagio; and IV, Finale; but on seeking the advice of [Anatoly Konstantinovich] Lyadov and others I did not do so. My aversion for seeking too definite a program in my composition led me subsequently (in the new edition) to do away with even those hints of it which had lain in the headings of each movement. . . .

The first movement takes the sonata form of a "short" overture (which omits the development section; see Table 3.1) for its basis. The second movement stands in place of the scherzo, replete with trio. The third, slow movement follows a typical *AB AB* plan, and the last movement is the "finale as summary," recalling the themes of the earlier movements in the grand symphonic tradition that includes *Harold,* among many other pieces. The themes of Scheherazade and the Sultan recycle throughout.

It is the "oriental" stylistic aura surrounding *Scheherazade,* more than its form, however, that provides its distinctiveness. Orientalism in Russian music came to be represented by a complex of features initially expressed in a series of vocal pieces, most notably Glinka's opera *Ruslan and Lyudmila* and significantly in Borodin's *Prince Igor,* the opera Rimsky-Korsakov was orchestrating when he conceived *Scheherazade.* The features include melismatic text setting, chromatic passing and neighbor tones, and especially a tendency to raised "fifths and flatted sixths" that lend an uncertain major-minor modal quality to the music. Richard Taruskin links all these traits to fantasies of an alluring "oriental" sexual licentiousness. Enter Scheherazade, seductress of the harem, whose theme as played by the solo violin comes as close to implying vocal melismas as instrumental music can suggest. "Slinky" oriental chromaticism yielding uncertain mode weaves itself throughout the whole composition, with a classic example appearing in the theme of the "Young Prince" at the opening of the third movement (Example 7.4). Here we have "melismatic" embellishments in measure 3, raised fifth scale degree in measure 5 turning to lowered sixth scale degree in measure 7, combined with ever present open fifths in the lowest bass voices that

EXAMPLE 7.4   Beginning of the third movement of Rimsky-Korsakov's *Scheherazade*

connote folk or "primitive" music throughout the classical canon. The composer adds these "oriental" features to other unusual sonorities, such as the octatonicism that threads its way through the second movement of the piece. The West came to think of Russia as a land of pagan barbarism closely associated with the musical exoticism that marks all of Rimsky-Korsakov's *Scheherazade*. Rimsky's pupil Stravinsky would mine precisely this vein of fairy-tale primitivism when he made his debut in Paris with *The Firebird* during the same 1910 season that featured his late mentor's piece.

Tchaikovsky

Pyotr Il'yich Tchaikovsky (1840–93) rarely indulged the orientalism that marked Rimsky-Korsakov's works, and he had much more formal training as a musician than any of Balakirev's group. But Tchaikovsky was every bit as Russian a composer as any of the "mighty little group"; he simply proceeded from a more cosmopolitan national tradition.

Tchaikovsky came from a middle-class family, the son of a metallurgical engineer and manager. His father switched jobs frequently, but the young Pyotr gained some measure of stability by attending first the Schmelling School in St. Petersburg and then, from the age of ten to the age of nineteen, the School for Jurisprudence there. He studied piano all the while, and even tried his hand at composition, but when he graduated in May 1859, he took a civil-service position in the Ministry of Justice and put aside his desire to become a professional musician. He still found time, however, to take classes in thorough bass and composition at the Russian Musical Society, which became the St. Petersburg Conservatory in 1862 under the leadership of Anton Rubinstein.

In 1863 Tchaikovsky resigned his position at the Ministry of Justice to pursue study at the conservatory full-time. He graduated in 1865 with a silver medal in composition, and he immediately assumed a post teaching harmony at the Russian Musical Society in Moscow, which in turn became the Moscow Conservatory in 1866 under the direction of Rubinstein's brother, Nicolay. During Tchaikovsky's tenure there he composed his First Symphony, op. 13, which included some Russian folk songs as themes; he began an opera, *Voyevoda;* and he wrote a harmony textbook.

In 1868 Balakirev drew Tchaikovsky into his circle, influencing him to compose the concert overture *Romeo and Juliet* and also prompting a period of intense interest in folk material on the younger man's part. In the following years Tchaikovsky composed settings for a group of Russian folks songs; a Second Symphony, op. 17 (1872), based on Ukrainian folk songs; and his first complete opera, set amid the political upheaval surrounding Peter the Great, *The Oprichnik* (1872). Two string quartets and yet another opera, *Vakula the Smith* (1874), followed, as well as a host of other pieces. Though Tchaikovsky lost contact with Balakirev in 1872, his brush with the kuchkists left a lasting impression. Many of his subsequent pieces bear the imprint of Russian folk song.

The year 1874 marks the beginning of Tchaikovsky's maturity as an artist in many ways. It began with the First Piano Concerto, op. 23 (1875), rejected as unplayable by Nicolay Rubinstein, but then adopted wholeheartedly by Hans von Bülow, who premiered it in Boston. The exquisitely beautiful *Variations on a Rococo Theme* for cello and orchestra, op. 33 (1876), followed, and the milestone of classical ballet, *Swan Lake,* op. 20 (1876). Tchaikovsky displayed an immense range of talent across many genres with a Fourth Symphony, op. 36 (1878), suites for orchestra, and two more operas, *Eugene Onegin* (1878) and *The Maid of Orleans* (1879). His wide-ranging output began to gain him international recognition as Russia's greatest composer, in certain ways the counterpart of Brahms (whose birthday, May 7, he shared coincidentally). Eventually he would be recognized by the tsar with the Order of St. Vladimir (1884) and a permanent stipend, at the same time receiving support from a wealthy patroness, Nadezhda von Meck.

Although his professional life flourished, however, Tchaikovsky lived a stormy and often unhappy personal life. He agonized over his homosexuality, and when an admirer, Antonina Milyukova, wrote him with a declaration of love and threatened suicide if he would not see her, he capitulated. In July 1877 he married Antonina, a match so unsuitable that the composer had a complete emotional collapse. His brother Anatoly escorted him on a lengthy tour of Switzerland, France, and Italy, but when he returned, his wife refused to dissolve their relationship. Not until 1881 would Tchaikovsky secure a divorce, and the emotional turmoil of the marriage took its toll on the quality and the quantity of his work.

Beginning in 1884, however, Tchaikovsky regained some of his confidence, settling outside Moscow for the rest of his life. He renewed contact with Balakirev and began work on his greatest pieces. These include *The Sleeping Beauty* (a ballet; op. 66; 1889), *The Queen of Spades* (an opera; op. 68; 1890), the Fifth and Sixth Symphonies (opp. 64 and 74; 1888 and 1893, respectively), *The Nutcracker* (op. 71; 1892), and a host of other pieces. In 1887 he undertook his first foreign tour as a conductor, directing his own works in Leipzig, Berlin, Hamburg, London, and Paris and meeting composers such as Brahms and Grieg. An American tour followed in 1891, when Tchaikovsky was guest of honor at the inaugural concert of Carnegie Hall. The next year he was elected a corresponding member of the French Academy and also awarded an honorary doctorate at Cambridge in 1893.

Though a number of lurid stories surrounding Tchaikovsky's death have made their way into the scholarly literature, there seems to be little basis for thinking that he committed suicide. Family and friends around him during his last days witnessed the composer in a good mood with many plans for the future. He came down with cholera while visiting St. Petersburg. But how precisely he contracted the disease remains a matter of conjecture (most probably from poor sanitation at a restaurant). His Sixth Symphony served as memorial, conducted by Edward Nápravnik at a St. Petersburg hall draped in black, with a bust of the composer mounted on the stage. This last gloomy composition does not mean, however, that the composer met an untoward fate.

Tchaikovsky inclined very much as a composer to neoclassicism. Some of his earliest musical impressions came from an orchestrion (an elaborate sort of music box) in his family's home that played excerpts from Mozart's *Don Giovanni.* Tchaikovsky's veneration of music history runs as a theme throughout his life, and manifests itself audibly in pieces such as his *Variations on a Rococo Theme,* op. 33, for solo cello and orchestra (1876); his First Suite, invoking Bach (op. 43; 1879); and his Fourth Suite, op. 61, based on pieces by Mozart (1887). This affinity for the techniques and styles of earlier music has much to do with the traditional phrase structure, extraordinarily controlled counterpoint, harmonic incisiveness, and formal clarity of all Tchaikovsky's works. His carefully crafted phrases and thorough command of harmony in particular account for his success in ballet, where *Swan Lake, The Sleeping Beauty,* and *The Nutcracker* still constitute the benchmark for classical dance.

Nowhere is Tchaikovsky's command of music for the dance so clear as in *The Sleeping Beauty,* arguably his finest ballet and one of his favorites among his own works. The director of the Imperial Theaters, Ivan Alexandrovich Vsevolozhsky, commissioned the work and wrote the scenario based on a fairy tale by Perrault. As the story unfolds, the birth of the young princess Aurora occasions a celebration from which the evil fairy Carabosse is inadvertently excluded. She appears anyhow, enraged at this slight, and condemns the child to eternal sleep the first time she pricks her finger, but the Lilac Fairy alters the spell so that her sleep will last only until a prince comes to kiss her on the brow and to take her for his bride (Prologue). The ensuing episodes, translated into a set of dances by Marius Petipa, include the princess's coming of age and the prick of the needle (both in Act I), the arrival of the prince and reawakening after one hundred years (Act II), and the celebration of the young couple's union (Act III).

Tchaikovsky bound this sequence of events together by means of extensive thematic and tonal interconnections in order to overcome the episodic nature inherent in ballet. The composer relates the music of the evil Carabosse (Example 7.5a) at the beginning of the Prologue, for example, to the "dream music" (b) that descends on the royal court as it falls dormant. But Tchaikovsky recasts Carabosse's motive of scalar chromatic ascent by reharmonizing it. The bass in the "dream music" now descends primarily by thirds to reflect the Lilac Fairy's magic transformation of Carabosse's curse into a more beneficent and sublime enchantment. The two interrelated motives recur in various guises throughout the ballet, reinforced by a nexus of keys revolving around E major,

EXAMPLE 7.5   Tchaikovsky's *Sleeping Beauty:* (a) Opening of the Prologue; (b) "Dream Music" from Act I, motive taken from opening of the Prologue

E minor, and C major-minor. Many other melodies add to the interconnected web of motives and keys.

Just as Tchaikovsky articulated the interrelated action of *The Sleeping Beauty* by means of musical structure, so his highly defined phrases provided an ideal platform for the dance. In the "Pas d'Action," no. 8 in Act I, for example, the opening flourish affords the dancers (four suitors of Princess Aurora in this case) time to come forward and assume their initial positions on stage. The heart of the dance, in which each suitor admires a medallion of the princess, begins at the *adagio maestoso* in 12/8 time (Example 7.6). The composer first introduces a layer of accompaniment to establish the meter, and he then floats the melody over this substrate as a Beethovenian Satz to lend the feeling of what Petipa describes as "tender agitation" to the music. Measure 2 of Example 7.6 contains the first cell, measure 3 reverses melodic direction, and measures 4

EXAMPLE 7.6   Pas d'Action, no. 8 from Act I of Tchaikovsky's *Sleeping Beauty*

through 6 develop fragments of the two cells in ever accelerating motion. It seems uncanny that so unbalanced a phrase construction could result in such poise. But Tchaikovsky somehow managed to satisfy the need for symmetry with his six-measure phrases, at the same time producing the mood Petipa required. Equally uncanny is the composer's ability to turn a simple arpeggiated accompaniment into counterpoint by means of orchestration, the melody in the upper strings added on top of the woodwind choir's slower figuration. Stravinsky certainly came to know and employ this kind of layered, additive structure in his ballets twenty years later.

Lest we believe that *The Sleeping Beauty* lacks distinctive national flavor, we can always turn to the spirited "Polacca" in Act III. This number underlies a "Procession of Fairy Tales" in which figures from various Perrault stories (Pussin-Boots, Goldilocks, Little Red Riding Hood, and so forth) make their entrance to provide entertainment for the reawakened court. But the fantastic nature of the characters appearing on stage cannot obscure the associations of the polonaise, which "often replaced the march where a specific overtone of official pomp was wanted," as Taruskin observes. "Tchaikovsky's 'imperial' style was virtually defined by the polonaise." What could be more Russian, then, than this "characteristic" dance accompanying a fairy-tale court's celebration, commissioned by the Director of the Imperial Theaters for the entertainment of Alexander III himself. The composer was miffed when he heard the tsar murmur faint praise of *The Sleeping Beauty* after attending its dress rehearsal. But imperial poor taste cannot diminish the nationalistic splendor of Tchaikovsky's polonaise or the faultless periodic structure and brilliant instrumentation that render it so apt to the dance. *The Sleeping Beauty* is a masterpiece of dramatic cohesion, piquant characterization, and fitting musical stagecraft throughout.

Tchaikovsky's extraordinary compositional technique comes particularly to the fore in his symphonies. Though the first three have much to recommend them, the composer attains complete mastery in the last three. The Fourth Symphony includes Russian folk material, whole-tone scales, octatonic harmonies, novel orchestral effects, and a great deal of rhythmic ambiguity, especially in the first movement. The Fifth Symphony features more pervasive thematic cyclicity than the Fourth and the same progression from minor mode at the beginning to triumphant major mode in the finale. The Sixth Symphony, however, presents Tchaikovsky's most original orchestral thoughts, and it ranks as one of the late nineteenth century's greatest musical works.

By the end of the century composers had begun to search for an alternative to the plot of triumph over struggle inherited from Beethoven's Fifth and Ninth Symphonies. Tchaikovsky's answer was a tragic symphony beginning with a first movement in minor mode, followed by two buoyant inner movements, dying away in a pessimistic finale. Tchaikovsky provided coherence among the movements by means of understated thematic relationships. He reworks the ascending scalar motive of the first movement's main theme as the initial "waltz" in the second movement and also as the beginning episode of the third movement. The first movement's descending second theme transforms into the minor-mode "trio" of the second movement, which in turn generates the material for the slow finale.

Throughout these thematic manipulations Tchaikovsky retains absolute command of structure. The first movement displays all the plasticity of late-nineteenth-century sonata form (Table 7.1). The composer reuses material from his second theme in the closing area to balance the weight of the main theme and a first transition that features melodic material of its own. Because he focuses so heavily on the main theme in the development, Tchaikovsky dispenses with its return later. Instead, he limits the recapitulation to the closing area, which rehearses the secondary thematic material. By the end of the century sonata

TABLE 7.1   Schematic for Tchaikovsky, op. 74, mvt. I

SECTION	SUBSECTION	KEY	MEASURES
Introduction		b: i	1–18
Exposition			
	Mth	i	19–29
	trans.	i→III	30–88
	Sth	III	89–100
	trans.	x	101–129
	Closing	III	130–160
Development		X	
	bridge		161–170
	core		
	model 1 (mth)		171–174
	sequence		175–178
	sequence		179–182
	frag. (3×2)		183–189
	dissolution		190–201
	model 2		202–205
	frag. (2×2)		206–209
	dissolution		210–213
	model 3		214–217
	repeat		215–218
	dissolution		219–230
	model 4 (mth)		231–236
	frag.		237–238
	dissolution		239–244
	varied		245–248
	frag. (5×2)		249–258
	dissolution		259–262
	frag. (2×2)		263–266
	retran.	V pedal	267–304
Recapitulation			
	Closing	I	305–334
Coda		I	335–354

forms increasingly followed a three-part dramatic model: Conflict of themes in the exposition built to a crisis in the development and arrived at a denouement (or "winding down") in the recapitulation. Tchaikovsky emphasizes the central crisis in this tumultuous movement and abbreviates the denouement in keeping with his tragic theme.

The tensions of sonata form suit the composer's antitriumphant finale perfectly. Although this movement lacks a true development section (see Table 7.2),

TABLE 7.2 Schematic for Tchaikovsky, op. 74, mvt. VI

SECTION	*SUBSECTION*	*KEY*	*MEASURES*
Exposition			
	Mth	b: i	1–18
	trans.	i–III	19–38
	Sth	III	39–70
Bridge		III–i	71–89
Recapitulation			
	Mth	i	90–102
	trans.	i–i	103–147
	Sth	i	148–163
	codetta	i	164–171

the composer explores the qualities of his material through variation. The descending scalar motives of the main theme appear fragmented over prominent appoggiaturas in the secondary theme. The bridge between exposition and recapitulation also fragments the secondary theme very slightly at the end, and the transition in the recapitulation displays the transformation of main thematic motives into the motives of the second theme. What serves Tchaikovsky best in this movement, however, is the classic tonal plan of a minor-key sonata form, with the transposition of the secondary theme from major to minor for the recapitulation. For at least a century it had been customary in minor-mode symphonies to end in a major tonic, but Tchaikovsky reverses the trope, converting triumph into tragedy.

Combined with its neoclassical heritage, the Sixth Symphony displays prominent "Russian" traits. The 5/4 "waltz" of the second movement invokes the pentasyllabic meters of Russian folk song (see Example 7.3 and attendant discussion). And in one of the most intriguing displays of heterophony ever crafted, the composer apportions the opening phrase of the finale's main theme *between* the first and second violins (see Example 7.7), making it literally impossible to determine which part carries the melody. This novel orchestration also represents a sonic tour de force: When the symphony is played by an orchestra deployed in customary nineteenth-century array, the first and second violins on opposite sides of the podium yield an antiphonal effect at the beginning of the main theme.

We cannot view the entire range of Tchaikovsky's talent here, encompassing as it does chamber music, song, opera, ballet, concerti, and symphonic music. Suffice it to say that he was one of the nineteenth century's greatest composers, one whose national roots remain evident throughout his works.

EXAMPLE 7.7   Heterophony in the first and second violins at the beginning of the fourth movement of Tchaikovsky's Sixth Symphony

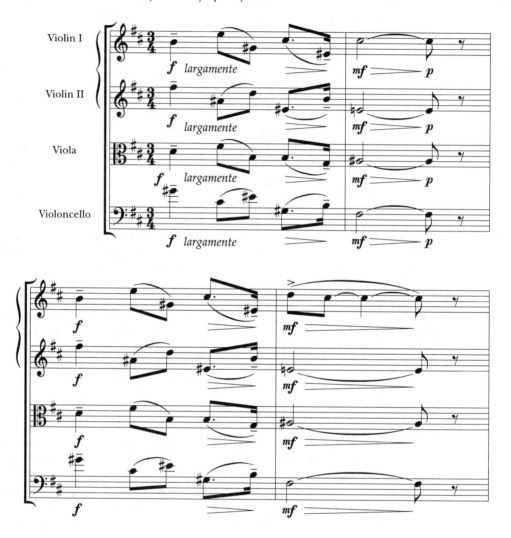

CENTRAL EUROPE AND SCANDINAVIA

Czech Music

During the nineteenth century much of central Europe fell under the dominion of the Hapsburg monarchy, which reigned over a relatively decentralized empire extending from present-day Bosnia in the south to parts of present-day

Poland in the north. The many ethnic groups under Hapsburg rule tended to move away from one another by an almost centripetal force. The German-speaking areas no less than the Poles, Czechs, Slovaks, Hungarians, Serbians, and many others strained against the concept of a multinational polity governed by a hereditary aristocracy and constitutional monarch centered in Vienna.

Prague and the ethnically Czech areas surrounding it reflected the peculiar cultural paradoxes of the Hapsburg Empire, where groups found their identity by pulling against a German culture that nonetheless formed one of the central threads of intellectual life. This ancient Czech city, located only a few hundred miles from Vienna, conducted much of its daily life in German. And the most famous Czech composers of the nineteenth century, Smetana and Dvořák, wrote pieces located firmly in the German musical tradition, even as they invested them with aspects of local color.

Smetana

Bedřich Smetana (1824–84) typifies the combination of German education and nationalist sentiment common to many Czech artists. Born in eastern Bohemia to a German-speaking father who worked as a master brewer in the service of several noblemen, Bedřich studied piano as a youth but gave up music for a classical education. Eventually he made his way to the Academic Gymnasium in Prague, where he heard a concert by Franz Liszt that persuaded him to become a musician. After completing his academic education in Pilzen, he returned to Prague in 1843 as a piano teacher, and there he studied harmony, counterpoint, and composition with Josef Proksch.

Smetana spent much of his early career teaching piano to the children of the nobility and heading a music institute he had founded. The Prague Revolution of June 1848 moved him to compose nationalistic music, though at this time he still spoke German exclusively. Disappointed in the failure of political liberalization and in the poor financial performance of his music school, he eventually took a position teaching piano in Göteborg, Sweden, where he lived from 1856 to 1861. He also conducted several choral societies there.

In 1861 Smetana returned to Prague, spurred in part by a competition to compose a Czech national opera. This would mark the beginning of his most productive period, during which he composed no fewer than eight operas to Czech libretti, including *The Bartered Bride* (final version, 1866) and *Dalibor* (1868). He also composed a number of piano pieces, songs, and orchestral works, including the cycle of six nationalistic tone poems entitled *Má vlast (My Fatherland;* 1874–81). For much of this period Smetana held a position as principal conductor at the Provisional Theater in Prague.

The last decade of Smetana's life took a tragic turn. He contracted syphilis and was forced to give up his conducting position and eventually his residence in Prague. Living with his married daughter and suffering from deafness, he still managed to compose, most notably a series of string quartets and a piano trio. Eventually the progressive neurological symptoms of his disease overcame him, and he died in an asylum for the mentally ill in 1884.

Smetana may be best known in his own country as the composer of nationalistic operas, but in the rest of the world his instrumental music receives more exposure, especially *Vltava* (or *The Moldau)* from *My Fatherland.* Liszt and the New German School clearly influenced Smetana in composing this programmatic piece that takes a journey along the Moldau River for its subject matter. The various scenes unfold rather like the segments of a potpourri overture: first "the sources of the Moldau," beginning with a stereotypical "wave figure" in a single flute, adding a second "source" in the clarinet, and then forming a broad melodic stream with the entry of the strings in measure 40. The next scene features a "forest hunt," with the usual horn figures, followed by a "wedding celebration in the country," featuring a polka, an ethereal "elfin dance in the moonlight," and a stormy episode about "the rapids at St. John." The tone poem returns to the minor-mode theme of the river itself (m. 333) and ends finally in a noble coda. Though the melody associated with the river and the wedding polka may imitate folk music, most of the episodes draw on the repertory of conventions (wave figures, hunting motifs, and so forth) developed in German music before midcentury. But Smetana had a more intricate frame of nationalistic reference in mind. The first tone poem of *My Fatherland,* entitled *Vyšehrad* after the ancient seat of the Moravian empire, takes themes from Smetana's opera *Libuše* about a princess of the medieval Czech dynasty. These themes appear again in the coda of *The Moldau* as the river moves past the ruins of the Vyšehrad castle (Example 7.8). Of course, this extended frame of reference will be obscure to most listeners, for *Libuše* is rarely performed. And orchestras seldom play *The Moldau* in the context of the rest of *My Fatherland* to complete the link. Smetana was an important composer in the history of nineteenth-century Czech music, but he had his greatest impact locally.

Dvořák

It remained for Smetana's successor, Antonín Dvořák (1841–1904), to place his homeland securely on the international musical stage. Dvořák, unlike Smetana, came from a Czech-speaking family. He gained his initial background in music from playing violin in his father's inn, in local churches, and in the village band of the small northwestern Czech town where he was born. When Dvořák was thirteen his father sent him to Zlonice to learn the family trade of meat butchering, and there Antonín took lessons in violin, viola, piano, organ, and keyboard harmony with a German teacher who was also the church organist. He would later immerse himself in German for a year at a private school in northern Bohemia, and he continued his study of organ and harmony.

Eventually the young Dvořák chose to follow the career of a church musician, and he enrolled in the Prague Organ School in 1857. He also continued to

EXAMPLE 7.8   "Vyšehrad Motive" from the end of Smetana's *Moldau*

play viola, and after graduation in 1859 he joined a small orchestra that hired out for restaurants and balls. In 1862 this ensemble became the nucleus of the Provisional Theater Orchestra under the direction of J. N. Maýr and later of Smetana. Serving as principal violist in the orchestra brought Dvořák into contact with a great deal of opera and prompted him to begin serious composition of both instrumental and vocal music, including two symphonies, a group of songs, chamber music, and two nationalistic operas.

In 1871 Dvořák quit his orchestra position to devote more time to composition, and he supported himself during this period mainly by teaching piano and singing. In 1874 he submitted fifteen of his compositions for an Austrian State Stipend designed to support young artists. The committee, which included Hanslick and Brahms, awarded him the prize, and more important, Brahms began to take an active interest in the young composer's career. He recommended Dvořák to the Bonn publisher Simrock, who commissioned the first set of *Slavonic Dances*, op. 46, for piano, four hands, which appeared in 1878. These, along with the publication of a string quartet, a string sextet, a piano trio, some *Slavonic Rhapsodies* for orchestra, and an assortment of songs, brought the composer to international prominence.

Throughout the 1880s Dvořák's international reputation grew, and his music received performances in Germany, France, England, and the United States. He continued to compose Czech national operas, turned down a commission from Vienna for a German opera, and toured widely conducting his orchestral music (especially in England) and playing his chamber music. The London Philharmonic Society commissioned his Seventh Symphony, op. 70, in D minor (1885); he composed more *Slavonic Dances* (op. 72), choral works, and a widely admired Violin Concerto, op. 53 (1883).

In early 1892 Mrs. Jeannette Thurber, wife of a wealthy American wholesale food merchant, brought Dvořák to New York as director of her National Conservatory of Music. He was then at the height of his fame, holder of the Austrian Order of the Iron Crown, a member of the Czech Academy of Sciences and Letters, and an honorary Doctor of Music at both Prague and Cambridge Universities. His stay in America, lasting three years, included the composition of the *New World* Symphony (op. 95; 1893), an *American* String Quartet (op. 97), more chamber music, and his Cello Concerto (op. 104; 1895). After the National Conservatory fell on hard times, he returned to Prague and a composition professorship at its conservatory. Though the pace of his composition fell off during his last decade, Dvořák continued his interest in Czech national opera especially, and in his final years he produced his best work for the stage, *Rusalka,* op. 114 (1900).

Dvořák's instrumental music had the largest role in spreading his fame, and it continues to feature prominently in the concert hall today. He was in many ways a "pan-nationalist," believing that all music should be imbued with national character, but not necessarily just the local color of the composer's own background. He drew on his Czech roots most frequently, of course, and we can see these clearly in pieces such as his *Slavonic Dances,* op. 46, for piano, four hands (later orchestrated by the composer). The composer rarely included authentic folk material in his melodies, preferring instead to rely on his own imitation of the popular style he had learned while playing in village bands during his youth. The first number in op. 46, for instance, replicates the rhythms of a *furiant,* a vigorous dance in triple meter that plays on rhythmic hemiola (three beats in the time of two: the opening sounds like a measure of 3/2 rather than two measures of 3/4; see Example 7.9). The last dance in the first set of *Slavonic Dances* also adopts the rhythms of the furiant, numbers 4 and 6 assume the patterns of a "neighbors' dance" (*sousedská*), and numbers 5 and 7 imitate a "jump dance" (*skočná*). Dvořák also borrows from other Slavic traditions, including the polka (a Polish dance; no. 3) and the *dumka* (a Ukrainian lament; no. 2). The idiosyncratic rhythms and quickly changing moods of the various dances lend them their national character, rather than any unusual scales or harmonies.

Dvořák sometimes relied on unevenness and irregularity to convey a "characteristic" message of nationalism. " 'Characteristic' meant idiosyncratic rather than general or typical, the exception rather than the rule, 'interesting' and

EXAMPLE 7.9   Opening "furiant" from Dvořák's first set of *Slavonic Dances,* op. 46

'striking' rather than 'nobly simple,' coloristic rather than statuesque," we will remember Carl Dahlhaus writing (see Chapter 1). Nowhere is this so evident in Dvořák's output as in his *Dumky* Trio, op. 90 (1891), which finds him in a pan-national mode. A *dumka* is a Ukrainian lament that moves quickly between tears and laughter (an idiosyncrasy of local color). Its imitation in op. 90 produces the unusual effect of exposing a slow theme in minor mode juxtaposed directly with the same material in a major-mode allegro (compare Example 7.10*a* and *b*). In other sections of the piece the composer reverses this process, but however he arranges the contrasting tempi and modes, the constant stopping and starting makes for a highly unusual effect and an idiosyncratic form.

When Dvořák arrived in New York, he immediately seized on American music as the source of inspiration. An interview for the *Chicago Tribune* (August 13, 1893) reports him saying:

> Every nation has its music. There is Italian, German, French, Bohemian, Russian; why not American music? The truth of this music depends upon its characteristics, its color. I do not mean to take these melodies . . . and work them out as themes; that is not my plan. But I study certain melodies until I become thoroughly imbued with their characteristics and am enabled to make a musical picture in keeping with and partaking of those characteristics.

We know that the composer heard some African American spirituals sung by one of his students, Harry T. Burleigh. Later, during a sojourn in Spillville, Iowa,

EXAMPLE 7.10   Dvořák's *Dumky* Trio, op. 90: (*a*) Phrase from the slow introduction to first movement; (*b*) Motive from slow introduction reconfigured in faster tempo later in the first movement

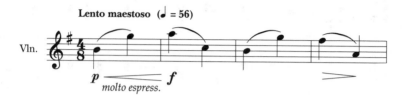

in the summer of 1893, he heard some music sung by American Indians (which tribe remains obscure), and he also obtained transcriptions of Indian songs. He came away with a curious impression of commonality:

> Since I have been in this country, I have been deeply interested in the national music of the Negroes and Indians. . . . I found that the music of the two races bore a remarkable similarity to the music of Scotland. In both there is a peculiar scale caused by the absence of the fourth and seventh, or leading tone. In both the minor scale has the seventh invariably a minor seventh, the fourth is included and the sixth omitted.

Whether spirituals and Indian songs held these features in common or not, Dvořák dutifully included them in his American pieces, the most famous of which is the *New World* Symphony. Stereotypical "tom-tom" motifs in conjunction with melodies leaping downward by fifths appear in the third movement, and the second movement's pentatonic English horn melody has often been taken for a spiritual (and used to appear under the title "Going Home"). In fact, the composer's own program for the second movement bore an Indian theme: "It is in reality a study or sketch for a longer work, either a cantata or opera which I purpose writing, and which will be based upon Longfellow's 'Hiawatha.'" But the authenticity of Dvořák's materials is beside the point. As a pan-nationalist he advocated art invoking either folk or popular material, and his music, Czech or "American," does just that.

German Music

Though we might tend to view the German-speaking parts of the Hapsburg Empire as part of the musical mainstream, politically these portions of the dual monarchy strained as much against the concept of multinational empire as the Slavic and Hungarian regions did. The "nation" of Austria came into existence only after the First World War; before that the German-speaking portions of Emperor Franz Josef's realm existed as separate principalities (upper Austria, lower Austria, Salzburg, Styria, and so forth) under the crown. Self-conscious pan-Germanism became an important cultural factor in the music of some composers living under Hapsburg rule.

The Strauss Family

The founder of the Strauss dynasty, Johann, Sr. (1804–49), came from a Jewish family of small-business owners in Vienna. Though he studied to become a bookkeeper, he soon evinced talent as a violinist and eventually studied theory with Ignaz von Seyfried, music director at the Theater an der Wien. Johann played in dance orchestras around the city, including those of Michael Pamer and Josef Lanner. But he soon formed his own orchestra and by the age of twenty-five was holding forth in the Sperl beer garden and dance hall. There he enchanted visitors ranging from Chopin to Wagner to Hans Christian Andersen with his music. In 1833 Strauss began taking his orchestra on tour abroad, where he won international recognition for the precision of his ensemble and the quality of his dances. In 1846 he was made Director of Music for Imperial Balls, for which he provided numerous compositions. His music proceeded from the tradition of light music (waltzes, *Ländler*, marches, and so forth) begun by Haydn, Mozart, Beethoven, and Schubert, with a healthy dash of elements from Austrian folk music for seasoning. Few of his dances retain currency today, but his *Radetzky March*, closely associated with the Hapsburg military, still appears as a regular feature of the Vienna Philharmonic's annual New Year's concert.

Johann Strauss, Jr. (1825–99), amplified the tradition begun by his father and achieved lasting international prominence as a composer of nationalistic Austrian music. His father had originally wanted his first son to become a banker, and to that end sent him to the distinguished Schottengymnasium to receive a classical education. But the younger Johann took violin lessons in secret, later studying theory and composition with Joseph Drechsler, choirmaster at St. Stephen's Cathedral and a theater composer. In 1844 Johann, Jr., set up as an orchestra director on his own, and he merged his orchestra with his father's in 1849 when the elder Strauss died.

The younger Strauss also became Director of Imperial Ball Music in time, and he eventually toured England and the United States (in 1872). His younger brothers, Josef (1827–70) and Eduard (1835–1916), joined him in the family business of composing and leading orchestras. Together they dominated the performance of dance music in Vienna during the last half of the nineteenth century. After Josef died, Johann gave direction of the Strauss orchestra over to Eduard and spent the rest of his life composing and touring as a conductor of his own music. Johann, Jr., produced upward of five hundred dances and a number of operettas, including the highly successful *Fledermaus* (*The Bat;* 1874) and *Zigeunerbaron* (*The Gypsy Baron;* 1885).

The music of Johann Strauss, Jr., invokes nationalism through a number of devices we have seen in other composers, partly by reference to traits from folk music, partly by a set of "characteristic" musical gestures. Many of the famous waltzes open with folklike sounds, such as the droning open fifths of *Morning Papers* (op. 279; 1864), *Tales of the Vienna Woods* (op. 325; 1868), *Du und Du* (op. 367; 1874; based on *Die Fledermaus*), and the *Treasure Waltzes* (op. 418; 1886; based on *Der Zigeunerbaron*). Pedal points can also suggest drones, as we find in the opening of *On the Beautiful Blue Danube* (op. 314; 1867) or *Roses from the South* (op. 388; 1880; based on *Das Spitzentuch der Königin*). Ostinati also fall into this family of folkish invocation, such as the one that opens the *Emperor Waltzes* (op. 437; 1889). In a piece such as *Tales of the Vienna Woods*, a multi-segmented composition portraying various local "stories," the rural scene evoked by folklike drones introduces material suggesting local color. The slow introduction in *Tales* features a cimbalom (a hammered dulcimer imported from Hungary) playing a *Ländler* (Example 7.11) that then becomes one of the ensuing waltzes. Other Strauss dances can feature imitations of Alpine yodeling or Austrian folk song.

In fact, the very titles of Strauss waltzes often evoke localities around Vienna or topics of the day. In a real sense the music of the Strauss family is so identified with Vienna and its surroundings, it has become an icon of nationalism itself. Hearing it played summons up German-speaking Austria at the end of the nineteenth century, a place that devoted itself heedlessly to its own local color as the Hapsburg Empire's many constituent parts spun away from one another.

EXAMPLE 7.11   Excerpt of *Ländler* from the slow introduction to Johann Strauss Jr.'s *Tales of the Vienna Woods*

Mahler

The pan-German nationalism that helped destroy the Hapsburg's multi-ethnic realm had one of its most ardent supporters in Gustav Mahler (1860–1911). Mahler spent his childhood in the small Bohemian town of Iglau, the son of German-Jewish parents who supported themselves by running a distillery and associated taverns. Gustav gave early evidence of musical talent, and his father hoped that his son would become a child prodigy on the piano, but this was not to be. His general abilities were such, nonetheless, that the young Mahler made his way to Vienna at the tender age of fifteen, where he enrolled at the conservatory. Though he did well in his study of the piano, composition and conducting soon became his favorite disciplines.

While finishing at the Vienna Conservatory, Mahler took courses at the university as well, and here in 1878 he joined the so-called Pernerstorfer Circle. This student group espoused a radical German nationalism guided by Richard Wagner's philosophy as elucidated in Friedrich Nietzsche's *The Birth of Tragedy from the Spirit of Music* (1872). During this period Mahler became friends with Victor Adler (father of Austrian socialism) and participated regularly in meetings at which he accompanied the group on the piano while they sang songs such as "Deutschland, Deutschland über Alles!" (the German national anthem) to the tune of the military song "O du Deutschland, ich muß marschieren!" The students advocated the unification of the German-speaking portions of the Hapsburg Empire with Germany and also socialism based on cultural nationalism.

(Adolf Hitler would imbibe this same philosophy in a later, more virulent form during his youthful sojourn in Vienna.) Mahler audited classes given by Anton Bruckner (darling of Vienna's Wagnerian faction), and in 1878 he published a reduction of Bruckner's Third Symphony for piano, four hands. During this period Mahler supported himself teaching piano and also began composing his first major piece, *Das klagende Lied,* a cantata with a text taken from a medieval German fable.

In 1880 Mahler embarked on a career as an opera conductor, taking the usual route of initial appointments at small, provincial theaters in places such as Bad Hall, Ljubljana, and Olmütz. Posts in larger cities followed, including Kassel, Prague, and Leipzig, until Mahler's talent gained recognition and he became first the director of the Royal Opera in Budapest (1888–91) and then chief conductor at the Stadttheater in Hamburg (1891–97). During this time Mahler also toured as a conductor throughout Germany and abroad. His extraordinary abilities brought him to the attention of the Viennese authorities, who hired him at the urging of Brahms and Hanslick (among others) in 1897 to conduct at the court opera in Vienna. Shortly after his arrival he was appointed director, a position he held for ten years often viewed as the Vienna Opera's golden age. He later went to America as a conductor at the Metropolitan Opera (1907) and of the New York Philharmonic (1908).

Mahler's demanding routine as a conductor permitted him little time for composition, and he restricted himself in his adult career to songs and symphonies. He took the vast majority of texts for his songs from an anthology of explicitly nationalistic German folk poetry published at the beginning of the nineteenth century, *Des Knaben Wunderhorn* (*The Youth's Magic Horn*). He also employed poems from the *Wunderhorn* in his symphonies, as well as borrowing melodies from his songs for various movements. As a result, writers speak of his first four "Wunderhorn" symphonies. They display the cultural nationalism that pervades his work before the turn of the century, as well as revealing his extraordinary command of orchestration, counterpoint, and the symphonic tradition.

We can find all these traits combined in Mahler's Third Symphony (1893–96), perhaps his most explicitly nationalistic work. He imagined it articulating a musical vision of all creation based on Nietzsche's *Birth of Tragedy*. Nietzsche saw two antithetical poles at work in art and the universe: the Dionysian (the instinctual, irrational, and populist) and the Apollonian (the intellectual, rational, and elitist). He argued that German art and politics had to restore the Dionysian to its proper role balancing the Apollonian. Accordingly, Mahler begins his symphony with a "Procession of Dionysios," using what the composer considered to be "popular" music, especially marches for brass band and trumpet signals (see Example 7.12 for the "reveille" opening the movement). In the first movement the two themes (sharing many melodic motives) present us with, respectively, a funeral dirge and a contrasting victory march arranged in a vast

EXAMPLE 7.12   "Reveille" from the opening of Mahler's Third Symphony

pageant that also contains all manner of pastoral references (birdsong, thunderstorms, horn calls, and so forth). For all its populist content, the movement still retains sonata form, but with a common Mahlerian twist of writing out an abbreviated repetition of exposition material (as opposed to the tradition of simply repeating the exposition whole; see Table 7.3).

Most of the remaining sections of the Third Symphony continue the populist mood established in the first. The second movement, marked as "in the tempo of a minuet," is in reality a folkish *Ländler* that intimates nature, according to Mahler's program ("what the flowers in the meadows tell me"). The "minuet" quotes from one of his earlier *Wunderhorn* songs, "The Heavenly Life." The third movement ("what the animals in the forest tell me") takes its melody from yet another of Mahler's *Wunderhorn* songs, "Ablösung im Sommer," and the fifth movement actually sets a *Wunderhorn* text using a folkish emblem heard in another nationalistic composer: a bell-like ostinato. Mahler, unlike Musorgsky, assigns this to a boys' chorus singing nonsense syllables. Even the concluding slow movement, for all its contrapuntal intricacy, runs in a populist vein by imitating a pious chorale (see Example 7.13).

Mahler, Third Symphony, mvt. V:
"Es sungen drei Engel" from *Des Knaben Wunderhorn*

Bimm bamm, bimm bamm!	Ding dong, ding dong!
Es sungen drei Engel einen süßen Gesang.	Three angels sang a sweet song.
Mit Freuden es selig in den Himmel klang.	That resounded blessedly with joy in Heaven.
Sie jauchzten fröhlich auch dabei,	They shouted gladly also,
Daß Petrus sei von Sünden frei.	That Peter was freed from sin.
Und als Herr Jesus zu Tische saß,	And as Lord Jesus sat at table
Mit seinem zwölf Jüngern das Abendmahl aß,	With his twelve disciples eating the last supper,
Da sprach der Herr Jesus: "Was stehst du denn hier?	The Lord Jesus said, "Why are you standing here?
Wenn ich dich anseh', so weinest du mir."	When I look at you, you weep."

TABLE 7.3 Schematic for Mahler, Third Symphony, mvt. I

SECTION	SUBSECTION	KEY	MEASURES
Exposition			
	Mth (reveille and dirge)	d: i	1–131
	trans. 1	I–♭I	132–163
	Mth (abbreviated)	i	164–224
	trans. 1′	I–III	225–253
	Sth (victory march including reveille)	III	254–322
	trans. 2	III–I	323–330
	Closing	I	331–363
Development			
	bridge		364–454
	core		
	model 1 (trans. & mth) sequences and fragments		455–529
	model 2 (sth) sequences and fragments		530–573
	model 3 (sth) sequences and fragments		574–604
	retransition	D♭ pedal	605–642
Recapitulation			
	Mth	i	643–736
	trans. 2	♭VI–III	737–749
	Sth	III	750–823
	Closing	III	824–857
Coda		♭I–III	858–875

"Ach, sollt' ich nicht weinen, du gütiger
  Gott?
Ich hab' übertreten die zehn Gebot.
Ich gehe und weine ja bitterlich,
Ach, komm und erbarme dich über mich!"

"Hast du übertreten die zehen Gebot,

So fall auf die Knie und bete zu Gott.
Liebe nur Gott in alle Zeit,
So wirst du erlangen die himmlische
  Freud!"

"Ah, why should I not weep, my good
  Lord?
I have broken the Ten Commandments.
I go forth weeping bitterly,
Ah, come and have mercy on me!"

"If you have broken the Ten
  Commandments,
Then fall on your knees and pray to God.
Love only God for all time,
And you will attain heavenly joy!"

EXAMPLE 7.13   "Chorale" from the beginning of the last movement of Mahler's Third
Symphony

Die himmlische Freud' ist eine selige Stadt,	Heavenly joy is a blessed city,
Die himmlische Freud', die kein Ende mehr hat.	The heavenly joy that has no end.
Die himmlische Freude war Petro bereit't Durch Jesum und allen zur Seligkeit.	Heavenly joy was prepared through Jesus For Peter and all in blessedness.
Bimm bamm, bimm bamm!	Ding dong, ding dong!

Mahler's remaining "Wunderhorn" symphonies often feature some combination of popular material and an almost obsessive preoccupation with folkish
piety and medieval religiosity. His Second Symphony (1888–94) includes a movement based on a funeral dirge; another based on a *Wunderhorn* song, "St. Anthony

Preaches to the Fish"; a setting of the *Wunderhorn* prayer, "Primeval Light"; and a choral rendition of Klopstock's "Resurrection Hymn." The Fourth Symphony (1892–1900), which begins with sleigh bells, takes Mahler's song "The Heavenly Life" for its finale. Mahler's First Symphony (1884–88), less explicitly religious, takes melodies from the composer's folklike "Songs of a Traveling Journeyman" and offers a funeral dirge based on "Frère Jacques."

The frequent appearance of folklike or popular style in Mahler's music often caused audiences and critics consternation, leading to charges of vulgarity. However, the presence of these elements not only made the composer's nationalistic point but also offered him a source of highly distinctive material that retained its identity in the midst of the most massive orchestral texture. Mahler possessed an exhaustive command of instrumental effects, and his non-imitative, spatial counterpoint and layering of instrumental choirs served to dramatize his populist message.

Scandinavia

It may seem odd to group Nordic composers with the central Europeans, but many of them took their instruction in German conservatories, especially Leipzig. One of them, the Danish Niels Gade (1817–90), actually served as chief conductor of the Gewandhaus Orchestra for a brief time after Mendelssohn's death. We hear Gade's work seldom in the modern concert hall, but the work of the other prominent composer drawn into the Leipzig orbit, the Norwegian Edvard Grieg, still has some currency today.

Grieg (1843–1907) was descended from a prominent Bergen family of merchants and diplomats. His mother had some reputation as an amateur pianist, and she gave Edvard lessons beginning when he was six. In 1858 the famous Norwegian violinist Ole Bull heard the boy play and immediately suggested he be sent to the Leipzig Conservatory. There Grieg studied with E. F. Wenzel, who instilled in him a love of Robert Schumann's music. Edvard also took courses in harmony and counterpoint with Moritz Hauptmann, among others. After graduating, Grieg eventually made his way in 1863 to Copenhagen, then the cultural center of Norway as well as Denmark. In The Danish Capital he met Gade, who encouraged him to develop his talent for composition.

Eventually Grieg fell in with Norwegian nationalists living in Copenhagen, and he dedicated himself to write classical music that would reflect the beauties of the Norwegian folk idiom. After a tour of Europe during which he met the poet Ibsen, Grieg returned to Norway in 1866, settling in Christiania, where he founded the Norwegian Music Academy in 1867. He busied himself composing, conducting, and giving piano recitals. His nationalist works focused on lyrical pieces for the piano, songs, and incidental music for plays such as Ibsen's *Peer*

Gynt. He also produced works in a more cosmopolitan style, including a famous Concerto for Piano (1872) modeled very much on Schumann's example, a string quartet, and sonatas for violin and cello.

In 1885 Grieg took up residence in a home he had built at Troldhaugen in western Norway. During his last two decades he toured Europe almost every autumn and winter as a pianist and composed during the spring and summer. In the 1890s he received honorary doctorates from Oxford and Cambridge, kept up friendships with the likes of Brahms and Tchaikovsky, and promoted Norwegian music and music making in his native country.

Grieg's "Norwegian" style surfaces most prominently in his collections of short, lyrical pieces and in songs. Both of these genres appear in the theatrical music that can serve as a prime example of the composer's artistic nationalism. Grieg wrote his most famous incidental music for Ibsen's *Peer Gynt* (op. 23; 1874–75), a play that dramatizes episodes from the life of a fictional Norwegian folk hero. Grieg's numbers accompanied the action, served as entr'actes, and also set songs sung on stage by characters in the drama. A selection such as "In the Hall of the Mountain King," from Peer's Act II encounter with the mythical king of the trolls, signals "folkish" style at the outset with an ostinato (see Example 7.14).

EXAMPLE 7.14   Beginning of "In the Hall of the Mountain King" from Grieg's incidental music to *Peer Gynt*

Having established folklike credentials with his opening gesture, Grieg adds an idiosyncratically "Norwegian" one, the use of a raised fourth scale degree in measure 2 of the melody, which then descends chromatically to the natural fourth degree just a moment later. The device translates the scale often used on the Norwegian Hardanger fiddle that includes a fourth scale degree lying between a perfect and augmented fourth. The drone created by the four sympathetic strings of the Hardanger fiddle influences the accompaniment of another number from *Peer Gynt,* "Solvejg's Song" from Act IV (see Example 7.15). If the open fifths here betoken a folk instrument, the melody itself derives by Grieg's own admission from an actual folk song, probably "Jeg lagde mig saa sildig" ("I lay down so late"). Later in "Solvejg's Song" the composer includes the same raised fourth degree resolving downward chromatically that we saw earlier.

In a letter from the end of his life (1897) Grieg writes, "I didn't want to be merely Norwegian, much less to be chauvinistically Norwegian. . . . I wanted to find expression for the best that was within me, which was something a thousand miles away from Leipzig and its atmosphere." Grieg's German conservatory training conditioned many aspects of his style, however, from its regular phrasing to its frequently conventional voice-leadings and harmonies. Grieg's "best" may have found its roots in the "melancholy scenery of western Norway," but he could never entirely suppress the polished technique that gave him the means to inscribe his love of homeland.

EXAMPLE 7.15   Excerpt from "Solvejg's Song" from Grieg's incidental music to *Peer Gynt*

ENGLAND AND THE UNITED STATES

Viewing the two English-speaking democracies together may appear a mere convenience at first glance, but they hold something in common about their approach to the art of music. Both of them tended to import a great deal of talent in the nineteenth century, England because it was an extremely wealthy nation and the United States in part because of its large immigrant populations and later because its wealth also became an artistic magnet. Many European composers who tended to overshadow the local talent spent a good deal of time in England. By the same token a number of composers considered moving to the United States (Wagner, to take just one example), and beginning in the last decade of the century some prominent ones did (Dvořák and Mahler, as we have just seen).

The two highly mercantile societies came to view music much more as a commodity than was the case on the Continent. In Germany, France, Italy, and Russia, governments at the central or local levels often supplemented the commercial support of art music. This was less true in England, and art music in the United States relied almost exclusively on commerce and private patrons for its existence. But although England and the United States "bought" much of their art music abroad, there are still some "nationalistic" composers worth noting.

England

Sullivan

As with the Scandinavian composers viewed earlier, English composers of the nineteenth century sometimes became satellites of the Leipzig school. The Leipzig influence resulted in part from the immense popularity in Great Britain of Felix Mendelssohn, who visited the country often as a conductor and whose works were held in high esteem by the royal family. Leipzig also exerted influence through the likes of William Sterndale Bennet, who had spent a considerable amount of time there during the 1830s and 1840s, becoming a great favorite of Robert Schumann.

We should not be surprised, then, that the most famous of nineteenth-century British composers during his lifetime, Arthur Sullivan (1842–1900), began as a chorister at the Chapel Royal, continued at age fourteen in the Royal Academy of Music with Sterndale Bennet, and then left for advanced study in Leipzig with Moritz Hauptmann, Julius Rietz, and Ferdinand David from 1858 to 1861. His classmates there included none other than Edvard Grieg. Through these distinguished beginnings, and also perhaps because his father was bandmaster at the Royal Military College, Sullivan was well connected with Britain's artistic elite. He numbered Charles Dickens, George Grove, and Tennyson among his friends and became close to members of the royal family.

Sullivan composed works that reflected the confident assertiveness of Britain during the last third of the nineteenth century, when Queen Victoria's empire had reached the peak of its influence. While in Leipzig he began with incidental music to Shakespeare's *Tempest,* and he continued with pieces such as a *Princess of Wales March* (1863), a masque on Henry Chorley's *Kenilworth* (1864), incidental music for Shakespeare's *Henry VIII* (1877) and *Macbeth* (1888), an opera based on Scott's *Ivanhoe* (1891), and a slew of hymns, the most famous of which remains the militant "Onward, Christian Soldiers" (hymn tune: St. Gertrude; 1871). There were also songs to texts by British authors, an *Imperial March* (1893), a ballet entitled *Victoria and Merrie England* (1897), and a host of other serious pieces that took a decidedly patriotic and nationalistic tone.

We remember Sullivan best for his comic operettas written in conjunction with William Schwenck Gilbert (1836–1911), the son of a naval surgeon who had turned first to the law and then to writing plays. Gilbert and Sullivan's collaborations often take up distinctly British subjects, and there may be no better example than *H.M.S. Pinafore, or the Lass That Loved a Sailor* (1878). Set on a ship of the line, the plot concerns Ralph (pronounced "rafe") Rackstraw's suit for the hand of his captain's daughter, Josephine. She in turn has been promised to Sir Joseph Porter, First Lord of the Admiralty. A relatively earnest subject belies Gilbert's verbal interplay and cleverness in handling this plot: England maintained its power by means of a superior navy, and class distinction preserved clearly demarked lines of authority in the fleet. Gilbert both approves and disapproves of the gulf that separates the lower classes (Ralph) from the middle classes (the captain and Josephine) and the aristocracy (Sir Joseph). Though all sing the praises of "A British Tar," Ralph can gain Josephine's hand only when it is discovered that he was switched at birth with his captain. Josephine's resultant decline in status makes her unsuitable, of course, for Sir Joseph.

For this romp Sullivan provides music that takes some cues from Offenbach's opéras comiques, while parodying the style of previous Italian composers and throwing in a dose of peculiarly "British" music. For an instance of the latter we can view "A British Tar," which Sullivan sets as a "glee," a kind of composition for three or more unaccompanied male voices developed by English composers in the seventeenth century. ("Glee" comes from the Anglo-Saxon *gliw* or "entertainment.")

"A British Tar" from *H.M.S. Pinafore* (1878), text by W. S. Gilbert

A British tar is a soaring soul, as free as a mountain bird.
His energetic fist should be ready to resist a dictatorial word.
His nose should pant and his lip should curl,
His cheeks should flame and his brow should furl,
His bosom should heave and his heart should glow,
And his fist be ever ready for a knock-down blow.

His eyes should flash with an inborn fire, his brow with scorn be wrung.
He never should bow down to a domineering frown, or the tang of a tyrant tongue.
His foot should stamp and his throat should growl,
His hair should twirl and his face should scowl,
His eyes should flash and his breast protrude,
And this should be his customary attitude.

The voices move in close harmony and often feature a section of canon or imitative counterpoint. The nationalistic sentiment is as unmistakable here as it is in the responsorial chorus "For He Is an Englishman," spoken in defense of Ralph when he dares to cast his "wormy eyes" on the likes of Josephine.

"For He Is an Englishman" from *H.M.S. Pinafore*

For he is an Englishman,
For he himself has said it,
And it's greatly to his credit,
That he is an Englishman!

For he might have been a Roosian,
A French or Turk, or Proosian,
Or perhaps Itali-an!
But in spite of all temptations
To belong to other nations,
He is an Englishman!

To set this number Sullivan supplies a stirring march (see Example 7.16) intimating the grand imperial style. It displays British power in four-square rhythms

EXAMPLE 7.16 Excerpt of "He Is an Englishman" from Gilbert and Sullivan's *H.M.S. Pinafore,* Act II

not unlike those in "Onward, Christian Soldiers." Nineteenth-century English musical nationalists did not rely so much on the coyly folkish as on militant emblems of the superiority to which they felt entitled.

Elgar

Edward Elgar (1857–1934) followed the alternative course of training available to nineteenth-century musicians and composers: apprenticeship. His father owned a music shop, tuned pianos, and served as a church organist. Edward took violin lessons, and he must have learned something of organ and piano from his father, who sent the boy to work in a law office at age fifteen. He rebelled after only a year and became a freelance musician for the rest of his life. At first he played violin in orchestras around his hometown of Worcester, and he soon succeeded to the directorship of the Worcester Instrumental Society (1877), conducted the Worcester Philharmonic (1879), and played in the local music festivals. In 1883 he joined the Birmingham Orchestra, which played some of the pieces he had begun to compose. He also supported himself teaching violin. Elgar moved briefly to London in 1890, but he was not at all well known, and he returned to the provinces after only a year.

Over the course of the 1890s Elgar's compositions began to earn him recognition. Soon the famous London publisher Novello accepted some of his works, and he finally hit on a major success with his *Imperial March,* written for Queen Victoria's Diamond Jubilee (1897). His arrival as an international composer came in 1899 when Hans Richter conducted the first performance of the *Enigma Variations* with the London Philharmonic. Soon after, Cambridge University conferred an honorary doctorate on the composer (1900), and he was awarded a knighthood and invited to become a chaired professor at Birmingham University in 1904. Elgar spent the remainder of his life composing and conducting in England and abroad, and during his last years he recorded a number of his own works to define his legacy.

Many of Elgar's best-known nationalistic pieces, such as the five *Pomp and Circumstance* marches, came after the turn of the twentieth century. But we can gain a taste of his national style by looking at the piece that established his reputation as a major composer, the *Variations on an Original Theme,* op. 36, also known as the *Enigma Variations.* Elgar gave a superscript for each section (rather like Schumann in his *Carnaval*) commemorating an assemblage of his idiosyncratically British friends. They included a number of amateur musicians the composer had tutored and friends such as Richard Arnold (son of the poet Matthew Arnold, V), George Sinclair (organist at the Hereford Cathedral, XI), A. J. Jaeger (editor at Novello, IX), and Lady Mary Lygon (XIII).

The theme of the *Enigma Variations* (Example 7.17) has occasioned extensive debate, since Elgar hinted that he had borrowed from a well-known melody, saying to his friend Dora Penny (variation X), "I thought that you of all people

EXAMPLE 7.17   Opening of the "Theme" from Elgar's *Enigma Variations*

should guess it." The most intriguing (and nationalistic) solution comes from Theodore van Houten, who suggests in *The Musical Times* (1976) that Elgar had quoted from the chorus of Thomas Arne's national ode, "Rule Britannia," the phrase setting the word "never." The link to Dora came, then, from the British penny of the composer's time, which portrayed the figure of Britannia on one side. Whatever the true "enigma," the melody suggests that Elgar was also well acquainted with Brahms. The theme begins with a series of "ever developing motivic variations" that immediately intrigued his German editor at Novello (Jaeger) and conductors such as Richter (an ardent Brahms supporter).

When it came time to characterize himself in the finale, Elgar chose an exuberant march in the British imperial style, with a melody punctuated by off-beats in the manner of his later *Pomp and Circumstance* march no. 3 (1904). The form of the last variation (XIV) runs parallel to that of Elgar's other nationalistic marches. It includes the feisty march proper, running from measure 544 to measure 582; a stately, legato trio from 583 to 624 (with an ending quotation from variation IX); a return to the march proper (mm. 625–659); and a last statement of the trio leading to a grand coda. Elgar's choice of a majestic imperial style to characterize his own aspirations has something quintessentially English about it. He became the court composer of a monarchy actively engaged in maintaining the aura of Britain's world domination.

The United States

Gottschalk

It was natural that the early days of the new North American republic saw a great deal of culture imported from foreign climes, if only because a substantial part of the population had immigrated. By the 1840s Americans could boast an increasingly vital indigenous popular and religious music, but art music still came from Europe. It arrived in the form of pirated sheet music (international copyright would come only in 1892), Italian singers, German instrumentalists, and French conductors.

It took some time for native-born Americans to make their name amid foreign competition, but a few did so in spectacular ways. One of the earliest was Louis Moreau Gottschalk (1829–69), son of a merchant who had immigrated from London and married the daughter of a well-to-do New Orleans baker. Young Louis studied music with the organist of the New Orleans cathedral, who soon urged the boy's parents to send him to Paris for professional training. Arriving in the French capital at age thirteen, Gottschalk was refused an audition at the Conservatoire because of his American nationality, but he took piano lessons privately with Charles Hallé and composition with Pierre Maleden. In 1845 he played his first recital in the Salle Pleyel to great acclaim, and he made his formal début in 1849 just before his twentieth birthday playing his own compositions. His virtuosic pieces for piano based on American popular and folk themes made a sensation in France along with his flashy technique at the keyboard. Hector Berlioz reflected Parisian sentiment when he wrote, "Mr. Gottschalk was born in America, whence he has brought a host of curious chants from the Creoles and Negroes; he has made them the themes of his most delicious compositions . . . in which the nonchalant graces of tropical melody assuage our restless and insatiable passion for novelty."

For several years after his Paris triumph Gottschalk toured the French provinces, Switzerland, and Spain, where he enjoyed the patronage of Isabella II. He augmented his American pieces, such as *Bamboula* (1845), *La savane* (1845), *Le bananier* (1846), and *Le mancenillier* (1846), with "Spanish" compositions, such as *El Zitio de Zaragoza* (1851), *Souvenirs d'Andalousie* (1851), and *Minuit à Seville* (1852). In 1853 Gottschalk returned to the New World, making a hit with concerts in the United States, Canada, and Cuba. From 1857 to 1862, burnt out by incessant touring, he lived reclusively in various Caribbean and South American countries, returning to North America for a new round of concerts from 1862 to 1865. After an affair in San Francisco with a female student caused a serious scandal, he left the United States for South America, never to return, and he died near Rio de Janeiro in 1869.

Not only did Gottschalk use folk and popular material in his nationalistic pieces, he could also imitate the sounds of American instruments on the piano, as he did in *The Banjo: An American Sketch,* op. 15 (1855). The designation of genre on the title page, "grotesque fantasie" (see Figure 7.1), suggests that the composer had minstrelsy in mind. American minstrels made use of exaggerated blackface makeup and a five-string instrument adapted from the original "banza" brought from Africa by slaves. Gottschalk's music alludes to the instrument's drone string by means of an incessantly repeated pitch, as well as reproducing the repetitive rhythmic strumming of minstrel banjo players. Toward the end of the piece the composer quotes Stephen Foster's recently popularized blackface tune, "De Camptown Races." (Allusion to the line "Gwine to run all

Figure 7.1 Cover of Louis Moreau Gottschalk's *The Banjo,* with the title spelled using "characteristic" emblems of minstrels, the stage banjo and the tambourine. Music Library, University of North Carolina at Chapel Hill.

EXAMPLE 7.18   Excerpt from the end of Gottschalk's *Banjo,* featuring quotation of Foster's "Camptown Races" in the middle voice

night!" appears in the middle voice; see Example 7.18.) For his second extended concert tour in the United States during the Civil War, Gottschalk offered audiences other nationalistic pieces, such as *Union: Paraphrase de Concert on the National Airs Star Spangled Banner, Yankee Doodle, & Hail Columbia,* op. 48 (1862). The composer dedicated this patriotic display to General George McClellan and performed it on one occasion to Abraham Lincoln's immense pleasure. Such effusive display may seem to us a product of the Parisian school's empty virtuosity, but Gottschalk was the first composer born in America to make a sensation at home and abroad with characteristically American art music.

Sousa

John Philip Sousa (1854–1932) was one of those composers of "light classical" music who become emblems of nationalism, in part by virtue of official associations with their music and in part through their wide appeal. John Philip came from quintessentially American beginnings, which is to say that his parents both immigrated from foreign lands, his father from Spain and his mother from Bavaria. Since his father played in the U.S. Marine Corps Band, Sousa attended Washington, D.C., public schools and also studied at the local Esputa Conservatory. He then followed his father as an apprentice in the Marine Corps Band, while studying theory and composition with a local orchestral conductor and learning the violin.

After completing his first tour of duty with the Marine Band, Sousa left for the Philadelphia Centenary Celebration in 1876, where he played in Offenbach's orchestra. He spent four years in Philadelphia as a theater violinist and conductor, but returned to Washington in 1880, this time as director of the Marine Corps Band. He raised the quality of playing greatly during the time he led the group, but in 1892 he resigned his commission to form his own ensemble, which he took on tour at home and abroad for the rest of his life. This was the heyday of the American brass band, when many small towns had bandstands located in the central square. Sousa's group represented the pinnacle of accomplished wind playing, and it reached many listeners by using the newly developed network of rapid and efficient rail travel spanning the country. Alumni of the band carried Sousa's high standards of performance throughout the country, making him arguably the most influential American musician of his time.

In the midst of all this performance Sousa found time to compose eleven operettas, seventy songs, and incidental music to six plays, as well as writing numerous articles on music and even three novels. But he is best known for his band music, including waltzes, fantasies, over 300 transcriptions of other composers' music, and above all, 136 marches. These often bear topically American titles, such as *The Washington Post, Semper Fidelis* (the Marine Corps motto), *King Cotton, The Liberty Bell, The U.S. Field Artillery,* and *The Stars and Stripes Forever.*

We have seen that a number of European composers wrote nationalistic marches, and so it would be appropriate to ask what distinguished Sousa's as particularly American. For one thing, Sousa tends to prefer vigor instead of pomp and grandeur. The active accompaniments of his marches often feature what might be designated "alternating bass," in which the lowest instruments move regularly between the fifth and the root of a chord while upper instruments play the harmony on the offbeats, an arrangement we find in *Semper Fidelis* (1888; see Example 7.19). This accompanimental pattern would provide the basis for ragtime, early examples of which often bore the label "characteristic march." The sprightly marking of the beat in this fashion made Sousa's

EXAMPLE 7.19   Beginning of march proper from Sousa's *Semper Fidelis* showing alternating bass and irregular melodic rhythm

EXAMPLE 7.20   Accentuation of weak beats at the beginning of Sousa's *Washington Post*

marches the perfect accompaniment for a dance called the "two-step," which replaced the waltz in popularity during the 1890s.

Sousa's melodies for his marches often reinforce the vigor of their accompaniments by accenting weak beats and using uneven rhythms, as we can see in the first strain of *The Washington Post* (1889; Example 7.20). Then, too, the composer did not hesitate to make the patriotic implications of his titles explicit in spin-off publications. For instance, he converted *The Stars and Stripes Forever* (1897) into a song for which he supplied the famous trio with the words: "Hurrah for the flag of the free,/May it wave as a standard forever,/The gem of the land and sea,/The Banner of the Right." In this form *Stars and Stripes* became an unofficial national anthem "sung in countless American schools," the composer claimed in his 1928 memoirs, *Marching Along.* The vigor of Sousa's marches captures the vitality and optimism of a republic in its youth, just as it was beginning to flex its considerable political muscle. The whole world rightly associates these pieces with the exuberance of United States nationalism at the turn of the twentieth century.

Beach

Amy Cheney Beach (1867–1944) cut a singular figure in late-nineteenth-century American music, belonging as she did to that most select minority of female composers. She was descended from an old New England family that had milled paper in New Hampshire for several generations. When the mill burned down in 1869, her father moved the family to Boston, where he earned his living as a paper stock salesman. Beach's mother taught her piano from age six, and she showed an immediate aptitude. In spite of recommendations to send her to the Leipzig Conservatory, however, Amy's parents decided she should stay in Boston and study piano privately; they looked askance at a public career for their daughter. But her talent could not be denied, and she played her first public solo recital in 1884 at Chickering Hall (maintained by the Boston firm of piano makers). By 1885 she was featured with the Boston Symphony and the Theodore Thomas Orchestra. Amy might well have become a touring soloist immediately, had she not followed the more conventional (and parentally endorsed) route of marriage to a prominent Boston surgeon, Henry Harris Aubrey Beach, in December of 1885. This halted her career as a pianist in its tracks; she gave only a handful of local concerts each year during her marriage and under agreement with her husband donated all the proceeds to charity.

Like many performers with thwarted careers, Mrs. H. H. A. Beach (as she now styled herself) found an outlet in composition. She had already tried her hand at a few minor pieces before her marriage. Encouraged by her husband, she taught herself the basics of harmony, counterpoint, and orchestration, largely by copying out pieces by composers such as Bach, Liszt, Dvořák, and Wagner. She also consulted editions of instrumentation treatises by Gevaert and Berlioz. She secured Arthur P. Schmidt of Boston as her publisher, and she began to produce works for piano, songs, sacred and secular choral music, chamber music, a Piano Concerto in C-sharp minor, and a *Gaelic* Symphony.

When her husband died leaving considerable debt in 1910, Amy Beach resumed concertizing. During each of the following years she spent lengthy periods in Europe, giving concerts in Dresden, Munich, Berlin, Hamburg, and Leipzig. She did well and received praise both for her playing and for her compositions. Eventually she returned to the United States, settling finally in New York, touring as a pianist, and enjoying recognition as a composer.

We could hardly call Beach a raging nationalist; she tried to cultivate a cosmopolitan musical style, which included occasional, not always American, nationalism as one of its stylistic choices. When she did choose a nationalist approach, she took a thoughtful position. To Dvořák's assertion that Americans should base their music on material from African American practice she replied:

> To those of the North and the West there can be little, if any, association connected with Negro melodies. In fact, excepting those especially interested in folklore, only very few of the real Negro melodies are even known. The songs with which we are familiar have been written by Stephen Foster and other song composers of our own race. . . . We of the North should be far more likely to be influenced by the old English, Scotch, or Irish songs, inherited with our literature from our ancestors.

Beach's answer to Dvořák's *New World* Symphony came accordingly in the form of her *Gaelic* Symphony (1897), based on Irish melodies she discovered in an 1841 edition of *The Citizen,* a Dublin magazine. For a resident of Boston this was a particularly appropriate choice of material in a nationalist work of art. The second half of the nineteenth century had seen an enormous influx of expatriate Irish into the city, where they formed the lowest tier of a hierarchical social order for a time. Though they gained in respectability in the last part of the nineteenth century and rose to power in the twentieth, the Irish certainly qualified as the most distinctive ethnic group in Beach's Boston.

The "Gaelic" nature of Beach's Symphony in E minor is not so evident in its outer movements, which the composer based on one of her own songs, "Dark Is the Night!" But the two inner movements quote folk songs quite literally, and they exhibit all the haunting beauty of Irish melody. The second movement borrows the traditional Gaelic tune of "Goirtin Ornadh," which Beach assigns to the oboe (perhaps recalling the English horn in the second movement of the *New World* Symphony), converting the rhythm into that of a *Siciliana* in place of the conventional scherzo (see Example 7.21). The hallmarks of Irish folk song include a large leap upward at the beginning of the first phrase, here a sixth in the first measure from the grace note F to D. Beach supports the oboe with the remaining woodwinds and horn, reinforcing the folk melody with folklike timbre. The ensuing "slow" movement intertwines "Paisdin Fuinne" with "Cia an Bealach a Deachaide Si," both melodies drawn again from music appearing in *The Citizen*.

Other American composers contributed nationalistic art music at the end of the nineteenth century, of course. George Whitefield Chadwick (1854–1931), German trained, occasionally used African American and Indian melodies in his pieces. German-schooled Edward MacDowell (1860–1908) contributed an *Indian Suite* for orchestra in 1897 and would go on to write nationalist piano miniatures and tone poems in the twentieth century. Eventually Charles Ives (1874–1954) would derive an original vocabulary from the syncopations and peculiarities of American hymnody and popular music (he backdated some of his pieces to the nineteenth century to appear more original). But there is something uniquely American about Amy Cheney Beach's pioneering struggle to attain equality with her music, and something tremendously honest about her eclectic approach to nationalism.

EXAMPLE 7.21   Quotation of "Goirtin Ornadh" at the beginning of the second movement in Amy Beach's *Gaelic* Symphony

FURTHER READING

Russia

For a general overview of current issues in Russian music, English-language readers could begin with Richard Taruskin's *Defining Russia Musically* (Princeton, 1997). Taruskin is highly opinionated, but his opinions are well worth considering, and his series of essays will lead to further bibliography on Russian music.

Modest Musorgsky

Here again Richard Taruskin's *Musorgsky: Eight Essays and an Epilogue* (Princeton, 1993) is well worth the effort. Caryl Emerson and Robert Oldani's *Modest Musorgsky and Boris Godunov* (Cambridge, 1994) gives a very solid account of the composer's masterpiece. And finally a good brief biography comes from Emerson in the form of *The Life of Musorgsky* (Cambridge, 1999).

Nicolay Rimsky-Korsakov

It would be appropriate to look at two classics, one being Gerald Abraham's *Rimsky-Korsakov* (London, 1949) and the other being the composer's autobiography, *My Musical Life,* trans. Judah A. Joffe (New York, 1942).

Pyotr Il'yich Tchaikovsky

The lengthy standard biography comes from David Brown, *Tchaikovsky,* 4 vols. (London and New York, 1978–91). Readers might supplement this with Alexander Poznasky's clear-headed and succinct *Tchaikovsky: The Quest for the Inner Man* (New York, 1991). For Tchaikovsky's classic dances, Roland John Wiley has contributed *Tchaikovsky's Ballets* (Oxford, 1985).

Central Europe and Scandinavia

Bedřich Smetana

Not much appears in English, but John Clapham's *Smetana* (London and New York, 1972) offers a reliable, if dated, introduction.

Antonín Dvořák

John Clapham again provides the standard biography, *Dvořák* (New York and London, 1979). More current scholarship can augment his excellent account, including *Dvořák and His World,* ed. Michael Beckerman (Princeton, 1993), *Dvořák in America,* ed. John C. Tibbetts (Portland, 1993), and *Rethinking Dvořák: Views from Five Countries,* ed. David R. Beveridge (Oxford, 1996).

The Strauss Family

Readers have almost nothing scholarly to choose in English about the Strausses, and even less that is recent. Hans Fantel's *Johann Strauss: Father and Son and Their Era* (London, 1971) or Joseph Wechberg's *The Waltz Emperors: The Life and Times of the Strauss Family* (London, 1973) supply popular accounts. For more critical insight on Strauss's works for the stage, see Camille Crittenden's *Johann Strauss and Vienna: Operetta and the Politics of Popular Culture* (Cambridge, 2000).

Gustav Mahler
Henry-Louis de La Grange has written a magisterial biography in his *Gustav Mahler* (New York, 1973–), an ongoing project of four volumes complete now to 1907. Readers might supplement this with Donald Mitchell's interesting but more scattered *Gustav Mahler: The Wunderhorn Years* (London, 1985). For a shorter biography, see Peter Franklin's *The Life of Mahler* (Cambridge, 1997). William McGrath's *Dionysian Art and Populist Politics* (New Haven and London, 1974) gives the best glimpse into the roots of Mahler's nationalism.

Edvard Grieg
Though it looks something like a coffee-table book, Finn Benestad and Dag Schjelderup-Ebbe's *Edvard Grieg: The Man and the Artist,* trans. William H. Halverson and Leland B. Sateren (Lincoln, NE, and London, 1988), provides a good account of both the composer's life and his works, interspersed with original documents. Readers might supplement this with *The Songs of Edward Grieg* (Aldershot, UK, and Gower, VE, 1990) by Beryl Foster and *Onstage with Grieg: Interpreting His Piano Music* (Bloomington, IN, 1993) by Einbar Steen-Nøkleberg, trans. William H. Halverston.

England and the United States

Arthur Sullivan
Arthur Jacobs has produced the most scholarly biography to date, *Arthur Sullivan: A Victorian Musician* (Oxford, 1984), and this might be supplemented with *Gilbert and Sullivan: The Creative Conflict* by David Eden (Cranbury, NJ, and London, 1986).

Edward Elgar
Robert Anderson's *Elgar* (New York and London, 1993) provides an excellent, thorough account of the composer's life and works. Anybody interested in op. 36 would profit by reading Julian Rushton's *Elgar: 'Enigma' Variations* (Cambridge, 1999).

Louis Moreau Gottschalk
S. Frederick Starr's *Bamboula! The Life and Times of Louis Moreau Gottschalk* (New York and Oxford, 1995) gives an exhaustive account of the composer's life. A wonderful sample of his music is available in *Piano Music of Louis Moreau Gottschalk: 26 Pieces in Original Editions,* ed. Richard Jackson (New York, 1973).

John Philip Sousa
Sousa has not attracted a great deal of scholarly attention in recent years, and so readers are left to consult Paul E. Bierley's *John Philip Sousa: American Phenomenon* (New York, 1973). Readers would also find Sousa's memoirs enlightening: *Marching Along, Recollections of Men, Women, and Music,* rev. ed., ed. Paul. E. Bierley (Westerville, OH, 1994).

Amy Cheney Beach
Beach's life and works receive thorough treatment in Adrienne Fried Block's *Amy Beach, Passionate Victorian: The Life and Works of an American Composer, 1867–1944* (New York and Oxford, 1998). Documents of her life appear in *The Remarkable Mrs. Beach, American Composer* by Walter S. Jenkins (Warren, MI, 1994).

CHAPTER 8

The New Language
at Century's End

The 1890s served as one of the pivotal nodes on which music history turned, a point of elision that summarized the preceding century at the same time it prepared the modern era. In one sense this last decade of the nineteenth century saw the consolidation of aesthetic trends that had occupied composers, performers, and critics since the end of the eighteenth century. The constant demand for musical originality that found expression in Beethoven's music joined with the diversitarian possibilities disclosed by nationalism to overthrow the strictures of the musical common practice. Although composers continued to draw on reflexes conditioned by two centuries of relatively consistent tonal usage, they discarded the actual "rules" of harmonic precedence and voice-leading. From here on, it would be every composer for himself or herself. Pragmatism (using sound exclusively for its practical effect) and empiricism (achieving sonic goals by trial and error) replaced the old tonal order.

At the same time as the tonal common practice unraveled, legal and technological developments established a new framework for the purveying of music that lasted (with certain modifications) to the end of the twentieth century. The elevated notion of artistic creativity and its associated premium on originality finally effected universal recognition of intellectual property in the form of an international copyright union in 1886. This agreement (signed by all major European countries except Russia; the United States recognized the union in 1892) stipulated that a copyright established in one member nation would be valid in all the others. Mechanical reproduction of music also enjoyed phenomenal progress in the 1890s. More or less elaborate music boxes had existed for a long time. But the invention of the pianola (an early player piano) meant that keyboard pieces and reductions of other works could now appear in the homes of those with no musical training. Sound recording served the same end: Invented by Edison in 1877, it achieved mass commercial viability with Berliner's system of flat discs in 1896. In the realm of art music, mechanical reproduction meant that composers could abandon the last vestiges of a style accessible to amateur players. Now professional musicians could record extremely novel or complicated music for the listening public.

All these developments favored stylistic diversity and encouraged experimentation in the younger generation of composers. In many cases they created new musical languages from components of the old tonal practice combined with elements gleaned from various strands of nationalistic music. We cannot view all the new currents here, but just a few from France, Italy, Germany, and the United States will serve to illustrate developments in the last decade of the nineteenth century.

FRANCE

The new language in French music took the form of what contemporaries (and most historians afterward) called "impressionism" after the movement in painting. Impressionist paintings, originally deriving their name from Monet's canvas *Impression: soleil levant* (*Impression: the sun rising*), did not entirely dispense with representation, but they placed equal or even greater emphasis on the qualities of light, color, and paint in and of themselves. To borrow a phrase from a later time, the medium became an important part of the message.

Where painting abandoned photographic precision for the abstract play of light and color, music by analogy abandoned the strictures of tonal syntax for a fascination with the very sound of certain chords, textures, and colors in and of themselves. Of course, the roots of this abstraction lay as far back as pieces such as the last movement of Beethoven's *Waldstein* Sonata and his late works. But French composers were also influenced heavily by Russians such as Musorgsky in his nonfunctional use of familiar chords. We should not confuse abstract sonority, however, with "absolute music." Indeed, impressionistic composers adopted programmatic titles more often than not for their pieces, frequently invoking visual imagery such as "Clouds" or "Footsteps in the Snow" or "Reflections on the Water." Musicians first applied the label of "impressionism" to the works of Debussy in 1887, and Ravel would join him late in the century.

Debussy

Claude Debussy (1862–1918) followed a path familiar by now from previous review of French composers' careers. The son of distinctly middle-class parents (a shopkeeper-turned-clerk and a seamstress), Debussy took piano lessons from Madame Mauté, mother-in-law of the poet Paul Verlaine. Young Claude's promise on the keyboard led him to the Conservatoire in 1872, though he turned out to be more adept at composition than piano in the end. Under the instruction of Guiraud, he won the Second and later the First Prix de Rome (1883). He also came under the influence of Tchaikovsky's patroness, Nadezhda von Meck, during his student years.

Returning from Rome in 1887, Debussy encountered a variety of further influences, including Wagner at Bayreuth in 1888 and 1889 and Javanese gamelan music at the Paris Exposition of 1889. For much of the 1890s the composer led a hand-to-mouth existence, slowly forming his new style in a series of songs, a string quartet (1893), *Prélude à "L'après-midi d'un faune"* for orchestra (1894), the first version of his operatic masterpiece *Pelléas et Mélisande* (1893–95), and a handful of piano pieces. The bulk of Debussy's composition and success came in the twentieth century, with the premiere of a revised *Pelléas* (1902), pieces for orchestra such as *La mer* (1905) and *Images* (1912), two stunning sets of preludes for the piano (1910, 1913), and more songs. The roots of his "impressionism," however, lay in the last decade of the nineteenth century.

Debussy's first public acclaim came with the performance in 1894 of *Prélude à "L'après-midi d'un faune"* (*Prelude to "The Afternoon of a Faun"*). In certain respects this work proceeds from the nineteenth-century tradition of orchestral tone poems: Debussy based his piece on a famous text by Stéphane Mallarmé about the erotic reverie of a young satyr (a figure, half man and half goat, from Greek mythology). An early program note, endorsed and possibly written by the composer, invokes mostly visual imagery:

> The music of this *Prélude* is a very free illustration of the beautiful poem of Mallarmé. It by no means claims to be a synthesis of the latter. Rather the desires and dreams of the faun in the heat of the afternoon pass through successive scenes.

This last thought may account for the fact that the *Prélude* assumes no fixed form, though short segments return now and then in irregular patterns. The piece is episodic, like the progression of the faun's reveries. Debussy indulges some references to the imagery of the poem: The piping of the flute at the opening of the piece intimates the syrinx, or panpipe, and it is possible to hear the faun dropping off to sleep in the dying away of the last bars.

Definite reference and formal cohesion lie far from the point Debussy wants to make, however. Instead he covets indistinct shapes and boundaries.

Part of this indefinite quality results from the absence of pronounced, regular meter throughout much of the *Prélude*. The composer avoids melodic periodicity and strict use of tonal cadence in a way that leaves his listeners suspended in time. Though melodic motives and phrases often repeat, they seem static and unchanging as they float over a series of accompanimental ostinati. Rarely does Debussy "develop" his melodic ideas by means of that orderly process that lends German music (or even music of previous French composers such as Saint-Saëns) a sense of progression. The lack of regularity in meter and phrase structure lends a vague, elusive quality to *Afternoon*, summoning the label "impressionistic."

Debussy wants us to focus on a series of delicate sonic textures for which Mallarmé's poetry serves merely as pretext. If we go through the piece gathering various musical novelties, such as the whole-tone melody in measures 32–33 (Example 8.1) or the intimations of pentatonicism in the melody of measures 55–58 intermixed with an implied whole-tone collection (Example 8.2), we miss the point in a sense. The lack of any consistent "system" of pitch or form or melodic development is the remarkable thing about the *Prélude*. Example 8.2 presents us with an alternation of two sonorities to be savored for their own sake, for the delicacy of the texture and flavor of the harmonies fleeting by. The

EXAMPLE 8.1   Excerpt from Debussy's *Prelude to "The Afternoon of a Faun"* using whole-tone scale

EXAMPLE 8.2   Excerpt from Debussy's *Prelude to "The Afternoon of a Faun"* using various pentatonic combinations

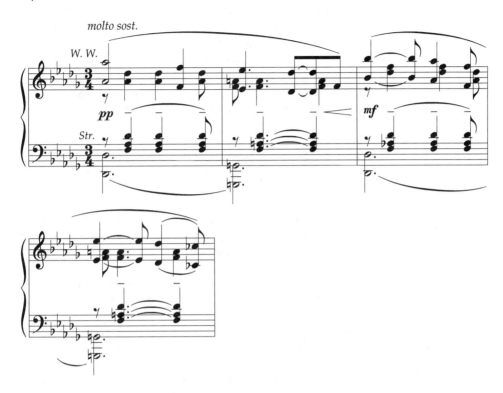

very lack of harmonic and melodic progression in this passage facilitates immediate focus on the sound itself. If Debussy wants to invoke dominant–tonic cadences, as he sometimes does in the *Prélude,* he feels free to do so. But these vestiges of the common practice also become abstract sonorities, because the composer does not bind himself to their regular use. This approach elicited frustration and consternation from the older generation of French composers such as Saint-Saëns: "The *Prélude à 'L'après-midi d'un faune'* is pretty sound, but you find in it not the slightest musical idea properly speaking. It is as much like a piece of music as the palette a painter has worked with is like a painting."

The vague, inchoate nature of Debussy's style ("he has cultivated the absence of style, of logic, and of common sense," Saint-Saëns fumed) supplied the perfect vehicle for setting Maurice Maeterlink's *Pelléas et Mélisande,* a play about the mysteries of uncontrollable sexual attraction and consuming jealousy. Maeterlink had been heavily influenced by the French vogue for Wagner in the late nineteenth century, and his drama concerns a Tristanesque or Arthurian love triangle between the prince Golaud, his youthful bride, Mélisande, and his young half brother, Pelléas. Golaud suspects the young pair of infidelity, and when he finds them kissing, he slays Pélleas and wounds Mélisande. Synopsis of the plot, however, hardly conveys the symbolist imagery of the play, representing sexuality and death in terms of sight and blindness, light and dark, heat and cold, and other elaborately extended metaphors. *Pélleas,* like *Boris Godunov,* unfolds as a psychological drama in a series of somewhat disconnected scenes tracing the tentative nature of the lovers' growing passion intertwined with the insistence of Golaud's mounting jealousy. Pélleas and Mélisande's exact relationship remains shrouded in a mystery never entirely revealed (like desire never fully expressed).

Debussy's love of *Tristan* and of Maeterlink's obscurity prompted the composer to combine Wagnerian features (leitmoifs and text declaimed over a symphonic texture) with an elusive musical vocabulary. Though Debussy did not finish the opera until 1902, he began writing it in 1893, and he had clearly determined many aspects of his new musical style by the time he completed the first version of the short score in 1895. To capture the dark, medieval aura of Maeterlink's setting, Debussy frequently adopts Lydian or Phrygian mode in place of conventional major, sequences of half-diminished seventh chords in place of common-practice progressions, and whole-tone or octatonic collections in place of diatonic ones. These exotic features intermingle with momentary references to more traditional cadential figures and more familiar tertian harmonies.

An example of Debussy's unusual amalgamation appears in Act V, where Mélisande lies dying while Golaud is overcome by remorse (yet still driven by jealousy). The act opens with an instrumental prelude that takes its pitches mostly from an octatonic collection (C♯ D E F G A♭ B♭ B; see Example 8.3) arranged revealingly in an ostinato. This mysterious and tonally ambiguous motif symbolizes the apparent mystery of Mélisande's rapid decline from her minor external wounds (she dies of an unseen psychic trauma). Later in the act the ostinato returns when, much to Golaud's consternation, the palace serving women unaccountably enter, sensing their mistress's impending demise. And eventually Mélisande expires to a fragment of the ostinato figure without ever having revealed to Golaud the secrets of her heart (the final, unresolved mystery of her love for both brothers).

In spite of the melodic and harmonic motifs that pervade *Pélleas,* however, the piece does not leave the impression of a rigorous system in the manner of Wagnerian music drama. Debussy seems to use whatever techniques and sonorities fit the emotion of a particular moment, and the ever changing harmonic palette and scales defy a strictly systematic analysis. In this Debussy may owe much to Musorgsky's *Boris Godunov,* which the French composer probably knew. Using some of the same techniques to quite different effect, Debussy's music lends atmosphere to a series of discrete instants that slip away as elusively as the undefined passion of the two young lovers. By combining recurring motifs with

EXAMPLE 8.3   Excerpt from the opening of Act V of Debussy's *Pelléas et Mélisande* featuring mostly an octatonic collection

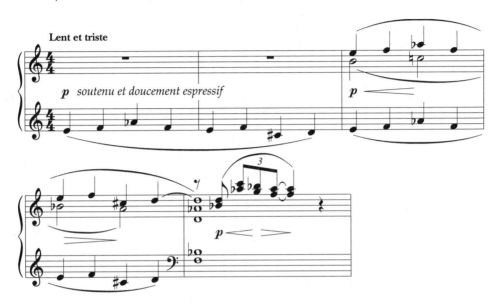

pragmatically conditioned musical language, the composer effects coherence without blatant rigor. Thus, a darkly sensuous, artistically satisfying impression lingers, without a revelation of the mechanism for achieving it. Debussy's technique is highly refined, and it possesses an elegance beautiful in its own right.

Ravel

Highly refined sonic elegance also marks the music of Debussy's fellow traveler, Maurice Ravel (1875–1937). Like Debussy, Ravel was a product of the artistic establishment. His father, a highly cultured engineer, actively encouraged his son's artistic proclivities. He secured the best Parisian teachers of piano, theory, and composition for young Maurice, setting the stage for the boy's entry into the Conservatoire in 1889. Like Debussy, Ravel fell under the spell of the Javanese gamelan, and he evinced the same enthusiasms for Wagner, Russian music (especially Rimsky-Korsakov), and the poets Baudelaire and Mallarmé. Though Ravel left the Conservatoire in 1895 without having won any of its major prizes, he continued to audit classes with Gabriel Fauré. About the same time, Maurice published several compositions, among which were some short piano pieces that gained the attention of Debussy.

Whether justifiably or not, critics often regarded Ravel's early music as derivative: "[He is] obviously under the influence of a musician whom one should esteem but not imitate, Claude Debussy," Pierre Lalo wrote petulantly in an 1899 review for *Les Temps.* The resemblance between the two composers' styles and their shared techniques may have resulted as much from common musical stimuli (the Russians, gamelan music, and Wagner) as from any direct emulation by Ravel. The younger composer possessed a distinctive personal idiom from the very beginning of his career. His music tends to be more periodic in its melody, more clearly directed in its harmonic rhythm, and less mellifluous than Debussy's. But the two artists' writing evinces just enough kinship to justify grouping them together as "impressionists."

Ravel composed his most important pieces in the twentieth century. (He was thirteen years younger than Debussy and would outlive him by almost two decades.) But we can catch a glimpse of his version of the new French musical style by viewing his first big hit, *Pavane for a Dead Princess,* which appeared in 1899. Ravel must certainly have drawn his inspiration for writing an antique "pavane" from works like Fauré's minuet for "Clair de lune" (see Example 6.13). But where Fauré had flirted with nonfunctional harmony a decade earlier, Ravel embraces it fully, as in the cadence preparing a return to the *Pavane*'s first phrase (Example 8.4). The initial ninth chords move in parallel motion. And the ensuing E minor ninth chord in first inversion progressing to the cadential dominant seventh can also sound ambiguously as a tonic major-minor seventh in G with added sixth (this would become a favorite twentieth-century device). Although the harmonies for the ensuing tune are conventional enough, the attendant parallel fifths obviously give Ravel no pause whatever. In fact, the open fifths lend the piece its antique patina.

Theorists sometimes call the impressionists' penchant for rich harmonies played in parallel motion "planing," and it is a common feature of much late nineteenth- and early-twentieth-century avant-garde music. The technique shifts focus away from the traditional function of chords to their intrinsic sonorities. Ravel's preference for more complicated harmonies (seventh and ninth chords) augments the opulence inherent in treating them as sound divorced from syntax. *Pavane,* like *Afternoon of a Faun* or any number of other impressionist works after it, exuded an agreeable and open sensuality (not to be confused with expressiveness) that awoke a prudish suspicion in an older generation of both critics and composers.

ITALY

Where French composers cultivated a cool, almost impassive sensuality by means of their new tonal freedom, Italian composers at the end of the century produced a new intensity of passionate expression called *verismo* (Italian for "realism"). In its strictest sense veristic opera placed characters from lower social classes in a context of local color and violent passions such as lust and hatred to produce tales of

EXAMPLE 8.4 Excerpt from Ravel's *Pavane for a Dead Princess* "planing" back to a return of the opening melody

betrayal and murder. A forerunner of the type would certainly be Bizet's *Carmen,* and Italian examples still in the repertory include Pietro Mascagni's *Cavalleria rusticana* (1889) and Ruggero Leoncavallo's *I Pagliacci* (1891). If we widen the definition just slightly to include other naturalistic operas as well, we come upon works as various as *La bohème* (1896) and *Tosca* (1900) by one of the most performed and beloved opera composers of all time, Giacomo Puccini.

Puccini (1858–1924) came from a long line of musicians, mostly church organists and choirmasters, who lived in and around Lucca. His family assumed Giacomo would follow in the tradition, and so he trained by singing in choruses as a boy, took organ lessons, and started playing in churches in his early teens. At seventeen he began writing pieces for the organ, and in 1876 he heard a performance of Verdi's *Aida* that persuaded him to become a composer of operas. Supported by a slender scholarship, Puccini entered the Milan Conservatory in 1880, remaining there three years. During his studies he evinced a talent for writing beautiful melodies, and he also mastered all the various shades of modern orchestration.

Encouraged by the opera composer Amilcare Ponchielli, Puccini began composing an opera based on a supernatural tale by Heine, *Le villi* (the same story used by Adolphe Adam for his ballet *Giselle*). The one-act opera eventually won a hearing at Teatro del Verme in Milan (1884), where it made such a hit that Giulio Ricordi, the famous Italian publisher, decided to print it in a revised version. Ricordi also commissioned a second opera, *Edgar* (1889), which had little success. Puccini followed this with an opera on a story of his own choosing, *Manon Lescaut* (1893), that established him as the heir of Verdi. After *Manon* Puccini collaborated exclusively with Luigi Illica and Giuseppe Giacosa to produce three of his greatest operas, *La bohème, Tosca,* and *Madama Butterfly,* all of which have become staples of the operatic repertory.

The three collaborators turned first to an opera based on a series of short stories by a nineteenth-century French author, Henry Murger. Published initially in *Le Corsair,* the stories were turned first into a play, *La Vie de bohème* (1849), written in collaboration with Théodore Barrière. Murger then rewrote them as a loosely structured novel, *Scènes de la vie de bohème.* The novel attracted Puccini, who detected a certain resonance with his own impoverished student days.

Illica constructed a scenario for *La bohème* from selected episodes of Murger's novel, and Giacosa then fashioned appropriate verse. The main plot concerns the poet Rodolfo and his affair with the seamstress Mimi, their separation and eventual reconciliation just as Mimi dies of tuberculosis. These events bear some similarity to those in Verdi's *La traviata,* but whereas Verdi's foray into early realism takes place among the rich and powerful, *Bohème* focuses on people living at the margins of society. Illica set his scenes variously in a cold artists' garret, in a Parisian café, and before one of the city gates of Paris. Giacosa often uses colloquial phrases, and his verse frequently has no regular syllable count, stress, or rhyme. This naturalism reflects both the proletarian nature of the characters in *Bohème* and their anti-authoritarian values.

The new freedom of musical language suited the libretto, and Puccini avails himself of this license with an unerring instinct that avoids any fixed system. We can hear many conventional features, to be sure: tonal progressions and cadences that rely on tonal reflexes, aria-like sections that have become extremely well known (Rodolfo's and Mimi's monologues from Act I, Musetta's Waltz from Act II), returning motives that pervade long stretches of the opera and link various episodes separated in time. Yet Puccini is not constrained by any tradition in a systematic way. He favors (without imitating) the pedal points, ostinati, and parallel motion that contemporary French composers employed to suspend the common practice. Commentators most often cite the opening of Act III as a display of these impressionistic features (see Example 8.5). But the composer uses parallel progressions at the beginning of Act II, and he employs them together with other modernist devices throughout the opera as they suit his expressive purpose. The various musical reminiscences are more like the

EXAMPLE 8.5   Excerpt from the opening of Act III of Puccini's *La bohème*

punctuating gestures found in late Verdi, rather than a consistently developed web of leitmotifs such as Wagner employed. For instance, the so-called love theme that marks the climax of Rodolfo and Mimi's first meeting in Act I ("Ah! tu sol comandi, amor!") returns to preface Mimi's last moments with Rodolfo in Act IV ("Sono andati?"). But Puccini hardly weaves his entire musical fabric from such motifs, nor does he fragment and develop them. As poignant as such recollections are, they proceed from the dramatic demands of the moment, which the composer addresses with unfailing instincts.

Puccini supports his dramatic instinct in *Bohème* with an unrivaled command of orchestral technique. His instrumentation may not exhibit the sheer force of Strauss and Mahler or the fire of Rimsky-Korsakov, but its delicacy, clarity, variety of color, and sheer sensuous delight remain unsurpassed, even by Debussy and Ravel. This may account for much of Puccini's continued success: Musicians honor his discreet, restrained deployment of vast instrumental forces by treating them with a devotion accorded few other opera composers. *Bohème* unfolds with a gentle orchestral elegance that sustains its naturalistic plot effortlessly.

Puccini's last opera of the century, *Tosca*, concentrates on different aspects of *verismo* from those in *Bohème*. Based on Victorien Sardou's play of the same name, *Tosca* technically falls into the genre of a historical drama with distinctly upper-class characters. Its combination of torture, attempted rape, murder, execution, and suicide, however, play into the Italian tradition of realism. The plot revolves around the lust of the head of the Roman secret police, Baron Scarpia, for the famous opera singer Floria Tosca. She and her lover, the painter Mario Cavaradossi, in turn harbor antigovernment sympathies, and Scarpia uses these to torture Cavaradossi as a prelude to satisfying his desire for violent conquest of Tosca. But the opera singer stabs Scarpia to death as he is about to violate her, though she fails to prevent her lover's execution for political subversion and commits suicide rather than face punishment for Scarpia's assassination. All this violence occurs on stage, prompting one critic to call *Tosca* "a shabby little shocker." Shocking yes, shabby no. Puccini's opera has an existential message: Tosca's fame and good works cannot preserve her from a sordid fate any more than Scarpia's cunning and power can protect him. The universe does not deal in either justice or injustice, which are merely human illusions. To Giacosa, Illica, and Puccini, Tosca's and Scarpia's pride stamp different sides of the same worthless coin. The two foes spend their intense jealousy, piety, love, lechery, greed, and hatred for nothing.

Puccini responds to this combination of overt passion and philosophical skepticism with a tightly knit Wagnerian operatic structure. The parallel motion downward by tritone at the opera's outset (Example 8.6) not only stuns but also establishes a memorable leitmotif associated with Scarpia and his power. The motif returns in obvious places (Scarpia's first-act entrance or after his demise at the end of the second act) and also often reappears subtly developed. For instance, Puccini fills in the motif with a descending whole-tone bass to punctuate Scarpia's manipulation of Tosca in the second act at rehearsal 39 and when she agrees to Cavaradossi's mock execution (rehearsal 55 to 58). Interrelated leitmotifs like this create a dense orchestral texture in *Tosca* and displace the predominantly lyrical vocal writing heard in *Bohème*. Though *Tosca* does feature sections of "aria," they are neither extensive nor consistently lyrical. For instance,

EXAMPLE 8.6   Scarpia's leitmotif at the opening of Puccini's *Tosca*

Tosca's "Vissi d'arte," the opera's most famous vocal excerpt, includes a fairly long section of declamatory writing for the voice. The solo cello carries the actual melody, Tosca's leitmotif played over a dominant pedal (see Example 8.7).

The combination of new musical vocabulary, leitmotif, and intricate orchestral texture in the service of the graphic plot make *Tosca* a truly modern work. The apparent sentimentality of Puccini's opera tends to mask its advanced vocabulary, but we need not be fooled simply because he constructs dramas with visceral impact. Indeed, the measure of his technical mastery lies in the fact that it draws so little attention to itself as it elicits a strong emotional response. This ability would later form the basis of that quintessentially twentieth-century art, film.

EXAMPLE 8.7   Excerpt from "Vissi d'arte," in Act II of Puccini's *Tosca*

GERMANY AND THE UNITED STATES

We generally think of German modernism as proceeding from the hyperchromaticism of Wagner's *Tristan* (see Example 4.11 and the discussion surrounding it). German composers such as Strauss in *Salome* and the "second Viennese school" (Schoenberg and Berg) in their early works pushed the limits of functional harmony until it became a chromatic abstraction. The "rules" of chord progression and voice-leading still applied technically, but the resulting harmonic ambiguity threatened tonal collapse. Yet at least one German composer, Gustav Mahler, initially blazed quite a different path away from the common practice. It is worth glimpsing how he experimented briefly with a musical language quite similar in some respects to that employed by French impressionists and Italian realists.

We have already seen in the previous chapter how Mahler's pan-German nationalism influenced his late-nineteenth-century songs and symphonies. At one point Mahler's proclivity for folklike style began to pull him away from the common practice altogether. The most obvious and significant example occurs in "Das himmlische Leben," which he wrote as an independent song in 1892 and later tried as the finale of his Third Symphony before placing it at last at the end of his Fourth. This song had a seminal influence on two of his four "Wunderhorn" symphonies, playing an immense role in their melodic content and style.

Wir genießen die himmlischen Freuden,	We relish the heavenly joys,
D'rum tun wir das Irdische meiden.	And therefore avoid earthly things.
Kein weltlich' Getümmel	No worldly tumult
Hört man nicht im Himmel!	Can be heard in heaven!
Lebt alles in sanftester Ruh'!	All live in gentlest calm!
Wir führen ein englisches Leben,	We lead an angelic life,
Sind dennoch ganz lustig daneben!	Yet are quite merry besides!
Wir tanzen und springen,	We dance and leap,
Wir hüpfen und singen,	We skip and sing,
Sankt Peter im Himmel sieht zu!	Saint Peter in Heaven watches!
Johannes das Lämmlein auslasset,	John lets the little Lamb out,
Der Metzger Herodes drauf passet!	The butcher Herod watches for it!
Wir führen ein geduldig's,	We lead a patient,
Unschuldig's, geduldig's	A blameless, patient
Ein liebliches Lämmlein zu Tod!	Dear little Lamb to its death!
Sankt Lukas den Ochsen thät schlachten,	Saint Luke doth slaughter the ox,
Ohn' einig's Bedenken und Achten.	Without the slightest thought or care.
Der Wein kost' kein Heller	Wine costs not a farthing
Im himmlischen Keller.	In the heavenly pub.
Die Englein, die backen das Brot.	The cherubs bake the bread.

Gut' Kräuter von allerhand Arten,	Good herbs of every sort,
Die wachsen im himmlischen Garten!	Grow in the heavenly garden!
Gut' Spargel, Fisolen,	Good asparagus, beans,
Und was wir nun wollen,	And anything we want,
Ganze Schüsseln voll sind uns bereit!	Whole platefuls stand ready for us!
Gut' Äpfel, gut' Birn' und gut' Trauben,	Good apples, pears, and grapes,
Die Gärtner, die Alles erlauben!	The gardeners provide everything!
Willst Rehbock, willst Hasen,	Should you want venison or rabbit,
Auf offener Straßen sie laufen herbei.	They run through the open streets.
Sollt ein Fasttag etwa kommen,	Should a day of penance come along,
Alle Fische gleich mit Freuden angeschwommen!	The fish gladly come swimming right up!
Dort läuft schon Sankt Peter,	There runs Saint Peter,
Mit Netz und mit Köder,	With his net and bait,
Zum himmlischen Weiher hinein.	Into the heavenly fish pond.
Sankt Martha die Köchin muß sein.	Saint Martha must be the cook.
Kein' Musik ist ja nicht auf Erden	There is just no music on earth
Die uns'rer verglichen kann werden.	That can compare to ours.
Elftausend Jungfrauen	Eleven-thousand virgins
Zum tanzen sich trauen!	Give themselves over to dancing!
Sankt Ursula selbst dazu lacht!	Saint Ursula herself laughs at it!
Cäcilia mit ihren Verwandten	Cecilia and her relations
Sind trefflichen Hofmusikanten!	Make splendid court musicians!
Die englischen Stimmen	The angelic voices
Ermuntern die Sinnen,	Lift our spirits,
Daß alles für Freuden erwacht!	So that all awakens for joy!

Mahler was well aware that "Das himmlische Leben," with a text taken from *Des Knaben Wunderhorn*, was not only folkishly nationalistic but also highly subversive in its poetic and musical content. It paints a folkloric "world upside down" that presents a surreal theology. For instance, Herod the butcher of innocent children somehow dwells among the blessed. He accomplishes in heaven what he was denied on earth, slaying the lamb (Jesus) with the unexpected aid of John (Christ's favorite apostle or the Baptist—we never know which). The evangelist Luke slaughters his own symbol (the ox), as earthly pleasures (game, good vegetables, fine fruit) and appetites dominate heavenly pursuits (Saint Peter catching cheerfully cooperative fish, Martha cooking). Cecilia makes music, fittingly enough, but Saint Ursula enjoys a macabre joke at the expense of the eleven thousand virgins who danced with her to their watery martyrdom. "What roguishness, combined with the deepest mysticism, hides there," Mahler reportedly quipped to Natalie Bauer-Lechner about the text. "Everything is turned on its head, causality is absolutely invalid! It is as if you were suddenly looking at the dark side of the moon!"

"Invalid causality" might describe some aspects of Mahler's setting of "Das himmlische Leben" as well. Mark Evan Bonds has pointed out in his book *After Beethoven* the various surreal formal features of Mahler's song, its irregularity in beginning in G major but ending in E major, its sudden frenzied outbursts amid the heavenly calm, its dying away at the end just when everything supposedly awakes. This subversion extends to Mahler's musical vocabulary itself. To forestall normal tonal motion, Mahler indulges the pedal points and ostinati that became the stock-in-trade of early modernism, especially at the opening of the song and throughout the last double stanza (beginning significantly "Kein' Musik ist ja nicht auf Erden"). Parallel progressions that break the "rules" of voice-leading abound, most obviously in the slow refrain that ends each double stanza and in the final movement to E major (Example 8.8). Moreover, the "open fifths" here (lacking the third that completes conventional triads) not only result from Mahler's attempt to create an atmosphere of folkish primitivism but also deprive us of the most traditional sonic comfort of common-practice tonality. Mahler's transgressive eccentricities in "Das himmlische Leben" are all the more subversive for the apparently straightforward diatonicism that pervades the song. Its folklike tone tends to disguise its radical nature.

After 1900 Mahler did not pursue the brand of modernism that marks "Das himmlische Leben" and its related constellation of "Wunderhorn" symphonies. Instead he returned to the Wagnerian orthodoxy of using chromatic motion to push the tonal system to its limits in pieces such as his *Kindertotenlieder* and Ninth Symphony. But we can occasionally hear vestiges in some of his remaining "Rückert Lieder" and in *Das Lied von der Erde* of his earlier German impressionism. It was more radical conceptually in its departure from the common practice than the "logical historical progress" of hyperchromaticism during the early twentieth century.

If Mahler eventually shrank from the abyss, his closest American counterpart, Charles Ives (1874–1954), hurled himself right into it. Ives came from a musical family that prided itself on its Yankee independence. Charles's father was a bandmaster who led wind ensembles, orchestras, and choirs in and around Danbury, Connecticut, and his mother sang in local choruses. The young Ives learned the fundamentals of music from his father, began composing at age twelve, and became a salaried church organist by age fourteen. His father hoped Charles would become a concert pianist, but the boy evinced more interest in baseball than in concertizing. A late bloomer, he entered Yale just before his twentieth birthday and studied there with the German-trained Horatio Parker, who introduced a measure of discipline into his composing. Ives's First Symphony, written during these years, shows the unmistakable influence of Tchaikovsky and Dvořák, but it also includes bits and pieces of hymn tunes. Concluding that church organists made a poor living, Ives eventually joined the

EXAMPLE 8.8   Excerpt from Mahler's "Das himmlische Leben"

actuarial department of the Mutual Insurance Company through the good offices of one of his father's cousins. His real talent, however, lay in sales, and he eventually set up a highly successful agency that provided him a business career during the day and allowed composing evenings and weekends.

Ives's financial independence of professional music making in later life reinforced his separation from the decidedly conservative academic musical traditions that marked his college training. He had already absorbed a youthful skepticism of conventional musical practice from his father. Not only did the young Charles include a great deal of popular music in his "classical" compositions, he also questioned the basic rules treating dissonance, harmony, and counterpoint. The result of his iconoclasm appears in compositions begun during the last decade of the nineteenth century, such as "The Circus Band," a song Ives later published as part of his collection *114 Songs* (1922). The composer dates this song to 1894, though we should treat this with some care, for he was known to backdate compositions or revise them subsequently over a period of years. Still, the style of this song, which Ives claims to have taken from a march for brass band, would tend to place it sometime in the 1890s. It much resembles a two-step dance (literally marked "in quickstep time"), and it has some of the syncopation associated with ragtime (which originally developed from the march; see Example 8.9). This appropriation of popular style (ragtime march or two-step) finds its reflection in the song's text, with vernacular phrases apparently written by the composer himself:

> All summer long, we boys
> Dreamed 'bout big circus joys!
> Down Main street, comes the band,
> Oh! "Ain't it a grand and glorious noise!"

EXAMPLE 8.9   Excerpt from Ives's "The Circus Band" in ragtime

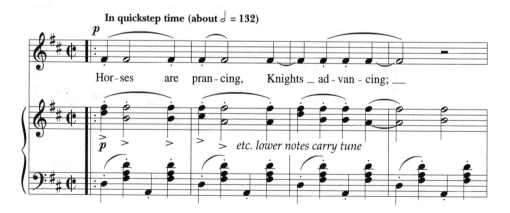

Horses are prancing, Knights advancing;
Helmets gleaming, Pennants streaming;
Cleopatra's on her throne!
That golden hair is all her own.

Where is the lady all in pink?
Last year she waved to me I think,
Can she have died! Can! that! rot!
She is passing but she sees me not.

Aside from the popular stylistic elements, we find dissonant chord-clusters in the name of realism (imitations of drum cadences; see Example 8.10), passages of planing (parallel motion) that suspend normal tonal progression (Example 8.11), and a general tendency to subvert the common practice even while alluding to its clichés.

EXAMPLE 8.10   Imitation of drum cadences from Ives's "The Circus Band"

EXAMPLE 8.11   Excerpt featuring "planing" from Ives's "The Circus Band"

Though pre-1950 modernism tended to call tonal language into question, it never entirely abandoned tonality's rhetorical gestures. During the first half of the twentieth century composers and critics frequently viewed musical modernism as a rejection of the nineteenth century, but we can see it in a different light. "Modern music" intertwined older threads of Romantic diversitarianism with newer threads of historicism, realism, and naturalism to produce an art that perpetuated many nineteenth-century aesthetic premises. If we recognize this underlying kinship, we begin to understand why nineteenth-century music still maintains its intense relevance to present-day audiences and musicians. We hear it constantly, in concert halls, on operatic stages, through radio broadcasts, and especially in scores for film and television. Music of the nineteenth century represents one of Western musical culture's highpoints, when intellectual control and human imagination melded to form a synthesis of extraordinary contrast and depth.

FURTHER READING

France

Debussy

The standard biography by Edward Lockspeiser, *Debussy, His Life and Mind* (London, 1962–65), has aged well, but readers might want to refresh it with Roger Nichols's *The Life of Debussy* (Cambridge and New York, 1998). William W. Austin provides a wonderful compilation of material on *Prelude to "The Afternoon of a Faun"* (New York, 1970) as part of his edition of the score, and Roger Nichols and Richard Langham Smith give a fine account of *Pelléas et Mélisande* in the Cambridge Opera Handbook series (1989).

Ravel

Arbie Orenstein's *Ravel: Man and Musician* (New York, 1975) can be supplemented by his *A Ravel Reader: Correspondence, Articles, Interviews* (New York, 1990) and also Gerald Larner's *Maurice Ravel* (London, 1996). Stephen Bauer has contributed an excellent article recently on "Ravel's 'Russian' Period: Octatonicism in His Early Works, 1893–1908," *Journal of the American Musicological Society* 52 (1999), 531–92.

Italy

Puccini

Puccini's most dedicated biographer is Mosco Carner in *Puccini: A Critical Biography,* 2nd ed. (London, 1974). He supplements this with a Cambridge Opera Handbook on *Tosca* (1985), and readers should not miss another book in this series dedicated to *La bohème* and written by Arthur Groos and Roger Parker (1986). More recently William Weaver and Simonetta Puccini have compiled a series of articles in *The Puccini Companion* (New York and London, 1994).

Germany and the United States

Mahler

For further reading, see Chapter 7.

Ives

Henry Cowell offered the pioneering *Charles Ives and His Music* (New York, 1955), to which Vivian Perlis added *Charles Ives Remembered,* an oral history (New Haven, 1974). Since then J. Peter Burkholder has become one of the best commentators on Ives's aesthetics and music in *Charles Ives: The Ideas Behind the Music* (New Haven, 1985) and *All Made of Tunes: Charles Ives and the Uses of Musical Borrowing* (New Haven, 1995). More recently Jan Swafford has published an extensive biography, *Charles Ives: A Life with Music* (New York, 1996). No student of Ives should omit Maynard Solomon's "Charles Ives: Some Questions of Veracity," *Journal of the American Musicological Society* 40 (1987), 443–69.

*I*ndex

Nineteenth-Century Music:
The Western
Classical Tradition